Slovenia

Over the past century Slovenia has rapidly developed from being a collection of provinces in the southern part of the Habsburg Empire, to a republic within Yugoslavia, to establishing itself as an independent state and becoming a member of the European Union.

This scholarly work provides a concise introduction to contemporary Slovenia, offering an overview of Slovenia's historical background and intellectual history, and detailed analyses of the major political, economic, and cultural developments since 1991. Portraying Slovenia as a distinctive state that paradoxically resists cultural homogenization, while moving beyond the national and towards Europe, John Cox examines this unique Eastern European nation as an extremely successful example of postcommunist transition and focuses on:

- the establishment of national sovereignty after splitting off from Yugoslavia and the country's recognition by the international community in 1992;
- political democratization and the creation of a highly successful market economy in Slovenia;
- Slovenia's accession to both NATO and the EU in 2004;
- the gradual development of a national program and the development of a sense of national identity and self-confidence among the Slovene people.

This up-to-date text will be of particular interest to students of East Central Europe, modern European history, and postcommunist democratization.

John K. Cox is Associate Professor and Director of the honors program at Wheeling Jesuit University. He is the author of *The History of Serbia* (Greenwood, 2002) and his current research interests include literary translation and the life and works of the Albanian writer Ismail Kadare.

Postcommunist states and nations

Books in the series

Slovenia

Evolving loyalties

John K. Cox

Routledge
Taylor & Francis Group

LONDON AND NEW YORK

First published 2005
by Routledge
2 Park Square, Milton Park, Abingdon, Oxon OX14 4RN

Simultaneously published in the USA and Canada
by Routledge
270 Madison Ave, New York, NY10016

Routledge is an imprint of the Taylor & Francis Group
© 2005 John K. Cox

The right of John K. Cox to be identified as the Author of this
Work has been asserted by him in accordance with the Copyright,
Designs and Patents Act 1988

Typeset in Baskerville by
Florence Production Ltd, Stoodleigh, Devon
Printed and bound in Great Britain by
Antony Rowe Ltd, Chippenham, Wiltshire

British Library Cataloguing in Publication Data
A catalogue record for this book is available from the British Library

Library of Congress Cataloging in Publication Data
Cox, John K., 1964–
    Slovenia: evolving loyalties/John K. Cox.
        p. cm – (Postcommunist states and nations; v. 18)
        Includes biblographical references and index.
    1. Slovenia–History.   I Title.   II. Series.
    DR1385.C69 2005
    949.73 – dc22

ISBN 0–415–27431–1

This book is dedicated to Lilly,
for her quick, knowing smile

Contents

Preface

Historians of nations other than their own always have a dual task: they must present to their readers both what is unique and what is universal about the country under study. All cultures possess both of these aspects, and exploring them both is necessary for differing reasons. Explanations of uniqueness intrigue us and lead us to sharper understandings of our own culture. Examinations of what is universal tend to de-mythologize ideas and practices and enable us to dispel stereotypes. The combination of these two modes of inquiry is not only satisfying; it is also intellectually necessary to present, or represent, a country in a three-dimensional view.

That the anglophone world is in need of these types of discussion of Slovenia, a small Central European country that only ten years ago emerged as independent for the first time in history, is patently obvious. The lack of knowledge about Slovenia in "the West" remains tremendous. This is, of course, the case with many other formerly communist countries of Central and Eastern Europe, too. Derek Sayer's recent work *The Coasts of Bohemia: A Czech History*[1] takes its title, indeed, from the Shakespearean world's shaky understanding of geography. Likewise, there is a rich and growing body of scholarly literature about a European variant of Edward Said's "Orientalism" which casts the Balkans as a primitive, fierce, and perpetual Other.

In 1974 the Slovene writer Drago Jančar wrote an essay entitled "The Hungarians Occupy Maribor."[2] He expresses his amazement that a publication as scholarly and as famous as the *Encyclopedia Britannica* could get so many facts about Slovenia grievously wrong. Most glaringly, the article on Maribor in the 1963 edition stated that the Hungarians took over the city during World War II. Although Hungary did annex a small part of eastern Slovenia known as Prekmurje, it was the Germans who occupied and abused Maribor, and the entire northern half of the country, in 1941. This, and the other errors Jančar found, led him to speculate on how insignificant the eastern half of the continent apparently seems to people in the West. This perception creates attitudes which then have negative political effects.

The author of this history recalls a somewhat similar episode from the summer of 1992 in neighboring Italy; a stubborn railroad clerk refused to issue a train ticket from Genoa to Ljubljana, maintaining that "the trains don't run there because there's a war on." (The brief seven-day war in Slovenia had been over for a year and the clerk was clearly thinking of the war in Bosnia. So this author rode to Trieste, had a nice cup of espresso, and bought another ticket there.)

Proof that this issue of ignorance maintains its relevance is provided by a recent misunderstanding involving the US government, in which the Bush administration listed Slovenia as a supporter of its war effort against Saddam Hussein; Slovenia was thus designated as a recipient of a significant aid package worth $4.5 million until – alas – someone remembered that the new ally Washington wished to reward was Slovakia, not Slovenia.[3]

Such issues are obviously not a thing of the past. In February 2004, the prime ministers of Slovenia and Slovakia issued a joint statement pledging to work to clear up their one bilateral problem: the fact that people from other countries (including sometimes postal officials) continue to mix up their countries. For some reason Ministers Anton Rop and Mikuláš Dzurinda feel that the mix-ups will cease once both countries are members of the European Union,[4] but there seems to be no reason to think that the level of popular confusion regarding (and hence lack of proper appreciation for) the two countries will change at all.

In our information-drenched but perspective-poor contemporary society, knowledge of Slovenia sometimes boils down in unpredictable fashion to tidbits of history (Friderik Baraga, the "Snowshoe Priest," was a famous missionary to the Native Americans and has been honored by the State of Michigan and the United States Postal Service) or to factoids from popular culture (Donald Trump has a Slovene girlfriend, the supermodel Melania Knaus). This book, one of several works on Slovenia to appear in the past few years, is intended to help deepen understanding of, and inform discussion on, the country of Slovenia, which is now a member of both NATO and the European Union. Simply put, this study tries to answer the question of how and why "the Slovenes" became "Slovenia." In more exacting terms, this book is meant as a cultural and political study of the growth of Slovene national consciousness and its gradual evolution into a force that produced statehood.

For historians, nothing is inevitable; it is the context of the past and the contingency of the present that are vital to understand. No single idea or movement in European history is more important than nationalism. This is still true today. All European peoples seem to have caught the nationalist virus at one point or another. And national identity is finding new ways to adjust to Europe's changing legal and economic life. But the force of nationalism does not exist in a vacuum. Its origins vary from country to country, the other political movements with which it bonds produce different cocktails of progressive and reactionary social structures, and it does not roll along invariably towards the foregone conclusion of a nation-state. Its investigators must peer behind the façade of inevitability and expose the mechanisms (even those as simple as the "demonstration effect," or one people copying the success of another) that produce change in identities, ideas, activities, and institutions. Along the way one must also account in some way for the wealth of possibilities that did not materialize.

The title of this volume, *Slovenia: Evolving Loyalties*, is not intended to be a reductionistic conceptual lens for viewing all of Slovene history. It is meant simply to pull together some of the many weighty themes dominating the common life of Europe's Slovene communities through the twentieth century. One of the great issues in Slovene history is the origin and spread of nationalism. Introduced via small groups of intellectuals, the idea of modern nationalism – a secular, mass movement with a strong connection to the idea of popular sovereignty – gradually took hold among Slovenes after 1848. The mechanisms for the spread of this idea are a very worthy topic of study, as is the ideological nature of this movement itself. Most observers agree that Slovene nationalism has been patient (or, in alternative parlance, pragmatic, evolutionary, gradualistic, or modest in its demands), has often accepted compromises, and thrived in multilateral environments such as the Habsburg Empire and the two Yugoslav states. Furthermore, it seems overwhelmingly to belong to the category of civic rather than ethnic nationalism. That is to say, although it is obviously founded on one culturally specific and historically attested group of people, and although the division between civic and ethnic nationalism is permeable, depending upon political and economic stimuli, Slovenes conceive of their territory and government as a political community. They are thus relieved of most of the intolerance and aggressiveness of states that seek to make their lands ethnically "pure." This relatively salubrious – though not immaculate – nationalism also deserves further study because the ethnic model has predominated in much of the Balkans and also helped bring about the fascist catastrophes in Italy and Germany, Slovenia's neighbors to the west and north. The issue of why Slovenes thought differently about the nation-state will be addressed explicitly in the conclusion to this book.

Unity and recognition are two other concepts that are very important in Slovene history. By "unity" is meant two things: achieving a common political unit, either autonomous or independent, for all contiguous Slovene communities in the Alpine–Adriatic region; and maintaining, even during the ever-slippery transition to a market economy, the social harmony that has often characterized Slovene political life. By "recognition" I intend more than just admittance to the international family of nation-states in 1992 or to the EU and NATO in 2004. What is meant is something more elemental: the spread of the idea of just who the Slovenes really are, how they are distinct from but connected to their neighbors, what they were doing for those eight decades in Yugoslavia, and the importance of the role they might play in the new Europe.

Many people helped with this book by means of their ideas, information, enthusiasm, and resources; they share the credit for whatever virtues this work possesses, but they are not liable for its faults. My gratitude goes out to Michael Biggins, Feliks Bister, Cathie Carmichael, Henry R. Cooper, Jr, Steve Fon, Denise Gardiner, Barb Julian, Fr Peter Lah, SJ, Barb Lahey, Josef Laposa, Betty Laughlin, Barbi Lehn, Fr George Lundy, SJ, Julianne Maher, Grace McInnis, Irena Milanič, Nick Miller, Mary Moore, Marian and Rich Mullin, Brian Požun, Bogdan and Svetlana Rakić, Carole Rogel, Gene Santoro, Katja Sturm-Schnabl, Barbara Šubert, Jera Vodušek-Starič, and the Wheeling Jesuit University Faculty Research and Grants Committee. And I owe a special debt of thanks, incurred over many years, to Anka and Božidar Blatnik, Murlin Croucher, Jeff Pennington, Tim Pogacar, Donald Reindl, Aleksandar Štulhofer, and Peter Vodopivec. As always, I thank Katy and Ethan for the sense of perspective that makes all of this worthwhile.

1 The Slovene lands and people to 1918

Introduction

The Slovenes were one of the first Slavic groups to be incorporated into the domains of the famous Habsburg Empire, and they were also one of the smallest. They were fairly slow to develop a national consciousness and clear political demands. This is partly due to their important strategic position in the Habsburg *Erblande*, or hereditary lands; historically, most Slovenes worked the land and were exposed to a great deal of Germanization. In addition, the Slovenes had little historical basis upon which to construct a modern people and state; thus, they moved much more slowly than, for instance, the Czechs, Italians, Hungarians, and Croats towards self-determination. But by the time of World War I, the Slovenes had produced several generations of renowned scholars who had cemented a national consciousness and begun to formulate political demands in the name of all Slovenes. The shape, extent, and success of the development of the Slovene national program are keys to the background of the first Yugoslavia.

Early Slovene history

The term "Slav" today refers to speakers of one of the Slavic languages. This branch of the Indo-European language family includes the sub-groupings East Slavic (including Russian), West Slavic (including Czech and Polish), and South Slavic (today's Slovene, Croatian, Serbian, Bosnian, and other tongues). The original Slavic tribes, numbering among themselves the predecessors of today's Slovenes, arrived in the Alpine–Adriatic region in the sixth century AD. Although the Croats, Serbs, Bosnians, and Bulgarians would all develop independent state structures and recognizable high cultures in the Middle Ages, Slovenes did not. They were, however, part of two limited political undertakings in capacities other than as merely subjects. From 627 to 658 they were part of a loose Slavic political entity under a partly mythological prince named Samo; this state, such as it was, extended from Saxony to the Adriatic. The main political fact of the time, though, was Bavarian and then Frankish sovereignty over the core Slovene lands. These lands, where Slovenes were numerous but not politically dominant, included the provinces known today as Carinthia, Carniola, and Styria, as well as the coastline along the northern Adriatic, the northeast corner of Italy. Christianization occurred around 800, and much power was wielded over Slovene lands from that point on by the Roman Catholic archbishoprics in Salzburg and Aquileia. German feudal lords moved in and Slovenes themselves remained mostly serfs, completing the political and cultural pattern that would long prevail. The main changes up to the period of the Enlightenment, with the exception of a brief flowering of Reformation culture discussed below, were provided by the consolidation of Habsburg power (by about 1400) and the incursions of the Ottomans, who had become a major force in the Balkans and then pushed on into Central Europe by about 1500.

There also exist some later Slovene political traditions, which indicate some degree of unity and local autonomy. Into the early 1400s, there was a principality (later, duchy) known as Karantanija; it was named for Carinthia, one of the northern Slovene regions. The local prince took his oath of office in Slovene, wore peasant clothes for the day, and was invested in a traditional ceremony on an outdoor stone throne just north of Klagenfurt. This throne, the *knježni kamen*, or, in German, *Kaiserstuhl*, was a remnant of an old Roman column; the accession was followed by a mass in the nearby church of Gospa Sveta/Maria Saal. From its origins in the 600s to the Frankish take-over in 820, Karantanija had its unique phase: the leader was elected by a limited franchise of freemen and had to agree to a "contractual" relationship with the people. It should be remembered, though, that the leader generally owed higher loyalties to foreign powers and that most Slovenes did not live in Karantanija. Nonetheless, this is as close as Slovenes got to a state tradition prior to 1991.

The famous Christian missionaries Cyril and Methodius, who brought both Christianity and literacy to several Central European and Balkan peoples during their ninth-century travels from their base in Thessaloniki, stressed the right of newly converted groups to worship, at least in part, in their native tongues. When European Christianity experienced its first great division in the eleventh century, this use of the vernacular, of course, would remain a part of the Orthodox tradition, but it would gradually fade in the Catholic world, to be replaced by the universal use of Latin. Evidence that the Slovenes originally worshipped in their own language is provided by the Freising Memorials (also known as the Freising Fragments, Texts, or Monuments; in Slovene *Brižinski spomeniki*). These manuscripts, discovered in Bavaria in 1807, are the oldest artifacts written in Slovene or, for that matter, in any Slavic language using the Latin script.

Like much of Europe, the Slovene lands were racked by peasant uprisings (*jacqueries*) in the sixteenth and seventeenth centuries. The biggest of the revolts, encompassing 80,000 peasant rebels at its peak, lasted for five months in mid-1515. Faced with ever-greater taxes being used to fight off the Turks, and with restricted use of common fields and forests, peasants demanded a return to their *stara pravda*, or traditional rights. They also demanded a role in determining future dues and duties. The situation in the countryside had recently worsened, since feudal lords were trying to increase production for export and there was a switch to a monetary instead of natural economy. A war with Venice and higher tolls imposed by cities shut down much of the peasants' economic activity. Thus, the peasantry organized into leagues and attacked and plundered castles. The nobility sought refuge in cities but finally called in some imperial troops and raised a mercenary army. Dozens of rebel leaders were executed, while taxes and the *corvée* (labor dues) were increased even more to pay for the damage that had occurred. The famous Croatian uprising (1572–1573) led by the ill-fated Matija Gubec also spilled over into parts of Slovenia, while the year 1635 saw another major uprising in the central Slovene lands. Although only involving about 15,000 rebels at its peak, this revolt also resulted from domestic and external causes. Erosion of traditional rights and increases in feudal dues and duties combined with higher imperial taxes and obligations to quarter ill-behaved imperial troops during the Thirty Years' War.[1] After the suppression of the second revolt, fewer leaders were executed but many more were sent to the galleys or into other types of forced labor.

From 1000 AD up to the time of the Reformation, however, an enormous gulf swallows up Slovene high or official culture. We know, of course, that there was no independent Slovene state or even administrative unity in these five-plus centuries; the Habsburg feudal system had sunk deep roots into the Slovene provinces and the area's cities became increasingly Germanized, in terms of both new population and diluted local loyalties of the resident Slovenes. It has been correctly asserted that in this long period "no writing, let alone literary creativity, took place in any of the numerous dialects of Slovene before the middle of the sixteenth century."[2] What then happened, during the Reformation, was remarkable, but, like a spark quickly extinguished, Slovene was destined to go underground again during the exigencies of the Counter-Reformation and the Thirty Years' War. Despite the occasional work of non-fiction in Slovene or in German about Slovenia, it was only in the nineteenth century that the Slovene language would begin, again, to take firm shape and to gain in self-confidence and acceptance. The long history of the language, then, is burdened with a remarkably slow beginning. Slovene survived through these centuries as a peasant language, in family and village use among one of Europe's smaller ethnic groups.

The Reformation was truly a seminal time for Slovene culture. Primož Trubar (1508–1586) is a figure of such importance in Slovene history that he has been called both the "father" of Slovene literature and the founder of the Slovene literary language. A Catholic priest who adopted Protestantism, he holds the first designation because his primer of 1550, entitled *Abecedarium*, was the first printed book in the Slovene language and because he is the first named poet in Slovene. He bears the second appellation because of his success in beginning the standardization of the Slovene language; his works follow, at least partially, a pattern common to English and German in this same era: the impact of Protestantism was registered as a spur to popular national culture, and great religious undertakings such as Martin Luther's Bible (1534) and the King James version (1611). (Dante's works had had a similar, if earlier, effect on standardizing the Italian language.) Although Protestantism all but disappeared from the Slovene lands during the ensuing Counter-Reformation, the works of Trubar and the men such as Jurij Dalmatin and Adam Bohorič who continued his work through about 1600 gave the Slovene language a much-needed injection of energy and status. Nothing approaching significant political change occurred in this time, as the Slovene lands remained firmly under the Habsburg scepter, even despite Turkish incursions; and even economic change had not yet permeated the region, since Slovene feudalism was able to suppress a series of violent peasant uprisings in this period. But one can speak of a revival, or an incipient modernization, of Slovene national consciousness through the rudiments of standardization and the beginnings of a wider literacy occasioned by Trubar's work, which flourished with help both from urban humanist circles (pressing for educational reform and the use of various vernaculars) and from German Protestant patrons, thinkers, and printers in Tübingen and Urach.

The supradialectal version of Slovene created by Trubar contained many Germanisms, which began to be purged (along with Protestant theology) by the authors of the Catholic Counter-Reformation. Trubar, of course, although writing for all Slovenes, had mostly an urban following and the Germanization of the language was most advanced in cities. Although Trubar sometimes used the words "Slovene" and "Slav" interchangeably (foreshadowing a major set of issues in nineteenth-century Illyrianism and Yugoslavism), he evolved a clear sense of who the Slovenes were and he eschewed pan-Slavic borrowings that would have made his writings intelligible to other Slavic peoples.

In total, Trubar published thirty-one books. They were all of a religious nature. Among them were translations of Gospels and the Psalms from the Bible, many pedagogical materials, music, and liturgies. Among the achievements of his immediate successors, Dalmatin's 1584 complete Bible translation (not surprisingly, from Luther's German version) and Bohorič's grammar (also of 1584), dictionary, and alphabet provided the greatest anchoring of the peasant-based Slovene national culture. Trubar's reputation remains so great that even modern Slovene writers such as Aškerc, Cankar, and Kosovel paid homage to him. His reverent but imposing likeness appeared on Slovenia's ten-tolar banknote after independence, a position of everyday prominence that can be likened to the image of George Washington on one-dollar bills in the US. Trubar, himself, seems to have known full well the momentous nature of his cultural undertakings:

"In the history of the planet this has never happened before, since the Slovene language was not written till now, much less printed."[3]

In the long centuries of high-cultural silence following the Reformation, written works from the Slovene perspective or on Slovene affairs were extremely rare. One exception to this tendency is the encyclopedic four-volume *Die Ehre des Herzogthums Krain* (The Glory of the Duchy of Carniola) by a nobleman and scholar named Janez Vajkard Valvasor (1641–1693). This work was published in 1689; the fact that it was written in German foreshadows the overlapping cultural identity of Slovene intellectuals that will continue into the decades of the great linguistic works of Kopitar and Miklošič. Such was the cultural power of the Habsburg metropole, Vienna, or, in this case, such was the degree of Germanization in the Slovene cities that produced Valvasor. Valvasor's name, fittingly, is found today in many variants, involving various combinations of Ivan, Johann, Weikhard, and Valvazor.

Valvasor was born into a Germanized aristocratic family in Ljubljana and received a Jesuit education there. Interested in the natural world and science, he traveled widely across Europe and North Africa and fought as a volunteer against the Turks. Upon settling down he began an energetic and comprehensive investigation of the life and countryside of his home country. He collected a library of thousands of volumes and drawings and he wrote and printed a total of nine volumes about Carniola and the surrounding areas. They were lavishly illustrated and most had Latin titles. His collection *Die Ehre* was the peak of his investigations into topography, history, technology, and ethnography. His enthusiasm for study was so great that, in addition to his three castles, Valvasor even bought a house in the city of Ljubljana so that he could be close to the archives.

Valvasor, in the fashion of the Baroque culture of the day, sponsored a group of artists who left renderings of some notable Slovene buildings of the time. The general intellectual setting of the time was rather thinly populated, with Jesuit high schools throughout plus a scientific association called the Academia Operosorum Labacensium and public library in Ljubljana. He is an individualistic phenomenon, although in some ways a breathtaking one, since he was also an inventor and architect and even a member of the Royal Society in England. Valvasor's work is of tremendous value to historians of many types. He provides detailed information on economic life, everyday customs and popular culture, heraldry, language, folklore, and military affairs. Valvasor depicts a great economic bustle and exploitation of natural resources – coal, timber and charcoal, ironmaking, agricultural products, wool, mercury – in the Slovene lands. Trade with German and Italian lands brought imported goods and a higher standard of living than in more remote, more predominantly agricultural regions of the inner Balkans. The assertion that the production and trade created a Slovene middle class which then, open to European ideas and eager to share political power, acted to introduce the ideas of nationalism into the society is disputed by many historians, however. This model certainly seems to hold for many Western European and some Central European peoples, but it has been argued that the bigger spurs to Slovene nationalism were provided by intellectuals (including churchmen) and the Habsburg government itself, which promoted education and the vernacular to mobilize the population and better centralize the government. At any rate, two things are certain: the intense economic activity of the early modern era provided for the emergence of a Slovene bourgeoisie that would, eventually, challenge the German supremacy in urban areas, and the highways (and eventually railroads) connecting Vienna to Trieste pulled the Slovene lands together and helped build an awareness of common identity across the regions.

Valvasor was one of the few Slovenes (the musician Jacobus Gallus and the scientist Jurij Vega being others) who was known outside his home region. He thus helped bring some knowledge or awareness of Slovenia to the outside world, and he confirmed the necessity (and possibility) of Slovenes maintaining intellectual contact with the rest of Europe and producing work up to international scholar standards. It has even been remarked that "he advocated the peaceful coexistence of peoples and was aware of the interdependence of humans and nature," which would make him an even more admirable figure by the standards of today.[4] Ultimately, in terms of nationalism, Valvasor was a chronicler of Slovene life, and not a deliberate promoter of national consciousness, but his work constitutes a vital catalog of, or voice for, Slovene culture and history.

The lands inhabited by Slovenes had been incorporated into the *Erblande* in the fourteenth century; under the organizational pattern of the Habsburg Empire, these particular Slavs lived in six different territorial units: they predominated in the historic province of Carniola and also were present in Styria, Carinthia, Istria, and Gorizia; in Slovene these regions are known, respectively, as Kranjsko, Štajersko, Koroško, Istra, and Gorica. In the Hungarian part of the Empire lived a smaller number of Slovenes – about 45,000 – in the nineteenth century, and even more Serbs and Croats. (Much later, in 1866, Italy would remove some of these Slovenes from Austrian rule by annexing territory north of Trieste that contained some 27,000 Slovenes.) The Slovene position between the German hinterland and the Adriatic made their territory of crucial importance to the Habsburg Empire; thus German superiority in the region, or at least an absence of Slavic particularism, was very important to Vienna.

For a number of reasons, the Slovene lands did, in fact, remain largely loyal to the Habsburgs – or quiescent, one might say, in the face of overwhelming pressure. One reason was that the German commercial class was dominant in the cities well into the nineteenth century. Another reason was the fear of Italian irredentism in Istria, the Trieste region, and Gorizia. The Slovenes in Carinthia and Styria also looked to Vienna for protection against German nationalist sentiment in the nineteenth century.[5] The first postwar generation of Slovene and Yugoslav leaders, who matured in the interwar period, when Italy had annexed a large portion of Slovenia, Istria, and Croatia, would be faced with a recurrence of this problem after World War II.

The bond of Catholicism was another source of Slovene loyalty. A nascent Slovene Protestant movement in the sixteenth century, which brought advancement in local literacy and the publication of the first studies of the Slovene language by men such as Primož Trubar, Jurij Dalmatin, and Adam Bohorič, disappeared during the Counter-Reformation, to which the Catholic Habsburgs lent strong support. Thus the basis for Slovene particularism had to be, in effect, largely reconstructed during the nineteenth century. In the words of the English historian A.J.P. Taylor, the Slovene national movement was "respectably clerical and conservative, a last echo of the alliance between dynasty and peasants."[6]

The Habsburg nineteenth century

For Slovenes the modern era dawned during the Enlightenment. This era also brought Revolution and the ascent of Napoleon, sometimes called "the Enlightenment on horseback," to France. The political philosophy and military campaigns of that country would in turn have great significance for Slovenia. But first, there was an indigenous Enlightenment. Its catalyst was a wealthy Baron named Žiga Zois (1747–1819). He was a major patron of the arts and learning, cultivating both European trends and the Slovene language itself. The Augustinian monk Marko Pohlin wrote an important grammar at this time, and the philologist Blaž Kumerdej (1738–1805) helped design and run an elementary school system initiated by Empress Maria Theresa. Since modern nationalism requires widespread literacy, the standardization and spread of Slovene is of great importance. The other artists and scholars whom Zois supported founded libraries, theaters, and newspapers.

During the Napoleonic wars, the Austrian Empire was often pitted against France. During an invasion of the Habsburg territory, the French organized some of their captured territory into the Illyrian Provinces. Although they only lasted from 1809 to 1814, the Provinces were important to Napoleon because they deprived the Habsburgs of key coastal territory. But they also gave a great shot in the arm to Slovene nationalism. In point of fact, they rested on a regional identity and did not represent a Slovene nation-state, since they included large numbers of Croats and not insignificant populations of Serbs and Italians as well. But Ljubljana was the capital city, and many Slovenes gained experience in politics and administration, and – perhaps most importantly – the Slovene language was in official and educational use. A French diplomat posted to Ljubljana also wrote a novel about the area, especially the coastline; Charles Nodier's *Jean Sbogar* (1818) is one of the first modern fictional representations of Slovenia by a non-Slovene.

A prominent figure in the Provinces was Valentin Vodnik (1758–1819). He was a newspaper editor, scholar, school administrator, and textbook writer. His work, on topics from grammar and geography to folk poetry work, contributed significantly to the maturation and unification of Slovene society. But he is also remembered for his poetry. One of his works, "Illyria Resurrected," serves an important triple function in Slovene history. First, it emphasizes Slovene statehood, or the governmental (as opposed to simply the cultural) aspects of nationalism. Second, the poem symbolizes the beginning of a more overt movement of regional cooperation between the Slovenes and their neighbors; both cultural and political cooperation, specifically with Croats, would later bloom at mid-century in the Illyrian Movement, as dialog and mutual assistance with other South Slavs such as the Serbs would do, in a more diffuse way, in the Yugoslav movement by the outbreak of the Great War. Third, the poem demonstrates the increasing connectedness of Slovenes to the ideas and trends of the broader world; here it is the Napoleonic wars and the ideas of the French Revolution that have come crashing into the country.

The poem is also a paean to Napoleon and captures the invigorating, liberating atmosphere of the confluence of the Enlightenment and Romanticism:

> Napoleon says,
> "Illyria, arise!"
> It arises, it breathes:
> And who calls you to life?
>
> O beneficent knight,
> You who awaken me!
> You extend your mighty hand,
> and pull me up . . .
>
> Since ancient times
> the snow-covered mountains have been our patrimony.
> Our honor comes echoing back
> to us from there . . .
>
> Over hundreds of suns
> moss grew to cover us;
> now Napoleon's decrees
> clear out the dust.
>
> The Napoleonic spirit
> is marching into the Slovenes,
> and a generation sprouts
> reborn completely new.[7]

Ideas about Slovene nationhood in the 1800s were largely bound up with the field of linguistics and the domain of literature. The Slovene approaches to national issues at the time fit onto a sort of spectrum. They are personified in three of the most important figures of the century: Jernej Kopitar on the one hand, and France Prešeren on the other, with Franc Miklošič somewhere in between. Such an approach to their ideas at any rate certainly helps to clarify the nature of the various "national programs" that developed between the French Revolution and the Great War. (This paradigm has, of course, its limitations, not least because the public discourse about nationalism was evolving at the time. After all, Slovene society was changing and these new ideas had sequential, not simultaneous, impacts.) The first group saw the assertion of Slovene identity in a multilateral or regional context, building on the original, powerful idea of Austroslavism in the works of the late eighteenth-century historian and dramatist Anton Tomaž Linhart; Kopitar's Enlightenment-era thinking would later be echoed in point of origin and in many essentials by Croatian "Illyrians" and Serbian "Yugoslavs." The second group saw Slovene national identity in the typical context of Romantic nationalism: unique, individual, autonomous, and ultimately independent.

Jernej Kopitar (1780–1844) represented basically an Austroslavist stance. This trend, later embodied by the long-term mayor of Ljubljana, Ivan Hribar, prevailed until World War I; after that time, another and more contested multilateral framework would replace it: Yugoslavism. Its main principles were that the Habsburg Empire was a unique state, with a common civilization across its many ethnic groups, that provided an indispensible haven for peoples like the Slovenes, Czechs, and Croats, sandwiched into "the lands between" the large German and Russian realms. Although talk of Slavs within the Empire banding together as a "third force" (trialism) or counterweight to the influence of Vienna and Budapest would remain unsettling to conservative officials, the Austroslavs did lend vital support to the throne at times of crisis, such as in 1848 against the rising tide of German unification. Under the leadership of the Czech historian František Palacký (1798–1876), it became an even more powerful force.

Kopitar's other main concern had to do with the cultural identity and cooperation of the Habsburg South Slavs. From our perspective today it might seem ludicrous to maintain that different Slavic peoples could or should fuse themselves together or even sacrifice some of their sovereignty through extremely close cultural or political cooperation. But one should remember that the linguistic and cultural lines between many Central European and Balkan Slavic groups were not yet clearly drawn in Kopitar's day, or even in the heyday of the Yugoslavist ideal in the early twentieth century; seen historically, with an eye to context and contingency, it is less profitable to think of today's nation-states than of the significant variations that existed in the 1800s between the customs and dialects from region to region in Italy or in Germany. Those countries had developed "big" nationalisms and created large states, and many Slavs wondered if they should do the same. The common ethnic or linguistic origins of the Slavs were also stressed, so that Austroslavists (and proponents of other kinds of fusion) saw themselves as advocating a return to something natural and powerful, not a renunciation of a laboriously protected kinship circle or zealously resuscitated cultural patrimony. Kopitar promoted mostly linguistic reform. He wanted the Slovenes and the Croats to build a new language with popular roots, based on the similarities between Slovene and one of Croatia's three main dialects, the kajkavian variant of north-eastern Croatia. He also wanted Serbs to steer clear of Russia's cultural orbit and make common cause with the Habsburgs.

Kopitar was educated in Ljubljana and Vienna and worked at first in the circle of the Enlightenment scholar and patron Baron Zois. In 1810 he took his first government job in Vienna, where he would be active, until his death, as an Imperial censor, Court librarian, and member of many European scholarly academies. Kopitar is often remembered for the huge boost he gave to the career of the young Serbian scholar Vuk Karadžič, even making Goethe aware for him of Serbian folk poetry; Karadžič would go on to produce invaluable collections of Serbian folk songs and epics, to reform the Serbian language, and to generate a lasting (if controversial) definition of Serbian nationalism as the identity of all people who speak the stokavian variant – including, as we know today, many Croats, Bosnians, and Montenegrins. Kopitar arranged for a great boost in the Slavic holdings of Vienna's libraries and for better printing facilities for Slavic books. It is often also recalled that Kopitar wrote his Slovene grammar, *Grammatik der slavischen Sprache in Krain, Karnten und Steyermark* (1808), in German, a reminder of where the cultural center of gravity of the Slovene intelligentsia still lay; Valvasor, Linhart, Matija Čop, and others had also written many key works in German. Although this grammar is important historically as a link in the chain of cultural preservation for Slovenes extending back to Bohorič and ahead, through the "alphabet wars," to the work of Miklošič and others, it is also noteworthy because it is the first to contain reflections on the history of the language and literature. Along with the Czech Josef Dobrovský, then, Kopitar was one of the founders of the field of Slavics; in the political course of Slovene nationalism, his systematic Austroslavism actually opened a new chapter as well.

Several forces kept Kopitar's ideas from taking the day. One of them was another regional or supra-ethnic linguistic movement called Illyrianism. This force, under the guidance of the publicist Ljudevit Gaj, heralded the beginning of the Croatian national renaissance; it later split into a straightforward Croatian nationalist trend and the Yugoslavism of Bishop Juraj Strossmayer. Croats, like Slovenes, were a Habsburg people; most Serbs at this time lived either in the Ottoman Empire still or in the small but growing principality around Belgrade that had rebelled against Istanbul in 1804. Although Illyrianism (or Illyrism), like Kopitar, stressed the close similarities between Slovenes and Croats, it was based on the stokavian dialect of Croatian, which is much closer to Serbian than Kopitar's kajkavian. This concern with unity with non-Habsburg South Slavs was one of the reasons Illyrianism was never very popular in Slovenia, despite the Croat–Slovene cooperation in the Napoleonic era and the enthusiasm of a few writers (and the youthful Miklošič). Another reason was that Slovenes suspected in Illyrianism a "greater Croatian" assimilation of their own small group; one should note here that this caveat is the same as that applied, later, by the Croats to Serbian ideas about "Yugoslav" cooperation or common identity. Shortly before the Great War, another manifestation of Illyrianism was triggered by the Habsburg annexation of Bosnia–Hercegovina. This was actually a kind of Yugoslavism and was adopted by leading figures in the socialist and youth movements, as well as the cultural world. Serbia had grown into a powerful Balkan kingdom and, in the Balkan Wars of 1912–1913, it conquered a great deal of land, including Kosovo and much of Macedonia. The influx of so many more Slavs into the Empire seemed to present a great opportunity but, again, the idea of assimilation – this time at the hands of an even more powerful Serbo-Croatian grouping – left most Slovenes cold.

An even more powerful movement, stressing Slovene uniqueness, proved to be romantic nationalism. Just as Austroslavism was a variant of a general European trend known as pan-Slavism, so Slovene Romanticism fits into the broader tradition of other European "national poets." It is here that we encounter two works by the man widely acclaimed as the Slovene national poet, France Prešeren (1800–1849). Largely outré in his own day, due to his bohemian lifestyle and his liberal, secular, vehemently anti-German political views, his modern and individualistic approach to poetry brought him increasing fame after his death. Trained as a lawyer in Vienna, he also wrote in German, but he conceived his mission as the creation of a modern consciousness among the growing Slovene middle class. Many of his works were overtly aimed at raising Slovenes' ethnic consciousness and self-confidence. Prešeren was actively involved in the linguistic and political debates of his day. He militated against Kopitar's idea that peasant speech was the only "pure" and worthwhile form of Slovene, and he worked to modernize the language and alphabet. He also rejected the Illyrianism of the poet Stanko Vraz and others, vehemently defending the integrity and uniqueness of the Slovene language and culture in the face of assimilation from whatever quarter.

Prešeren's longest poem "Krst pri Savici" (The Baptism on the Savica) was intended to be, and has become, the Slovene national epic, despite its contemporary vintage. It is set in the eighth century (actual Christianization began after 745) and depicts the bloody battles between the "pagan" or pre-Christian Slovenes and invading Germanic warlords who bring

Christianity in tow. The last leader of the valiant Slovenes is Črtomir, who while in retreat falls in love with the beautiful maiden Bogomila. She is the daughter of the keeper of a pagan shrine (to the goddess Živa, representing both Venus and Shiva) on the island in the middle of storied Lake Bled, in the midst of the wild Slovene Alps. While Črtomir is once again off doing losing battle with the brutal Valjhun, Bogomila and her father convert to Christianity – significantly, of the Italian and not the German variety. When they meet again, his love becomes decarnalized and transformed into a holy mission at her insistence; Črtomir is baptized and then sets off for ecclesiastical training at Aquileia, after which he, himself, becomes the chief missionary to the Slovenes and other nearby Slavs.

This epic embodies many important symbolic elements. First, it stresses the importance and long pedigree of the Slovene language and identity. Second, it memorializes the introduction of the Slovene culture to the broader world of Latin Christianity which would bring literacy, literary models, classical learning, and, of course, political ties. Third, its depiction of Germans as brutal and essentially deviant in their Christianity reflects Prešeren's concern over both Germanization at home and the rising political power of the nascent German state in Central Europe. Finally, it has been pointed out that in valorizing Črtomir's tactical retreat from his pagan ways, Prešeren was admonishing Slovenes to learn to be adaptive and proactive rather than always defensive and traditional-minded to the death when encountering superior force.[8]

The other important work by Prešeren is the shorter poem "Zdravljica" (A Toast). The national anthem of independent Slovenia is based upon part of this poem. Although many of Prešeren's most famous works are melancholy – if exquisitely beautiful – sonnets, this 1848 poem is full of quintessential patriotic hopes and, less typically, praise of the virtues of his homeland's human landscape. Most interestingly, the patriotic or nationalistic elements are balanced by the desire for freedom and peace for all peoples, and even for close ties with "Slava's every child," or other Slavic peoples.

Prešeren's fame grew to European proportions, and his works remain beloved in Slovenia today. His adult home in Kranj is a major museum. The Slovene-American journalist Louis Adamič summed up his impact in these terms:

> Prešeren was a lesser Goethe, a contemporary and spiritual kin of Pushkin and of Adam Mickiewicz . . . Prešeren was the first major – and remains the foremost – Slovenian poet. His verse and biography are one of the firmest cultural bases of Slovenian nationhood.[9]

His works have also been compared in their effect to Shakespeare, Racine, and Dante.[10] Today, the most prestigious Slovene literary prize bears his name, as do a famous publishing house and many other geographical sites and cultural institutions. His face also appears on the 1,000-tolar note. His cultural significance rests in the twin achievements of proving the maturity and artistic capacity of the Slovene language and pushing Slovene literature into the European mainstream by adopting international themes and techniques. Although he did not often use the word "Slovenija," relying more often on "slovenstvo" (Slovene speakers and cultural patrimony), Prešeren nonetheless aimed his works at the united readership of all Slovenes and he held a dim, unsympathetic view of the Habsburg Empire;[11] these two facts combine to make him a nationalist.

Two important works by the scholar Franc Miklošič (1813–1891; also frequently spelled Miklosič) deepen our understanding of the growth of Slovene national consciousness. All things considered, he was closer to Prešeren's emphasis on Slovene consciousness than to Kopitar's emphasis on Slavic consciousness. Miklošič's magisterial work was his four-volume *Vergleichende Grammatik der slavischen Sprachen* (Comparative Grammar of the Slavic Languages), published between 1852 and 1883. This work put the Slovene scholar, who got his PhD in Graz and then went on to a brilliant, wide-ranging academic career which peaked in his position as rector of the University of Vienna, at the front of the ranks of international Slavists. Such massive fame was good for all Slovenes, and all Slavs, as the Croatian politician Jelačić noted when Miklošič was promoted to rector in 1853.[12] The *Grammatik* is an interesting work because it at once reaffirms both the uniqueness of Slovene and its close relationship to other languages. In this latter way, and through his close cooperation with many Serb and Croat scholars as well as through his signing of the Vienna declaration of 1850 endorsing the existence and importance of a common Serbo-Croatian tongue, Miklošič's actions reflect the Illyrian idealism of the early nineteenth century.

The second of his works here under consideration, however, removes all doubt of his political loyalties. In his one foray into politics, during the revolutionary period 1848–1849, Miklošič was co-author of the famous political program *Zedinjena Slovenija* (United Slovenia). This work constitutes the Slovenes' first ever political or nationalist program. Although these were revolutionary times, the document called upon Slovenes to remain loyal to the Habsburg crown, which is a reason Miklošič remained in favor with the Austrian authorities and was eventually even knighted. But *Zedinjena Slovenija* did call for many other far-reaching, modern changes. The first, as the title suggests, was the administrative unity of the Slovene lands. The second was the replacement of German with Slovene as the local language of education and administration. Third, Austria should sever its ties to the German Confederation to its north and west. The Slovenes knew that a modern German liberal state was arising on the ruins of the old Holy Roman Empire (abolished in 1806) and that the Habsburgs were going to be under great pressure to join it. This anti-German stance in the program sounded an important new note in Austroslav Slovene thinking, since earlier thinkers such as Kopitar had concentrated more on the Russian threat.

From the midpoint of the nineteenth century on, there was an increasing amount of unrest among the Slavs of the Habsburg Empire. Although Slovenes played a part in certain key controversies in these decades, the main centers of agitation were elsewhere, among the Czechs, Slovaks, Poles, Croats, and Serbs. The Empire itself faced its greatest threats from increasingly virulent Hungarian particularism, from the Czechs' ever more strident demands for autonomy, from controversies regarding the expansion of suffrage, and, of course, from foreign encroachment (especially from Italy and Germany). The Slovenes played a relatively minor role in the potentially revolutionary movements within the Empire. Ideas of Slavic cooperation and autonomy or independence, such as pan-Slavism, Austroslavism, neo-Slavism, Illyrianism, and Yugoslavism, are explained below in the Slovene context.

In June 1848, delegates at the Slavic Congress in Prague attempted to deal with the centripetal forces coming from several quarters within the Empire. The Hungarians, led by the fiery separatist Lajos Kossuth, wanted to reduce their ties to Vienna simply to a personal union at the level of the crown; radical Germans sought inclusion in the new, unified Germany that was taking shape in the formerly fragmented lands to the north and west of the Habsburg realm. The Slavs themselves were divided on how to react to these developments. On the one hand, the Poles resented the inclusion of the Ruthenians (or Ukrainians, who were present in sizable numbers in the region where Poles had political and economic predominance, Galicia) in the discussions; the Poles also had little objection to Kossuth's separatist plans because they foresaw such an arrangement for themselves in Galicia. The Czechs opposed the Great Austrians (centralists who wanted to hold the Empire together in the face of both German and Slavic nationalisms) because they dearly wanted a sort of third, Slavic center of power based in Prague. On the other hand, though, for the Czechs to support Hungary's anti-centralist drive entailed abandoning large Slavic groups (Slovaks and Croats) to possible Magyarization (Hungarianization). Ultimately, the Slovenes joined in the triumph of Austroslavism, which stressed the significance of unity and cooperation among the Slavs but also recognized the importance of the continued existence of the multinational Habsburg Empire as a bulwark against German expansionism. Their interests meshed with those of the Czechs, Ruthenes, and "Great Austrian" Germans in opposing the separatism of both the Hungarians and the Poles. Like the Croats and the Serbs, the Slovenes remained loyal to the Crown during the revolutionary insurrections of 1848–1849; shortly before the war, the Slovenes in the diets of Carinthia and Styria had even voted to retain the historic provinces rather than carve them up and create bigger all-Slovene units. By 1850, the *status quo ante* had returned to Slovenia. To restore order, the government in Vienna pursued a decade of absolutist policies under Alexander Bach, who was Emperor Franz Josef's "right-hand man for almost all domestic questions."[13] During this period the oft-quoted lament of the South Slavs arose, to the effect that they had been rewarded for their loyalty to the Crown with the same harsh new regime that had been thrust upon the Hungarians for their perfidy.

The 1840s also brought very significant economic change to Slovenia. Feudalism was definitively abolished, and the construction of rail-roads began. The imperial port of Trieste had been a major stimulus to Slovenia's export economy since it was upgraded in 1719, and now Slovenia became linked to Vienna and the rest of the Empire through railways as well as roads. This allowed the traditional non-agricultural pursuits – timber, textiles, iron production, and the mining of silver, coal, mercury, and iron ore – to increase. A Slovene middle class gradually began taking its place next to the German-speakers in the cities. By World War I, the literacy rate was quite high and Ljubljana, with a total population of about 42,000, was half Slovene. Its mayors were regularly Slovene from the 1880s on.

After the "Springtime of Nations" of the 1848 era, the period of Habsburg absolutism shut down most expressions of nationalism and autonomy. For several years in the late 1860s, thousands of Slovenes gath-ered in a series of open-air meetings, called *tabori*, to demonstrate unity and cultural pride and press again the original demands of the United Slovenia program. These gatherings were banned in 1870, and again there was little movement on the Slovene national issue for a decade. It was under the premiership of Edward Taaffe (1879–1893), the so-called "Iron Ring" period, when important concessions were again made to Slovenes. Taaffe was not interested in obliging the national demands of *Zedinjena Slovenija* or any other such program within the Empire. But the Slovenes, along with other Slavic groups, nobles, and clerics, were allied with Taaffe and Emperor Franz Josef (1830–1916) against the rising tide of German nationalism. (This ironically cast the nascent Slovene liberals' lot in largely with conservatives, even though the German nationalists were mostly liberals as well.) The Slovenes benefited at the level of the Parliament in Vienna and also in terms of local administration. But perhaps the most significant gains were in the advances of Slovene as the language of an increasing amount of local education. In areas where Slovenes lived mixed with large numbers of German-speakers, the choice of instructional language often unleashed bitter controversies. This was especially true after secondary schools were created in 1869. Slovenes agitated vigorously for a Slovene-language classical high school (*gimnazija* or *lycée*) in the eastern Slovene town of Celje in the 1890s, precipitating a government crisis in Vienna that brought down their allies, the Taaffe government. It was not until 1905 that Slovene *gimnazije* were approved.

Another vital role in education was played by Anton Martin Slomšek (1800–1862), the Bishop of Maribor. Although earlier Jesuit control over many schools had been abolished in the eighteenth century, there was a great deal of ecclesiastical schooling again by the 1840s. The considerable growth of literacy among the rural population, both boys and girls, and the corresponding growth in national consciousness, owes a great deal to the work of the Catholic Church at this time. In 1842 Slomšek authored a widely used reader for young people, *Blaže in Nežica v nedeljski šoli* (Blaže and Nežica in Sunday School). The Bishop also started a seminary in Slovenia's second city, Maribor, and helped found the Družba svetega Mohorja (Society of St Hermagoras) in Klagenfurt in 1851. This organization, which still exists, promoted literacy, published Slovene works, and tried to supply books to Slovenes in Italy and Austria after the appearance of fascism. The use of Slovene in everything from courts to local elected assemblies varied from region to region, although it enjoyed a status in Austria as one of several "official languages." As a general rule, one can say that by the late 1800s it was more and more widely used across the spectrum of public life, but it never became the language of command in the military; that role continued to fall to German, just as in the Kingdom of Yugoslavia that role would belong only to Serbo-Croatian. Specifically in the domain of education, which vacillated between public and Church control, there was also a gradual expansion of the use of Slovene.

The first Slovene newspaper was *Kmetijske in rokodelske novice* (Agricultural and Handicraft News), guided to prominence after 1843 by its editor, the doctor and veterinarian Janez Bleiweis (1808–1881). An urban counterpart to such rural programs were the reading societies (*čitalnice*), which stimulated national consciousness and political activities as well as literacy in Slovene cities from the 1860s to about 1900. Also figuring prominently in Slovene developments in this era were gymnastics societies and savings and loan associations. The former were really patriotic organizations on the German model and, ironically, they were originally organized to combat Germanization. The *Sokol* (Falcon) was founded in 1863 and became associated with political liberalism; the clericalist *Orel* (Eagle) was founded in 1906. The combined effect of these trends, including the Tabor movement, was to help nationalism develop a mass base. It is instructive to note that by this period, even Slovene immigrants to America were founding cultural groups, mutual aid societies, and publications. In 1894, the Carniolan Slovenian Catholic Union (usually known as KSKJ) was founded, and ten years later the Slovene National Benefit Society (SNPJ) followed. Both groups still exist today. So do a number of other Slovene groups in cities such as Pittsburgh, Cleveland, Chicago, and Indianapolis, as well as newspapers such as the conservative *Ameriška Domovina* (American Home) and the more liberal *Prosveta* (Enlightenment).

In the post-revolutionary period, the Slovenes began to find themselves more often at odds with the central government. The Minister of the Interior, Anton Schmerling, instituted a highly centralized government with the February Patent of 1861. Conservative and clerical forces were united in their desire for a more federalist system, one that would leave more power in outlying regions of the Empire. Other groups in this camp were the conservative German Catholics, Italians, Czechs, and eventually, the Poles. The Slovenes joined the others in walking out of Parliament; the rump assembly was then named "Schmerling's Theater."[14]

The Slovenes stepped up their demands for a separate diet in the 1860s; the Maribor Program was a call, like *Zedinjena Slovenija*, for territorial unity and some degree of autonomy. But the chief concern for Emperor Franz Josef was the Hungarian situation. The *Ausgleich* (Compromise) of 1867 gave the Hungarians a great deal of autonomy; the Austrian and Hungarian parts of the Empire were linked only by the royal family and certain key ministries. These were more or less the demands the Hungarians had made in 1848. In Austria, the Liberals, also the heirs to much of the spirit of 1848, had the majority in Parliament. One of their key actions was to remove schools from clerical control. Freedom of expression for free-thinkers was strengthened and steps were taken to ease tension between various religious groups. Religious instruction for children was also made voluntary. This last step was an effort to augment the strength of the central government in building constructive educational programs; it also purported to reduce Austria's dependence on the "arbitrary pleasure of a foreign power," the Vatican.[15] Clericalists and federalists alike were opposed to this move, and the Slovenes and Poles both found themselves again in opposition to the government.

Slovenes had traditionally been little affected by pan-Slavism, which had been expounded by some Slavic intellectuals in the Empire, especially in Slovakia and the Czech lands, since the early nineteenth century. Pan-Slavism was both a literary and philosophical concept of unity among Slavs and, at the same time, a political belief that Russia would save the Slavic peoples, and indeed all of Western civilization, from Teutonic philistinism and aggression; it had grown in importance throughout the century. In the Great Eastern Crisis in the Balkans of the late 1870s, it flared up with even greater force. When Russia went to war with the Ottoman Turks in April 1877, most of the Slavs of the Empire looked forward to a Russian victory with delight. Owing to their historical animosities with the Russians, how-ever, the Poles were not very enthusiastic about the possibility of a Russian triumph. But the Czechs bestowed a sword of honor upon the Russian gen-eral, M.G. Chernyaev, while the Croats passed resolutions praising the Russian efforts on behalf of the Balkan Slavs. The Serbs of Hungary orga-nized military units under the nobleman Svetozar Stratimirović to fight against the Turks; however, Hungary wanted to go to war against Russia itself, so Stratimirović was arrested and tried for treason. The leader of the Old Czech political party, František Rieger, praised the Russians for battling for grand ideals and raising the dignity of all Slavs. The Slovenes joined in this movement and planned a pro-Bulgarian demonstration in Ljubljana, but the authorities banned it; Austria–Hungary was officially neutral in this war.

The next era of rule in Austria was known as the "Iron Ring" (1879–1893). Franz Josef's chief minister was now Count Edward Taaffe, who sought to form a non-partisan government bloc. He attempted to conciliate the nationalities to a certain extent in an effort to enhance the general feeling of loyalty to the Emperor. The Slovenes emerged as one of his favored groups. Although the Slovene intellectuals' dream of establishing a university in Ljubljana was not realized, Taaffe did see to it that Slovene became a language of instruction in the schools of Ljubljana, the Slovenes' cultural capital. More and more Slovenes were moving into administrative positions and the Carinthian capital Klagenfurt, where Germans outnumbered Slovenes by about eighteen to one, was classified as bilingual for administrative purposes. The effect on German-speakers living in the region was similar to that in Bohemia: they often felt that their culture and the province's efficiency of administration were being harmed by Taaffe's pandering to minority interests.[16]

In 1884 the Society of Saints Cyril and Methodius was formed in the Slovene lands. It was especially active in remote areas and sponsored Slovene-language schools, cultural societies, and economic cooperatives associated with the Tabor movement. In 1888 grammar schools in the Styrian city of Maribor (Marburg in German) introduced Slovene classes. This move did not seriously antagonize the local German population, which did not feel that its cultural superiority in Maribor was in danger. But Slovenes were moving into the cities in ever-greater numbers, gradually changing the traditional population structure of the region, according to which the countryside was largely Slovene and the cities mostly German. What is more, Slovenes began agitating for language rights in the schools of the next major Styrian town to the south, Celje (Cilli in German). This plan met major resistance among German-speakers, who feared that they stood to lose a southern outpost of German culture, since Celje was already much more Slovene than Maribor.[17] The Taaffe government fell in 1893 with the issue unresolved. Debate continued throughout 1894. Finally the *Reichsrat*, or Parliament, passed a bill authorizing the schools in June of 1895. Yet another government tumbled; this was the peak of publicity for the Slovene national issue. Concern over similar issues within the Empire was soon to shift to the Czech lands.

Two things are apparent from the Slovenes' nineteenth-century experiences, however. They came to link the fate of their national program with the spread of the franchise and participation in the parliamentary system in Vienna, messy as it could be; this fact meant that their movement towards claiming (not to mention achieving) self-determination was gradual. Some observers might call this movement patient, but that term implies that the goal of an independent state was already envisioned; one might also be tempted to use the term "modest," but that word implies that greater vigor might have been required. Royal and Titoist Yugoslavia would in some ways fray this connection between nationalism and democracy, but it would re-emerge in Slovene civil society by the 1960s and would play a large role in the breakup of socialist Yugoslavia. Second is the equally enduring connection in the Slovene mind between language and freedom. As two leading American historians of Slovenia have noted, Serbian or Croatian dominance "was just as deadly as succumbing to Germanization . . . a very worrisome fact of life for Slovenes in Austria. In either case, Slovene culture was threatened, resulting potentially in national extinction."[18] This starkly expressed and visceral preoccupation is also discussed further in the section on Oton Župančič below, but it was prominent in the 1980s and 1990s as well.

There were other literary works that helped mold the Slovene national consciousness as well. Janez Trdina (1830–1905) produced prose steeped in historical and folkloric themes. Fran Levstik (1831–1887) wrote a famous novella entitled *Martin Krpan*. This 1858 story, based on a folk tale, become a favorite of young readers across the Balkans but, of course, it deals with very serious themes. The story revolves around a powerful and huge Slovene peasant and his rocky relationship with the Emperor and his court; like Cankar's *Hlapec Jernej* of a half-century later, the metaphor here is one of humiliation and exploitation of the Slovene nation. It can be argued that Levstik's programmatic writings, even though he was not a political conservative, in some measure helped to condemn later Slovene writers to working on themes of localized, traditional "village" prose; certainly it took Slovene literature a long time to move its central focus from idealizations of peasant life to naturalistic analysis and interactions with the broader world. The writings of Prežihov Voranc, Oton Župančič, and Ivan Cankar were instrumental in furthering this process, which gained considerably in momentum as the twentieth century progressed. But Levstik's pedagogic and political contributions were significant, and it is also interesting to note that he encouraged other writers to treat themes from the period of warfare against the Ottoman Empire, a period in which "the Slovenes acted more independently than they ever have, before or since."[19]

In 1866 the first Slovene novel appeared. This work was *Deseti brat* (The Tenth Brother) by Josip Jurčič (1844–1881). It was a Romantic tale of village life with many folk motifs. Since the novel has been the dominant mode of modern writing, its introduction into a new culture is an important milestone for any language or national group; novels also provide the vehicle for exploration of important social and political problems, and they function as a kind of international "currency" of culture, representing one nation to another.

Jurčič was also a co-founder of the premier Slovene literary review of the nineteenth century, the *Ljubljanski Zvon* (Ljubljana Bell), in 1881. The journal was a vehicle for modern, post-Romantic tendencies and its list of editors and contributors reads like a "Who's Who" of Slovene culture in the period. It also ran articles on art criticism and, later, other topics from the humanities and social sciences, thereby greatly contributing to the modern consciousness of the Slovene nation. Ivan Tavčar, Ivan Cankar, Oton Župančič, and Srečko Kosovel were just a few of the eminent contributors. In September 1932, this journal would become a kind of vehicle for the Slovene national program. An essay on the *slovenstvo* of visiting American writer Louis Adamič (see below) unleashed a storm of discussion over Slovene national identity, the preservation of the language, the role of religion, etc. The pro-Yugoslav publisher refused to release the next issue, containing reactions to Župančič's essay. After some editorial and thematic shifts, the journal remained influential until it disappeared after the occupation of 1941.

The late Habsburg cultural scene was graced by the highly regarded and enduringly popular poet Oton Župančič (1878–1949), who struck a unique, prescient, and, perhaps, precarious balance in his works between cosmopolitanism and nationalism. On the one hand, Župančič was a convinced and successful modernist, in touch with pan-European trends and eager to push for their acceptance by other Slovene artists. But he was also extremely patriotic in terms of his deep personal love of his homeland and his preoccupation with it in many of his works. In "Duma," a sophisticated poem from 1908, Župančič combines graceful, poignant, "female" praise for the natural and familial beauty of Slovenia with anxiety over the fate of "male" emigrants who labor in mines abroad and under the "alien sky" of Germany and America. There is a third voice, a lusty, earthy Whitmanesque "soul" which has imbibed both the "delights" and the "miseries" of the native land.

The poem certainly contains praise for the broader world – in the urban and urbane fashion characteristic of Župančič – as in the lines:

> Here, here life's veins meet,
> The ways of the universe criss-cross here,
> I love them with their noise and sound, these great cities –
> The path to freedom goes through them, through them goes the path
>   to the future[20]

The main point of the work, though, rising above the embodied contradictions and varied voices or perspectives, is that the homeland is "holy." Thus, the poet rues the isolation of the Slovenes who have moved abroad; they will forget what the homeland means and will never return because they are "seduced by foreign glory."[21] Words such as "deracination" and "depopulation" are often used by critics to describe the state of Slovenia in the period of "Duma." Thus, Župančič's love of homeland is augmented by a growing sense of crisis on the eve of the Great War. Discussion of Župančič's concern with the preservation of *slovenstvo* (Slovenian culture and its imprint on the individual) is addressed below in the essay on Louis Adamič.

Another of the truly towering figures of Slovene literature was Ivan Cankar (1876–1918). He was one of the chief figures in the period of the

Moderna, an umbrella concept embracing Impressionism, Expressionism, and other movements in Slovenia. Taken together with the poetry of Lili Novy, Alojz Gradnik, Dragotin Kette, and Josip Murn and the paintings of Ivana Kobilca, Anton Ažbe, and others, this period before and after the Great War probably represents the golden age of Slovene high culture. Cankar was an extremely prolific writer of prose, drama, poetry, and essays. Many of his works drew the ire of conservative critics in his day, on account both of their sensuality and their progressive politics. But today Cankar is celebrated as a national treasure (and the leading cultural institution in downtown Ljubljana bears his name) due to his immense productivity, his openness to European trends, and his defense of Slovenia's cultural distinctness. This popularity comes despite the facts that the mood in many of his works is pessimistic and that his ideas of "Yugoslavist" political cooperation strike most Slovenes today as superannuated.

Two of Cankar's political statements are of special importance. In 1913 he wrote the essay "How I Became a Socialist." This piece is not only a poignant and articulate case study of the multifaceted appeal of socialism,[22] but its perception of injustice and advocacy of activism lay the foundation for Cankar's national views. As a student, Cankar found politics to be both distant and disgusting, and, in the last analysis, merely a distraction from the world of poetry. He attributes much of the blame for the quietest attitude to the Slovene school system, whose job it was to produce bureaucrats and automatons, and to the bland, undifferentiated "omelette" – presenting people with no real options – that was the Slovene political scene. Gradually he awoke, however, to the social misery of capitalism that he saw around him in the working-class district of Vienna where he lived. Awareness of this misery was linked from the very beginning to a profound antipathy for the lack of confidence and progressive ideas specifically of Slovenia's political leadership. He learned to combine literature and politics. He built on his visceral reaction to the current state of affairs by intellectual study. "Science and history," he wrote, "only provided me with the conclusive proof of what life itself had told me."[23] He also, without fail, combined his opposition to both social and national injustice, two concerns he also memorialized in his widely translated short novel *The Bailiff Yerney and His Rights*.

It is national injustice and the political future of Slovenia that are the topics of Cankar's most famous nonfiction work, a speech he gave in Ljubljana on April 12, entitled "Slovenes and Yugoslavs." This speech, highly dramatic in composition and incendiary in ideas, resulted in Cankar's brief arrest; he would face renewed imprisonment during the Great War. He noted that Austria–Hungary had forfeited its right to Slovenia's loyalty by denying it the basic rights of unification of lands and contact with other South Slavs, by keeping Slovenes in poverty and underdevelopment, by exposing them to assimilation, and by acting as a factotum for German imperialism in the Balkans. He made a very clear and courageous call for political unification, not just of Slovene lands, but of the combined Slovene lands with those of their South Slavic cousins. Hence, Cankar is a clear Yugoslavist and has rejected the Illyrianist idea – popular both in the 1830s and again in his day – of limited South Slavic cooperation under the Habsburg scepter. Although he derides Illyrianism as cowardice (in terms similar to those he uses to characterize the Slovene bourgeoisie in the first essay), he makes it very clear that his radicalism does not extend to the mistaken notion that Slovenes should be subsumed into any of the larger Slovene national groups or into a new Yugoslav identity, partly because none of the other groups is offering itself for such a process, either. Over and over he says that the important linguistic and cultural questions remain *Slovene* ones; only in political terms is Yugoslavism an option.

Cankar gave this talk just after the astounding Serbian and Bulgarian victories over the Ottoman Empire in the First Balkan War. A small group of students and the newspaper *Preporod* (Renaissance) were the only voices in Slovenia to echo Cankar's Yugoslav enthusiasm at this point. Slovenes were rejoicing at the Slavic victories, he reported, although they regretted the great bloodshed and wanted to remind the world that it could have been avoided if the great powers, especially Austria–Hungary, had taken a more active and fairer role in settling the national issue in the Balkans. Although Slovenia was weak compared to Serbia, their self-confidence was now growing and it was time for Austria–Hungary to take note that they were "a limb of a great family, which lives from the Julian Alps to the Aegean Sea."[24] This was the "Yugoslav Easter," meaning the resurrection of its peoples, or "tribes," which included Serbs, Croats, and Bulgarians as well as Slovenes. But not only was this Yugoslavism "exclusively a political issue" and a "political goal"[25] – among cousins, not brothers (and sisters) – but Cankar reminded his listeners in emphatic terms that this Yugoslavism entailed equal rights and equal powers for all equally valued members. Thus, Cankar crystallized both the hopes and the contradictions of most Slovene nationalists throughout both iterations of the future Yugoslav state.

In one of his most poignant poems, Cankar builds a parallel to his argument for the acceptance of Slovene equality. It is time, learns the reader, that Slovenia simply receive its due from the world of nation-states. The narrator in this untitled poem, usually known just by its first line ("They ride in rich carriages . . ."), is a poor debauchee who casts envious glances at rich libertines riding through town. He wonders how God can justify rewarding some sinners with wealth while letting others – equally sinful – languish in poverty. The reproach of the narrator is "As to others, so to me also!" Analyzed in the light of nationalism, Cankar cannot thus be accused of too much idealism; the behavior of nation-states and the politics of Slovenes might be corrupt but one must recognize in the speaker the strong proponent of the right to self-determination. In Cankar's work, we see Slovenes putting forth ever more concrete ideas of what it will mean to get "their place in the sun."

The early twentieth century brought more unrest to Slovenia. In 1905 the representatives to the Italian Parliament made reference to "our Trieste" and Italian irredentists sent money to Italians in that city, who then won local elections. These moves greatly disturbed the Slovenes, who felt Italian pressure mounting on their southern flank. The cabinet in Vienna also feared other Italian designs in the Balkans, such as the consideration of the Albanian port of Valona (Vlorë) as the Italian Calais, nicely complementing Italy's "Dover," Brindisi; these cities were used for the economic and cultural penetration of Albania. Italian theaters also showed plays with irredentist themes.[26] In 1908, at the time of the annexation of Bosnia, there was a week of confrontations in Slovenia, some of them violent, between police and demonstrators protesting Vienna's imperialism;[27] Slovene parliamentarians assaulted each other, sometimes with hydrogen-sulfide bombs; and Franz Josef refused to approve the fourth re-election of the pan-Slav mayor of Ljubljana.

A final note on the growth of Slovene political parties is in order. The Austrian sections of the Empire, where Slovenes lived, received universal male suffrage in 1907. The gradual extension of the right to vote had had two effects: Slovene representation in the parliament in Vienna grew, on the one hand, and political parties with different ideologies and platforms began to form in the Slovene lands and compete for the support of voters. The dominant party was formed in the early 1890s and was commonly called the Clericalist Party. The actual name of this conservative, Catholic group was the *Slovenska ljudska stranka* (Slovene People's Party) after 1905. The SLS, as it was known, stood for a close relationship with Vienna because it disliked German nationalism (of the time in Bismarck's Protestant-dominated Germany) and the growth of Serbian power in the Balkans; most of its members were thus very cool towards Yugoslav ideas. Its most famous figure was Monsignor Anton Korošec, who rose to prominence during World War I and subsequently became a major player in Yugoslav politics. But its somewhat earlier leaders included the conservatives Ivan Šušteršič, a lawyer; Anton Jeglič, the Bishop of Ljubljana; Karel Klun; and Fr. Anton Mahnič. A more liberal wing that ended up having a profound effect was led by Janez Krek, who differed from many in his party by being pro-Yugoslav and also very active in promoting labor unions and peasants' cooperatives. His minority position on cooperation with other South Slavic groups would eventually win out during the Great War, as we will see below. Meanwhile, Slovenes founded a Liberal Party in 1891, centered on the professional and middle classes in urban areas; distrust of great German nationalism made the Liberals well-disposed towards cooperation with other South Slavs inside and outside the Empire. In 1896 a socialist party was founded. Its leading figure was Etbin Kristan. It was eventually known as the Yugoslav Social Democratic Party, giving a good clue as to its internationalist positions; among other things, it was Austroslav and Yugoslav because its Marxist theoreticians held that larger states move more quickly along the dialectical path of economic and socio-political development. The socialists were strongest in the country's many mining areas and in the major cities of Trieste and Ljubljana.

One of the earliest activists for women's rights in the Slovene lands was Zofka Kveder (1878–1926). She was a newspaper editor and an author of several novels and volumes of sketches, notably *The Mystery of Woman* (1900). The first women's organization in the Slovene lands, founded in 1887, was the Slovene Teachers' Society. It was followed by several publications and then the major women's group in the entire period up to World War II: the *Splošno žensko društvo* (General Women's Society). Many of its members, such as Minka Govekar and Alojzija Štebi, advocated suffrage for women, but this was opposed by both major political parties. The conservative Clericals thought that women did not belong in politics, while the Liberals assumed that women – like peasants – would vote Conservative if they had the vote. The most productive area of public activity for politically minded women at the time was the field of Slovene national rights.[28] Later, some women were also active in workers', or proletarian, movements.

Slovenia in the Great War

World War I, or the Great War, as it is also called, marks an obvious turning point in Slovene history. As a result of this war, the Habsburg Empire would disappear from the map of Europe. Slovenia would not become independent as a result, but the contemporary mood and demands of nationalism, formulated as the "self-determination of nations," provided for Slovene accession to a South Slavic state inhabited mostly by closely related peoples such as Serbs and Croats. In addition, the war brought a clamoring for popular sovereignty and a sense of empowerment through military action to the masses of nearly all the countries that participated in it, including the colonies of the British and French. Before turning to the heady and controversial events of 1918, the year in which the new country of Yugoslavia was born, it is necessary to get a picture of what life was like for Slovenes during the war years.

In terms of the Habsburg army, Slovenes, like the Empire's other national minorities, served loyally throughout the war. The Habsburg military has a bad reputation to this day. Disasters on the Eastern Front against the ill-prepared Russian army played a key role in this reputation, but so did the agitation of many foes of the Austrian Empire who have exaggerated the rebelliousness of the national groups within its armed forces. The Austrians suffer, too, by comparison with the storied military prowess of their German allies; famous novels, such as Jaroslav Hašek's *The Good Soldier Schweik* – supposedly pacifistic but really more of an endorsement of individual contrariness and cynicism – have done little to enhance the Habsburgs' military reputation.

Most scholars, however, believe that it is a tribute to the Habsburg army that it held together as long as it did, given the pressure on the country from within and without. In terms of its armaments, other equipment, and numbers, the military actually grew stronger throughout the war. It is the ethnic composition of the army that has attracted the most attention of scholars, some of whom have assumed that its diversity must have led to its weakness. Like the general population of the Empire, there were ten major national groups represented in the army. Their ethnic identification did not, in actuality, translate into disloyalty to the government, although in many of their home regions separatist tendencies increased throughout the war. The diversity of the Habsburg Empire was almost mind-boggling, as the nationality statistics for the armed forces and the general population show. Slovenes made up only 2.6 percent of the Habsburg military, but they also comprised only 2.6 percent of the general population of about 52 million. The Habsburg military achieved a fairly even distribution of nationalities in its ranks. The following are the overall population statistics from the well-known 1910 census: Austrians (German-speakers), 23.9 percent; Hungarians, 20.2 percent: Czechs, 12.6 percent; Poles, 10 percent; Ruthenians (Ukrainians), 7.9 percent; Serbs and Croats, 9.1 percent; Romanians, 6.4 percent; Slovaks, 3.8 percent; and Italians, 2 percent. The casualty distribution was not to be even, however. The Empire mobilized nearly eight million men over the course of the war, of whom over one million lost their lives. The Slovenes lost tens of thousands of dead, reportedly the highest percentage of any nationality in the army.

Although the multinational army was not disloyal, its ethnic composition did affect policy in some other ways. There were some prominent figures in the high command, such as the Chief of Staff Conrad von Hötzendorff, who calculated that the Empire needed to get into a decisive war against Serbia quickly before the fault lines in the military deepened. The army also thought it best to deploy many units close to their home regions, for the sake of morale, although German, Hungarian, and Bosnian units were posted freely to various areas. By early 1917, in addition, commanders were trying to mix medium-sized units of various nationalities, with the aim of limiting the disaffection or disorder that might originate in large units of a single nationality. Although there were some problems with Czech troops throughout the war, both the French and the Russian armies had far greater problems with desertion and rebellion.

The Slovenes remained largely loyal to the government in Vienna during World War I. Their leading politician, the clericalist Anton Korošec of the SLS, promised loyalty to the death in 1914; the diet of Carniola, with Slovenes voting in support, condemned the activities of the Yugoslav movement, under the leadership of the Dalmatian politician Ante Trumbić, as treason.[29] When rumors began to spread in 1915 that the Allies had made significant territorial promises to Italy in hopes of bringing it into the fight against the Central Powers, Korošec and other Clerical leaders, such as

Ivan Šušteršič and Janez Krek, again expressed their hope that the Empire would protect them from Italian expansion.[30]

After the death of the tenacious and venerable Kaiser Franz Josef in late 1916, loyalty to the Empire began to weaken. This trend was bolstered, of course, by great material hardship, the poor leadership of several prominent generals, and the bloody inconclusiveness of the course of the war itself. The early successes on the Italian front were cancelled out by disasters against the Russians, and, by the summer of 1918, the army did begin to disintegrate. Large-scale problems emerged after the new emperor, Karl, announced that the country's subject nationalities had the right to seek independence and as the Italians finally breached the line along the Soča (Isonzo) river in the west. By 1918, the Habsburg Empire had five million men under colors at one time, but mutinies were beginning to occur. In that year, Slovene forces bound for the Russian front rebelled at Judenburg and other places in southern Austria, and South Slavic sailors, mostly Croats but including some Slovenes, mutinied at the prominent naval base of Boka Kotorska. Earlier in the war, numbers of Slovenes of fighting age had slipped across the border to join Serb forces, and many former prisoners of war in Russia – including the half-Slovene Josip Broz, the future Tito who would later rule Yugoslavia for over thirty years – joined the Bolshevik forces after the fall of the Tsarist regime.

This colossal war effort had a significant impact on the Slovene lands. The sense of urgency on the home front began right away, because Habsburg authorities imprisoned or executed hundreds of Slovenes whom they considered security threats; prominent writers, such as Cankar and the long-time Austrian civil servant Franc Maselj-Podlimbarski, were not excepted; even harsher measures were taken against Bosnian Serbs. Then the war against Italy, which started in 1915 when the Italians joined the Allies, heated up the home front even more because it took place on traditional Slovene territory. There was a consciousness among all the South Slavic soldiers of the Empire that the area along the Soča was "Slav earth"[31] and that they were fighting to protect their homelands from an expansionist Italy which had territorial designs on both Slovenia and Dalmatia (which was inhabited by Croats and Serbs). The Italians, not surprisingly, stressed the Italian essence of the city of Trieste and even of other coastal areas to its south, where Italians lived only in small numbers but where Italian (and before it, Venetian and Roman) cultural and economic influence had long been important. The Austrian province bordering Italy and the Adriatic was known as the *Küstenland* (the Littoral), and its population was 46 percent Italian, 31 percent Slovene, 21 percent Croat, and 2 percent German-speaking.

In the summer of 1915, the Italians struck at Austrian positions along the Soča river four times; in March 1916 the fighting started up again and lasted until late fall, with five more bloody but inconclusive "Battles of the Isonzo" taking place. In 1917, after two more Italian offensives, the

Austrians, reinforced by powerful German forces, struck hard at the town of Caporetto (Kobarid in Slovene) and managed a quick and decisive breakthrough on October 24. Tens of thousands of Italians were killed and over 200,000 were taken prisoner, and the Austrian and German forces pushed back the Italians almost to Venice. There the line stabilized for about a year; towards the end of the war, another Austrian offensive failed and the Italians began to recapture territory rapidly.

The long series of battles along the border had a significant effect on Slovenia. Of course many Slovenes died in the fighting; almost two-thirds of Austria–Hungary's casualties in the war occurred on this front. About 80,000 Slovene civilians were evacuated from the region as well, spending the remainder of the war in other parts of Slovenia or in refugee camps near Vienna.[32] A highly regarded Austrian poet, Franz Janowitz, died in the fighting here, and on the Italian side an even more famous poet, Scipio Slataper – born in Trieste to a mixed Slavic-Italian family – also fell. The American writer Ernest Hemingway, who was volunteering as an ambulance driver for the Italians, wrote his famous novel *A Farewell to Arms* about the fighting on this front as well. The writer Prežihov Voranc (born Lovro Kuhar, 1893–1950), who fought on that same front, later wrote an important anti-war novel entitled *Doberdob*, describing the life of Slovene soldiers. Other well-known Slovene works about the Great War include the novels *Hanka* by Zofka Kveder, *Prerokovana* by Fran Saleški Finžgar, and *Rdeči gardist* (The Red Guard) by Miško Kranjec, various short stories by France Bevk and Ivan Cankar, and the play *Kreature* (Creatures) by Bratko Kreft.[33]

By May 1917, a major mood shift was apparent in Slovene politics. All thirty-three parliamentary delegates in Vienna representing the South Slavic peoples of the Empire signed a declaration calling for their territorial unity and autonomy. Of course, the resolution did not pass the full parliament, but this represented a significant change of course for the Slovene Clericals. The door was now open for the Slovenes to cooperate fully with a body known as the Yugoslav Committee, which had been formed in November 1914 by both Croats and Serbs from the Habsburg Empire. This group, which included the famous Croatian politicians Ante Trumbić and Frano Supilo from Dalmatia as well as the sculptor Ivan Meštrović, had little credibility among Slovenes until late in the war, partly because its Slovene members were little-known figures such as Bogumil Vošnjak. Public demonstrations in Ljubljana, of an anti-Habsburg and pro-Yugoslav nature, also increased.

Trialism, the view that the Slavs of the Dual Monarchy should form a third internal power bloc as a counterweight to the Austrian and Hungarian administrative regions created in 1867, was essentially a domestic variant of Yugoslavism, which called for various kinds of cultural and political cooperation just among the South Slavs, either inside or beyond the Empire. Trialism among Slovenes and Croats gradually widened to include other Slavs such as the Czechs and Slovaks; but still, for most of the war, solutions were to be sought within the Habsburg framework. If only for patriotic and legal reasons, this was the approach of most Slovene intellectuals of the time. As the end of the war drew near, the conviction that the Habsburg Empire was going down in defeat grew, and this pushed ever more Slovenes, Croats, and Serbs into an "external" variant of Yugoslavism.

This was symbolized by the Corfu pact of July 1917, which united the Yugoslav Committee and the Serbian Prime Minister-in-exile Nikola Pašič in the effort to unite the South Slavs in an independent state. A Czech professor, Thomas Masaryk, who was a leading figure in winning international support for another new Slavic country, Czechoslovakia, also supported the idea of a "Yugoslavia," or Land of the South Slavs, as the term literally signifies. Unfortunately, key questions such as the relationship of Serbs, Croats, and other Slavic and non-Slavic nationalities on important issues such as language, cultural amalgamation, military affairs, and power-sharing within the federal structure were not resolved in advance, neither at the time of the Corfu Declaration nor when the state of Yugoslavia was proclaimed the next year. They would plague the new country throughout the interwar period. There were in place simply general statements of principle and a commitment to hold a constitutional convention to create the actual mechanisms of the state. The chief principles approved at Corfu, and embodied in later proclamations, were the equality of the three main South Slavic groups (no acknowledgment was made of the wishes or even identity of the Montenegrins, Bosnians, and Macedonians, not to mention non-Slavic peoples such as the Albanians of Kosovo), their essential unity, and the need for a constitutional monarchy under the current Serbian royal family, the Karađorđevićes. The Allies balked at these plans until January 1918, but then accepted the basic ideas of Yugoslavia and Czechoslovakia, ensuring that the Habsburg Empire would fully disappear at war's end.

As the Austrian government gradually lost control of its country, self-rule in terms of more or less day-to-day administration devolved onto the Slovene lands in October 1918. Korošec then steered Slovenia into a provisional government in Zagreb called the *Narodno Vijeće*, or National Council; it represented the South Slavic peoples of the crumbling Habsburg Empire. Also in October, in other parts of the Empire, a Czech government more or less began functioning in Prague, German-speakers declared their intention to create a new nation-state of Austria, and Hungary seceded altogether. The last gasp of the 650-year-old Empire came on October 16, when Emperor Charles proposed turning it into a federative state for the various national groups. On November 7, 1918, four days after Austria surrendered to the Allies, Korošec, acting on behalf of the National Council, signed an agreement with the Yugoslav Committee and Prime Minister Pašić of Serbia to approve the creation of a new country. Finally, on December 1,

Prince Regent Alexander of Serbia proclaimed the existence of the Kingdom of Serbs, Croats, and Slovenes. A vastly different historical epoch had now begun, with the voluntary association of Slovenes and their Balkan cousins in the hopes of achieving national self-determination replacing a medieval dynastic principle.

2 Slovenia in the two Yugoslav states

Slovenia in the interwar period

Although the interwar period was filled with controversy and unfulfilled potential, the new state of Yugoslavia (Kingdom of Serbs, Croats, and Slovenes until 1929) brought some benefits to Slovenes. In this period, there were about one million Slovenes, comprising 8.5 percent of Yugoslavia's ten million people. The country was 39 percent Serbs and Montenegrins and 24 percent Croats; Bosnian Muslims, Macedonians, Albanians, Hungarians, and other smaller nationalities received far fewer rights than the three biggest Slavic groups. A major issue for Slovenes right away was the disposition of their co-nationals in Italy and Austria. A plebiscite in the Austrian province of Carinthia in July 1920 determined that the border drawn at the Paris Peace Conference the year before would remain; in November 1920, the Treaty of Rapallo made permanent the Conference's decision to assign the Julian March (*Julijska krajina*), including the major cities of Trieste and Gorica, the Istrian peninsula, and northern Dalmatia to Italy. After the governments of Mussolini and Hitler came to power in those countries, Slovenes in Yugoslavia were greatly concerned over their political victimization and cultural persecution. The predatory Italian policies created support among Slovenes both for the Yugoslav idea and for the Communist Party, which emerged in the 1930s as the staunchest defender of that idea.

On the positive side of the ledger, Slovenes were protected from revanchist sentiments in Austria and Italy, the Slovene language was in official use, Slovene areas continued to live under their old Habsburg law code, their judicial system was reasonably fair and representative, Catholicism was given equal rights with Serbian Orthodoxy, and a concordat with the Vatican was even signed. King Aleksandar seemed serious about Yugoslavism, even though the whole country continued debating exactly what it meant: he gave his first son a family name, Petar, but then named his other two children Tomislav and Andrej to please his Croatian and Slovene subjects. Furthermore, industrial capacity expanded; the Slovene Academy of Arts and Sciences (SAZU) was established, as were the National

Gallery, an important scholarly institute devoted to Slovene minorities abroad, a radio network, and the first university, in Ljubljana; and communal assemblies (elected bodies in certain regions) were allowed some leeway for local self-rule in Maribor and Ljubljana. Monsignor Anton Korošec, though sometimes controversial, led the SLS to repeated electoral victories and was thus able to play a major role at the federal level in Belgrade. He was the only non-Serbian Prime Minister in the entire interwar period. By maneuvering his political machine in and out of coalitions necessitated mostly by the confrontational policies of the Croatian Peasant Party, he and some other regional figures – most notably the Bosnian leader Mehmet Spaho – engaged in enough horse-trading to win royal favor or at least benign neglect.

These must, of course, be weighed against the drawbacks of the twenty-three years under the Serbian Karađorđević monarchy. The Vidovdan Constitution of 1921, for instance, vexingly referred to the three main nations of Yugoslavia as constituent "tribes" of one "three-named people"; even though local affairs continued to be conducted in Slovene, the central government's emphasis on "unitarist" Yugoslav culture, by which it usually meant Greater Serbian culture, grew much more pronounced and threatening during the 1930s. In the 1920s the art historian Izidor Cankar and the famous painter Rihard Jakopič had already defended the distinctiveness and importance of a specifically Slovene culture in the face of external enthusiasm for new pan-Yugoslav ideas. Indeed, few Slovenes had ever desired either the assimilation of their language and culture into Serbian or Croatian or their amalgamation into a new mix; Slovenes understood Yugoslavism, in both its political and cultural variants, as more a matter of solidarity and affinity rather than identity. In 1932 the literary critic Josip Vidmar issued yet another resolute defense of an independent Slovenian culture with his book *Kulturni problem slovenstva* (The Cultural Issue of Slovenianness).

But another major problem in the 1920s was that no Slovene territorial unit was allowed. This signified the frustration of one of the most cherished nationalist goals since 1848. Obviously the more than 300,000 Slovenes living in Italy were not part of Yugoslavia, nor were the over 50,000 in Austria; but King Aleksandar also carved up the traditional territorial divisions inside the country and reallocated them among thirty-three new provinces. The borders were gerrymandered so that most areas had a Serbian majority. The territorial system for Slovenes, but not for the other groups, improved somewhat in the 1930s, when the King instituted a system of nine new provinces called *banovine*; these were designed to make economic sense and to split up Croatia even further, thereby promoting his vision of Yugoslav unity. Most Slovene areas were grouped together in the region called "Dravska."

Other problems included the unfair initial exchange rate for Habsburg currency; the Slovene perception that lower wages in southern cities such as Niš, Skopje, and Sarajevo hurt their industrial competitiveness; Serbian control of the army, police, and the offices of prefect (governor) in the thirty-three provinces; a transportation network that still tied Slovenia to Austria and Italy, not to the rest of Yugoslavia; lack of support for agricultural development which led to rural overpopulation and emigration; and the abolition of the patriotic organizations called *Sokols* in 1929. Unsavory business and governmental practices in Belgrade also alienated Slovenes: a "tightly knit clique of Belgrade financiers and businessmen" called the *čaršija* grew increasingly corrupt, while cabinet ministers – nearly all Serbs – made it easy for themselves to get comfortable pensions and kickbacks.[1] After the assassination of three Croatian deputies in Parliament in 1928, the King cancelled the 1921 Constitution and instituted an increasingly arbitrary and paranoid dictatorship; at the very least his insistence on more unitarist policies at the expense of federalism burdened the 1930s with more conflicts than the 1920s. Still, it could be argued that the biggest problems faced by the first Yugoslavia emerged right at its founding. Politicians like Serbia's Nikola Pašić and Croatia's Stjepan Radić were not up to the task of hammering out a workable power-sharing arrangement for the country; the former was used to steamrolling all opposition and the latter boycotted key proceedings and thus denied Croatia a voice at a key time.

To look more closely at some of the country's problems from the Slovene point of view, one can begin with foreign policy issues. Slovenes were forced to accept the losses to Italy and Austria of certain regions with strong Slovene-speaking minorities or even local majorities. In Istria, Dalmatia, the *Julijska Krajina* (Julian Alps or Julian March), and *Beneška Slovenija* (Venetian Slovenia), over 300,000 Slovenes and Croats came under Italian rule after World War I.[2] The Italian annexations arose largely from arrangements the Allies had made in 1915 in the secret Treaty of London, designed to ensure Rome's participation in the war on the Allied side. The claims to Dalmatia arising from this treaty were reduced somewhat in a compromise brokered by US President Wilson, but the Italians still controlled Zadar, its hinterland, and the islands of Cres, Veli and Mali Lošinj, Palagruža, and Lastovo. They also annexed the city of Rijeka (Fiume), after it was seized by an armed band led by Gabriele D'Annunzio, an Italian nationalist poet and political extremist.

This settlement was sealed in November 1920 by the Treaty of Rapallo. The one-sided territorial dispensation was followed by Italy's refusal to guarantee minority rights to its Slavs, although the Yugoslavs were forced to give such guarantees to their considerably smaller Italian population. After Benito Mussolini came to power in 1922, the Italian Slavs were also subjected to harsh Italianization measures.[3]

The other large Slovene setback in the arena of foreign policy occurred in the southern Austrian province of Carinthia (German *Kärnten*; Slovene *Koroško*). This region was one of the traditional units of the Habsburg *Erblande* which had a sizeable Slovene population. The neighboring state of Styria (German *Steiermark*; Slovene *Štajersko*) was split, with the southern half, including the regional hub of Maribor, awarded to the new Yugoslavia. But when Yugoslav troops occupied Carinthia, including its capital of Klagenfurt (Celovec in Slovene) after the war, the local government declared its allegiance to Austria. North of the border, Slovene- and German-speakers lived intermixed in many areas; the major cities of Villach (Beljak in Slovene) and Klagenfurt had a majority of German-speakers but also many Slovenes and they figured prominently in Slovene cultural life and their Slovene names are still used by all Slovenes today, inside and outside of Austria. The claims of the German-speaking population were backed up by the *Landwehr*, or local militia. An end to the stalemate was provided by the peace treaty for Austria, the Treaty of Saint Germain, which was signed in September 1919. Southern Carinthia was divided into two zones and a plebiscite was scheduled by Allied authorities and agreed to by the Austrians. The first, Zone A, had a Slovene majority. On October 10, 1920, this region voted by a ratio of 60 percent to 40 percent to remain in Austria; the plebiscite in Zone B, which included Klagenfurt, was then deemed unnecessary. The Yugoslavs were stunned, alleged fraud, and briefly invaded the area. But Great Power pressure soon forced the Yugoslavs to accept a boundary along the southern rim of the region, running through the Karawanken mountains. A significant Slovene population remains to this day in Kärnten, with smaller numbers in the neighboring Austrian state of Steiermark as well.

In the interwar period (1918–1939), Slovenes were unsuccessful in obtaining officially recognized cultural autonomy in Austria. They did, however, maintain their own organization, the "Political and Economic Association of Carinthian Slovenes." Some of their German-speaking Austrian neighbors were drawn to the Kärntner Heimatdienst, or the "Patriotic League of Carinthia," which pursued a German nationalistic agenda.[4] Slovenes were guaranteed two seats in the Carinthian *Landtag* (provincial assembly), but their political power was minimal.

The second set of issues that bears more exploration is the confused domestic situation in the new Yugoslavia. As British historian Fred Singleton has noted, the country faced massive problems of integration and consolidation because:

> [t]here were six customs areas, five currencies, four railway networks, three banking systems, and even, for a time, two governments until the Narodno Vijeće [National Council] in Zagreb and the Serbian government in Belgrade were merged into a single authority.[5]

The Slovenes made up 8.5 percent (1,019,997) of the total Yugoslav population in 1921. They held certain advantages over other regions of the country, such as a relatively low illiteracy rate of 9 percent, whereas the national average was about 50 percent. They also had the reputation of working with a sense of order that was "Central European" in nature, and for this reason they were valued by Belgrade as administrators.[6] In addition, relatively few non-Slovene bureaucrats were posted in Slovenia; the Serbian ruling circles did not feel as competitive with or as threatened by the Slovenes as they did by the Croatians and the national minorities on their own territory. This was because the Slovene language was indubitably distinct from both Serbian and Croatian, and because the Slovenes were several steps removed from the increasingly rancorous Serb–Croat territorial disputes in Croatia and Bosnia and their divisions over national and cultural issues such as the proper nature of the literary and political language.

There were, however, many domestic problems in interwar Yugoslavia. The most significant of these arose from the Serb–Croat rivalry, which was the moving force behind much of the country's internal politics. As the resentment between these two large groups sharpened and then culminated in the 1928 murder of Stjepan Radić, the leader of the Croat Peasant Party, the Slovenes attempted to immunize themselves from direct confrontation with the Serb central authorities by entering various coalitions in support of the Belgrade regimes. Other members of these coalitions included Muslims from Bosnia and the Sandžak region, Serb Radicals, and Serb Democrats. The Slovene leader of the time, Korošec, was able to secure some degree of autonomy for Slovenia in the first interwar decade. In fact, the Slovenes were able to make good use of their abilities as parliamentary bargainers from the Habsburg era to secure a degree of administrative "overprivilege" for themselves.[7]

Slovene agriculture was among the best developed in the country. Along with Slavonia and Vojvodina, Slovenia also had an effective system of agricultural cooperatives, which helped peasants gain access to modern equipment and supplied them with farming information and loans. But, in general, Yugoslav agriculture suffered from a great deal of surplus labor, with at least 44 percent overpopulation in the countryside. Peasants were often mistrustful of government intervention into their lives, since many of them conceived of officialdom as something alien and predatory. At any rate, government investment was pitifully low. In a country in which 79 percent of the population in 1921 earned its livelihood through agricultural pursuits, the government devoted only a little more than 1 percent of its budget to the Ministry of Agriculture. Shortly before the outbreak of World War II, the first figure had fallen only to 75 percent, while investment levels had fallen even more in proportional terms.[8] Other problems, such as "parcelization" (the deeding of ever smaller plots to multiple heirs) and usury, were also detrimental to agricultural production. Slovenia's position as a leader in the Yugoslav economy brought it both benefits and disadvantages, as it would during Tito's decades in power. On the one hand, Slovenes had a guaranteed market for their goods and a steady source of raw materials, but they were also saddled with high military expenditures and the costs of maintaining and elevating the standard of living of less-developed regions.

In addition to the prewar cultural figures mentioned above, many of whom were still active, three others from interwar Slovenia deserve special mention here. The first is Srečko Kosovel (1904–1926), who was an immensely talented and prolific writer in several genres. He died a tragically early death from meningitis just as he was hitting full artistic stride. Kosovel was far from being a realist like many of the writers mentioned thus far. Instead, expressionism and constructivism characterize his work, but there is considerable relevance to politics and national ideas because it is shot through with apocalyptic visions of the cruelty and decadence of contemporary society, as well as with the potential for renewal through technology and proletarian revolution. Further, many of his poems seem to ridicule nationalism as a lie or a fossil. The poetry collection *Integrali 26* is one of his most famous works. These poems, written in the mid-1920s, were published in full only in 1967, after much editorial wrangling and confusion over the manuscripts.

Kosovel hailed from the town of Sežana, in the haunting karst landscape of southwestern Slovenia. This region had, of course, belonged to the Habsburg Empire before World War I, but it was awarded to Italy after the Great War. Not only was all the Slovene littoral and much Croatian coastline denied to the new Kingdom of Serbs, Croats, and Slovenes for geo-strategic reasons, but the Slovene population there was harshly treated by the Italians and faced with assimilation under the Mussolini regime. Hence, in addition to poems that celebrate the spare beauty of his native karst region, Kosovel's *Integrali* is larded with single-line condemnations of Italian misrule. "They are burning down our Edinost (i.e. the Slovenian Unity Theater) in Trieste," a city that is "beautiful but sick." He notes further that the "Pseudochrist in Geneva,"[9] the sheepish League of Nations, is impotent to help. Authoritarianism carries the day in Europe, even after the war to end all wars: "The fist-bayonet keeps watch over us./And our faces are dead with dreams."[10]

Leaders are satirized as long-awaited saviors who arrive in "blood-stained feather headdresses," while the high culture of cathedrals, "museums to the Pharaohs," and "thrones of art" are simply the "white" and the dead who – again satirically – will guard and save Europe. Kosovel's caustic, ejaculatory critiques are even prescient in several ways.[11] Furthermore, Slovenes themselves are described as aimless and asleep, and Kosovel's worries over their future reach a climax in the poem "Genealogy," in which the progenitors of current Slovenes all bear names based on the word or concept of "servant." The multifaceted crisis of modernity finds expression in the aggressive nationalism of some states and in the incompetence or powerlessness of other peoples.

All told, these angry lamentations simply provide more fuel for Kosovel's conclusion that Europe was a lunatic asylum, a tired lie, slated for destruction; this civilization no longer has warmth in its heart or fire in its belly.

What would replace the old Europe, of course, is left vague enough in the poems to support various views. Certainly communists found much to admire in Kosovel's condemnations and calls for revolutionary rebirth. They could even argue that the nationalist oppression Kosovel describes had been resolved within federal Yugoslavia. But that is only one reading of his meaning. By the 1960s, when *Integrali* finally appeared, financial and administrative conflicts among the ethno-territorial units of Yugoslavia were producing a reappearance of nationalist tensions. It was possible to read in Kosovel a call for radical renewal of Slovene rights in the face of a new national threat: Belgrade.

Kosovel's reputation as a home-grown but left-leaning futurist was among the many factors leading to his enduring popularity. Other factors included the trenchant, ecstatic energy of his poetry, which dovetailed well with the artistic sensibilities of the 1960s; the natural beauty of some of his earlier work; and the volume and diversity of his writings. But a faith in the radical rejuvenation of the nation should not be omitted from a list of Kosovel's major characteristics.

Another very important cultural figure is the writer and journalist Louis Adamic (Adamič in Slovene). Adamič (1898–1951) was born in the village of Blato in Carniola and had emigrated to the US in 1913. He returned to Yugoslavia in 1932 on a Guggenheim Fellowship and published his most famous work, *The Native's Return*, in 1934. This book, which actually covers most of the other regions of Yugoslavia in addition to Slovenia, is important to the development of Slovene national identity for several reasons. Most importantly, it established a strong sense of connectedness between Slovene immigrant communities in the US and their old home-land; these connections continue to this day, although for much of the twentieth century there was a considerable gulf between conservative, Catholic-oriented Slovene-Americans and those of a more secular and politically progressive bent like Adamič.

Adamič's work combines journalistic reportage with emotional consid-erations. This has proven a potent combination for readers, many of whom were émigrés who shared his sense of isolation from his native language and family and his curiosity about the "old country." Adamič's work, here and in other books, is also interesting today because of the descriptions he provides, buttressed with photographs, of a now disappeared folkloric rural lifestyle in Slovenia; there are also vignettes of, and conversations with, politicians, writers, and other public figures. Not surprisingly, Adamič returned home to more fanfare than the average Slovene emigrant, due to his renown as a writer. He attributed this fanfare to Slovenes' desire to trumpet as loudly as possible the achievements of their native sons "to make the Serbs and Croats take notice."[12] Be that as it may, Adamič reminded his American readership that tiny Slovenia had no tradition of political or economic independence and hence Slovenes were "immeas-urably proud" of "two things which they felt were completely their own and which gave them the status of a nationality – namely, their language (which is similar to Serbo-Croat) and their culture."[13]

Adamič reaches interesting political conclusions in his book, written during the lead-up to World War II. By the end, he is convinced of three things: that the Serbian-dominated government in Belgrade consists of "gangsters" and "racketeers," that another world war was coming soon, and that a Russian-style socialist revolution was necessary to save Europe from poverty and misrule and to give average citizens (the Yugoslav versions of whom Adamič held in very high regard) the life they deserve. In a later, more complex and generally less sanguine work, *The Eagle and the Roots*, Adamič noted the grim effects of the tremendous fighting of World War II. The war and its terrors had taken a harsh toll on his family and on all parts of the country. Adamič balanced this darker mood and legacy of suffering with praise of the LCY's (League of Communists') struggle to remain independent from Stalin's Soviet Union, of Slovenes' efforts to educate themselves and modernize their land, and of Tito as an "eagle."

While Adamič's galvanizing effect on Slovene-American consciousness is clear, his reputation in Slovenia itself is somewhat more ambivalent and more of a victim of the left–right schism in twentieth-century Slovene society. Adamič's leftist credentials were established well before World War II. This occurred partly through his choice of themes, as in the subject matter of his first book, *Dynamite: The Story of Class Violence in America* (1931), and partly through his publishing contacts in Slovenia (with the liberal journal *Ljubljanski Zvon* instead of the conservative *Dom in svet*), and partly through his assessment of Yugoslavia's political crisis and its possible resolution. It should also be noted that Adamič made the first English-language translation of Cankar's *Hlapec Jernej in njegova pravica*, which appeared in 1926 as *Yerney's Justice*; he also published, in 1934, a translation of Edvard Kardelj's exposé on political oppression in monarchist Yugoslavia, *Struggle* (orig. *Boj*).

The poet Oton Župančič delivered a controversial assessment of Adamič after meeting him in 1932. The ensuing debate turned on the definition of *slovenstvo* (Slovenianness), which Župančič claimed Adamič had retained in full measure despite his Americanization. One point of controversy was whether Adamič was regarded by Slovene intellectuals as still truly a Slovene, given his purported loss of mastery over the language and his irreligiousness; the broader debate, which still has echoes today, concerned the nature of *slovenstvo* itself. Župančič characteristically argued that the narrow received definition of Slovenehood, centered on Catholicism, melancholy, and certain political or artistic movements, was egocentric and useless.[14] Adamič himself was even more concrete in his understanding of *slovenstvo*, noting that its insistence on doing everyday things "the Slovene way" and zealously guarding every aspect of Slovene history was an urgent, intense, and ultimately stifling type of nationalism that Americans had a hard time relating to. Today, as Slovenia joins the European Union, the world economy, and NATO, the debate continues on whether *slovenstvo* provides a bulwark against assimilation and homogenization or whether it is a hurdle Slovenes need to clear to become a cosmopolitan, integrated society.

Another significant cultural figure of the time was the architect Jože Plečnik (1872–1957). He was a student of the secessionist architect Otto Wagner and worked initially in Vienna. Then he worked on the Hradčany Castle complex and taught in Prague, and, later, across Yugoslavia. In Ljubljana he built a modern house and studio in the famous Trnovo district and had a most prolific career. His unique and much-loved modern style can be seen in the National and University Library, at the Žale Cemetery, in many church-related buildings, and in much of the infrastructure along the downtown river.

A warning sounded in the Slovenian underground as the 1930s advanced. The Communist Party of Slovenia, building on the foundations of earlier movements, was founded in 1937 in Čebinje. The party had close ties to the other parts of Yugoslavia and to Moscow. Its leading member was Edvard Kardelj, who in 1939 published the first version of his influential book *Razvoj slovenskega narodnega vprašanja* (The Development of the Slovene National Question). The book was reissued several times after World War II to accommodate it to changes in Yugoslav ideology, but its basic message remained the same. It was, first, an affirmation of the importance of the small Slovene nation, often treated dismissively by other Marxists. It also analyzed the way capitalism encourages the exploitation of minorities – especially such as the Albanians or Macedonians in Yugoslavia – in multinational states. And it proclaimed the end of centuries of exploitation and subjugation of Slovenes and stressed the vital, liberating role of the Communist Party. But it did one other important thing in its dialectical exposition of the course of Slovene history: Kardelj made a powerful acknowledgment of the importance of nationalism as one stage in social development. If nationalism is produced by certain forces, then it will disappear when society evolves: "It is precisely the complete liquidation of national oppression that will make it possible for the theme of common humanity to prevail in national cultures."[15] Kardelj's point is that as long as one people oppresses another, the victims will maintain their nationalism. In Titoist Yugoslavia, many Slovenes would argue, that is exactly what happened, even if it was not so much stronger peoples such as the Serbs, but rather the party itself, that in the final analysis would not relax its grip on their society.

In the wake of the Great War, of course, a new country of the South Slavs was formed. At first called the Kingdom of the Serbs, Croats, and Slovenes, it became known as "Yugoslavia" after the onset of the royal dictatorship in 1929. In some ways, the new country was constructed as an appendage of the rough-and-ready, previously independent – and recently very successful, at least until the ravages of the war – kingdom of Serbia; hence its capital was Belgrade, the rulers were the Karađorđević dynasty, and the powerful Serbian business and military elite held great sway in the country, with an admixture of administrative and parliamentary concessions held out to some of the other groups in the country to keep the social peace.

Contrary to the popular wisdom of the 1990s, Yugoslavia was not necessarily a doomed creation from the start, nor was its appearance solely due to the manipulations of the Great Powers or the thirst of Great Serbian nationalists; practical and idealistic considerations in favor of the new country were manifest in almost all regions. For the Slovenes, fear of Italian and Austrian-German revanchism, as well as widespread adherence to Yugoslav ideas and old traditions of making common cause with Croatia, spurred their inclusion, although the decision was an elite one: no plebiscite was ever held or constituent assembly elected. The Croats, who also had a considerable Yugoslav tradition, had pragmatic reasons for joining, in the fear of social rebellion posed by the "green bandits" (armed peasant veterans) roaming the countryside. Serbs were extremely eager to start the new state as a way of gathering all their co-nationals under one crown, even if this meant sharing the country with large minority groups; the royal family and political elites were also confident that they could use the vagueness of the original Yugoslav agreements to forge a state structure that suited their interests.

This said, it is fair to assert that royal Yugoslavia was a failed state. In concrete terms, law and order barely prevailed in terms of corruption and political violence; also, following the pattern in most of the new states created by the Versailles settlement, far too much money was spent on security and the military and far too little on infrastructure and, specifically, agriculture. Most ominously, the very justification for the state of the three related South Slav peoples (Serbs, Croats, and Slovenes, with not even lip service paid to the Bosnian, Albanian, Macedonian, Montenegrin, or Hungarian nationalities) was quickly called into question when most of the vague expectations of shared power and local autonomy, held by the Croats and Slovenes, were eroded.

Slovenia in World War II

Slovenia, like the rest of Yugoslavia, was invaded by powerful Axis forces on April 6, 1941. The Germans occupied the northern part of the country, inhabited by about 800,000 Slovenes. The Reich planned to annex this territory; while it never formally did so, the Germans did initiate vast "resettlement" programs that sent tens of thousands of Slovenes from both sides of the prewar border into exile or concentration camps. Their empty villages were then given to Germans from various areas. The Nazis, led by the notorious administrator Friedrich Rainer, considered Gorenjsko and Štajersko to be historically German lands and they attempted its "re-aryanization" by banning the Slovene language from official use, changing the names of people and places, and attacking Slovene culture. There were plans to rid the area of as many as a quarter of a million Slovenes.

Italy occupied the southern part of the country, including Dolenjsko, Notranjsko, and Ljubljana itself; the population of these areas was about 340,000. At least at first, until the start of the resistance, Italy's yoke was lighter than Germany's. Rome actually annexed its zone; of course, it also had already been in possession of large Slovene- and Croatian-inhabited areas since 1918; furthermore, the 1941 invasion also vastly expanded its holdings in Dalmatia, Croatia, Bosnia–Hercegovina, and Montenegro. Slovenes received Italian citizenship and a certain amount of autonomy. The Italians believed that their superior culture would eventually convert their Slavic subjects to proper Italians. By 1942, however, there were bitter fighting and vicious reprisals.

The Hungarians occupied the northeastern district of Prekmurje, with a population of about 100,000. This region contained most of Slovenia's small Jewish population, nearly all of whom were killed. The Hungarians also pursued assimilation policies, in part by splitting the Slovene population through assertions – like those of the Germans – that local "Wends" were a distinct nationality. Contacts between the three zones of occupation were difficult because of militarized internal frontiers and wartime destruction.

Slovenia had been ill-prepared to fight in 1941. The Yugoslavian army had not yet mobilized and the Communist Party (founded in 1937) had already stated that it would fight only when the interests of its ideological fatherland, the USSR, required it. Yugoslav forces quickly collapsed and the Axis met with little resistance especially in Slovenia and Croatia. The main opposition group in Slovenia, soon known as the Liberation Front (*Osvobodilna Fronta*, or OF), was founded in the Ljubljana home of the literary scholar Josip Vidmar on April 27. The importance of this Partisan organization cannot be overstated. Although it included a majority of non-communists, especially Christian Socialists led by the famous poet Edvard Kocbek and also members of the *Sokol* patriotic society, the OF would eventually become the vehicle by which Slovene and Yugoslav communists took over postwar political life. Key cultural figures, such as Juš Kozak, Mile Klopčič, and the great poet Oton Župančič, and some Catholic priests, most notably the Reverend Metod Mikuž, supported the Partisans. Tone Fajfar, a Catholic labor leader, wrote memoirs about the OF, as did dozens of male Partisans and such women Partisans as Božena Grosman, Nada Kraigher, Neža Maurer, Aleksandra Pirc, and Danica Vera Ribičič.

But many conservatives, especially from the SLS, decided to form an alternative organization in the spring of 1942, the *Slovenska Zaveza* (Slovene Alliance or Covenant). This group held resistance to the Axis to be futile and dangerous; they were determined to await an Allied victory and then re-establish the former Yugoslav government, but they were so virulently anticommunist that they were also willing to collaborate with the fascist occupiers. As a kind of umbrella organization, the Alliance galvanized resistance to the communist-led Partisans. Slovenes in the government-in-exile were torn between the two groups. Izidor Cankar, the respected art historian, urged the politicians at home in Slovenia to work with the Partisans.

The resistance war, which thus quickly became a civil war as well, was a tortuous affair. Much of it was fought guerrilla-style. The Partisans used hit-and-run tactics and maintained a large underground network of couriers, safe-houses, supply depots, radio stations, and printing presses. The Italians and Germans mounted major "scorched earth" offensives from time to time, but gradually their control was limited to the cities and main roadways. By late 1943 there were even uprisings in the prewar Slovene areas of Austria and Italy. The Italians encircled Ljubljana with a fence over forty kilometres long in order to isolate sympathizers there from Partisans in the countryside. The Nazis took over the former Italian areas in September, 1943. Up to that time, a number of anticommunist military organizations had been established by or for Slovenes, including the Italian militia known as MVAC, the Village Guards (*Vaške Straže*), and the Royalist Chetniks (also called the Blue Guards) of Karel Novak. Now the Germans made significant use of Slovene administrators and even security forces and tolerated more Slovene local government and language use than in the north. But at the same time the Nazi reprisals against the Partisans and their sympathizers were vicious, as they were also in Croatia and Serbia.

The man of the hour for the Germans – and for some, but not all, Slovene anticommunists – was Leon Rupnik, the mayor of Ljubljana under the Italians. He abhorred communism and believed in Hitler's eventual, if miraculous, victory and established the controversial military unit called the Home Guards (*Domobranci*). He wanted to fight against what he, along with some other prominent politicians in Catholic circles (such as the Bishop of Ljubljana, Gregorij Rožman) and in the government-in-exile, considered to be an important domestic enemy: the OF. The Germans funded and had operational control over his Ljubljana-based force of nearly 14,000; there were smaller similar forces of a few thousand men in other districts. Although Rupnik and his forces were collaborators, they were not Nazis; they conceived of their undertaking not along the lines of Croatia's fascist Ustaša movement but rather of the Serbian Chetnik leader Draža Mihailović or of Vichy France.

Within the OF, the Slovene communists were increasingly dominating affairs. Their most important leader was Edvard Kardelj, while Boris Kidrič, Franc Leskošek, and Miha Marinko also played leading roles at the local and federal levels. Leading Partisans included Dušan Kveder, Franc Rozman, Lidija Šentjurc, and Vida Tomšič. Rozman, also known as "Commandant Stane" was a veteran of the International Brigades in the Spanish Civil War, like so many other Slovene resistance fighters. He became head of the Slovene Partisans on July 13, 1943 but met an accidental death the next year. Šentjurc became a major party functionary after the war. Tomšič organized women in support of the OF; after she was captured by the Italians, she then played a significant role in organizing prisoners of war into fighting units and bringing them back to Slovenia after Rome's capitulation. Many Slovene military units were named after famous cultural figures, such as the writers France Prešeren and Ivan Cankar. In all of Yugoslavia, the Partisans and their active supporters eventually totalled about 800,000. The movement had a modernizing effect on many areas, since there were many active roles for women, including in combat. The Anti-Fascist Women's League was founded during the war and existed until 1953. It was a communist-run umbrella organization for women's political and social movements of various types, put into operation mostly to mobilize women but to some degree it also became a vehicle for their emancipation. Furthermore, great attention was paid to the inclusion of national minorities and to limiting the power of traditional Serbian and Croatian elites.

Communist naivety about a social revolution in Germany or the might of the Soviet armed forces rendering the Nazis impotent governed many decisions. At times this made the communists too passive, and at other times too aggressive. But at all times they had in mind reviving Yugoslavia as an entity and carrying out a social revolution to change the fundamental economic and political structure of Yugoslavia in addition to winning an anti-imperialist "war of national liberation." Likewise, when the anticommunist political forces – from the prewar parties who were determined to restore the old Yugoslavia, included by means of limited collaboration with the occupiers – believed that an Allied invasion of the Balkan coast was imminent in 1943, they moved more recklessly against their opponents.

During the war the Partisans assassinated two prominent politicians working against them. These were the former Royal governor, Marko Natlačen, and the Jesuit priest and professor, Lambert Ehrlich. They also executed hundreds of fighters and sympathizers from the various local groups arrayed against the Partisans and developed a reputation for forcibly requisitioning supplies from hard-pressed peasants. Their murders of members of what they disparagingly termed the *Bela Garda* (White Guards, a term from Russian history indicating reactionaries), as well as the Partisans' constant homage to the USSR, obvious distrust of allied Catholic groups, and ceaseless deprecation of the government-in-exile, cost the Partisans support. Still, in the eyes of communists and many other Slovenes, anyone who collaborated with the Axis for any reason was a national traitor, since the Germans planned to subjugate and exploit the Slovene lands fully and even depopulate and resettle large parts of it. Assimilation, expulsion, and mass murder were all tactics the Nazis used or planned to use to Germanize the Slovene lands. Despite the severe Axis reprisal policies, more and more Slovenes were determined to fight for their own liberation; many noncommunists joined the OF because it was the most effective resistance organization and because it pledged to build a more democratic and modern Yugoslavia after the war. This support grew tremendously in late 1943, after the Western Allies began to support the Partisans and the Italians withdrew from the war, leaving behind a great deal of equipment and weaponry.

The Partisans gradually developed stronger ties to the communist-led movements in the rest of Yugoslavia. They also gradually cemented their own hegemony within the OF. The Dolomite Declaration, signed on March 1, 1943, irrevocably gave the communists the leading position by obliging the other groups in the OF to renounce formation of separate political parties after the war. Although it promoted unity in a time of crisis, this Declaration proved to be a great source of consternation for noncommunists, most of whom shared the goal of national liberation but not social revolution with the communists; many OF fighters were not necessarily aiming for a transformation of the socioeconomic foundations and political system of the country.

The OF included fighting units, secret police, communist commissars for ideology and propaganda, and important supply and medical units. The Slovene resistance fighters met at Kočevje in October 1943, to establish the foundations of a new state and to pick delegates for the upcoming pan-Yugoslav resistance meeting in Jajce, Bosnia. It was the Slovenes' insistence and understanding that the postwar Yugoslavia, whatever else it was to be, would grant equal rights to Slovenes, provide a significant degree of local autonomy, and vouchsafe the right to self-determination; on this basis, the Slovenes were willing to commit their land to a revived Yugoslavia.

By the spring of 1944, emboldened by dilatory Soviet aid, the Partisans began setting the stage for their seizure of power after the Axis defeat. The ruling committee elected at Kočevje was, at an important gathering in Črnomelj, renamed the Slovene National Liberation Council. It took on a wide range of administrative functions beyond the military, including schools, but it also began to cut a sinister profile with its new security organs that now fell under the direct control of Tito's inner circle. By the middle of that year, Tito had an agreement with the London government-in-exile, led by the prominent Croatian interwar politician Ivan Šubašić; the two groups agreed, under Allied pressure, to work together after the war to form a new government, even though the Partisans intended to replace the traditional parties with the "people's power" ostensibly incarnated in their own movement. But the agreement at any rate brought an offer of amnesty for the *domobranci*. The Partisans also set up a commission to work chronicling the war crimes of the Axis powers and their collaborators; they also established another body under the guidance of the famous historian Fran Zwitter to fortify Yugoslav arguments for border modifications at the coming peace conference.

Despite fierce German resistance, the Partisan army grew to 37,000 by the end of the war. The Soviet army briefly helped in the recapture of Prekmurje, but the OF "liberated" the rest of the country itself, including Trieste. Rupnik was urged by the prewar SLS and Liberal Party leaders to step down and allow them to steer the country between the Nazi and Partisan extremes. But Rupnik intended to continue the fight however possible. He and Bishop Rožman fled Ljubljana on May 5, 1945, heading for Austria. A few days later Ljubljana was recaptured and the last Germans surrendered.

All told the war and its bloody denouement took about 80,000 Slovene lives. Over half of these were Partisans and their supporters. Close to 10,000 anticommunist fighters, civilians, and Axis draftees died as well. The German and Italian losses were 6,000 and 1,500 dead, respectively. Many thousands of Slovenes were sent to concentration and labor camps, deported, or held hostage. The country was economically exhausted by the years of fighting and much of its infrastructure damaged. Events in the rest of Yugoslavia were no less dramatic or important than those in Slovenia. Vast numbers of people died across the region. There were about one million deaths in all – nearly half of them Serbs, and most of those at the hands of the Croatian fascists known as the Ustaše. Bosnia–Hercegovina saw the heaviest fighting, since it was in the refuge of the mountains there that Tito's forces developed their base of operations.

Unfortunately, the German surrender did not bring an end to the suffering. Tito's forces massacred something in the order of 15,000 Slovene collaborators and civilians right after the war, as part of a still-controversial set of actions that took the lives of as many as 50,000 Croats and 5,000 Serbs and Montenegrins as well. When British forces in southern Austria refused to accept the surrender of large numbers of fleeing Yugoslavs, the Partisans were given the chance to "settle accounts" with large numbers of past and potential foes, some of whom had indeed pledged to keep fighting the communists; but Tito had them killed in summary fashion, with the injustice of extrajudicial executions heightened by the murders of panicked civilians. The fleeing Slovenes made it to the town of Viktring (Vetrinje in Slovene) near Klagenfurt before they were repatriated; many were sent deep into the interior of the country, executed, and buried in mass graves there. The place names associated with these sordid events, including Kočevski Rog and Teharje for Slovenes and Bleiburg for Croats, became in the postwar period neuralgic reminders of communist brutality, the ideological bitterness of World War II, and the smoldering need for reconciliation among various factions within the individual societies affected.

The most obvious legacy of World War II in Slovenia is the communist assumption of power at its end. Another is the set of civil wars that left scars remaining in Slovene, Croat, and Serbian society to this day. But some historians also see in the Partisan victory an indication of the inadequacy of Slovene political culture as it had developed prior to 1941.[16] The traditional-minded parties of the day failed to realize both the desire of the population for a fairer and more democratic Yugoslav federation and its willingness to fight against the Axis. Communist rule, which moderated in severity within a decade, also ended up being the motor of the industrialization, urbanization, and political modernization of the Slovene lands.

A major figure in the resistance, Edvard Kocbek (1904–1982), was also one of the leading figures in Slovene history and letters in the twentieth century. He was a writer, a political figure, and a Christian Socialist activist who left an important impression on Slovene culture and society through his life as well as his literary works. His essays, short stories, memoirs, and especially his poetry are still justifiably popular and highly regarded by critics. In 1940 he even wrote a short, but wide-ranging, essay entitled "Central Europe" in which he laid out the political, economic, and foreign policy challenges facing Slovenia in an analysis that is still relevant today.[17] His principled commentary on politics, especially the bloodshed and atrocities of World War II, galvanized and polarized Slovene society, even as he won a place as an enduringly popular public intellectual. Kocbek also signed the *Dolomitska izjava* discussed above. He noted in his diaries that "something strange, and dangerous, was seething in the atmosphere" on the day of the declaration; he "sensed non-Slovene and non-democratic intentions" in the air.[18]

After playing an important role in the resistance for three years, Kocbek became embroiled in controversy with the Communist Party (CP) shortly after the war. He got a reputation for asking touchy questions; his zeal for change was coming into conflict with his understanding of political ethics and procedural democracy, especially as they applied to his native Slovenia. In 1945 Kocbek essentially asked the CP who had given it the right to introduce a "party state"; indeed, although Tito was very popular, no elections were ever held confirming the CP's mandate to rule. Then, two years later, he asked the CP leadership another tough question: what had been the fate of the tens of thousands of collaborators (Whites, Croatian fascists known as Ustaše, and Serbian Chetniks) and others who fled towards the advancing British and American armies in the spring of 1945? Kocbek was told that these people were being detained for "re-education"; in reality, they had been executed by the Partisans and buried in mass graves. Kocbek soon found this out.

By 1952, Kocbek had been forced out of all political offices. In the 1960s his works began coming back into print. His sixtieth birthday in 1974 proved to be the main milestone in his later life, and an important year for Slovene civil society. One could pick any number of works from his large corpus to highlight Slovene national issues, but we shall focus here on a short story from his highly controversial and highly praised collection, *Strah in pogum* (1951; Fear and Courage). Kocbek wrote very few stories, but even these have unfortunately been translated into English, and neither have his lengthy autobiographical writings from the 1940s and 1950s.

One of the stories, "Ogenj" (The Fire) takes place in a small Slovene village under Italian occupation. It contrasts the attitudes of two priests towards resistance against the Italians. The parish priest, Fr Jernej Amon, is sympathetic to the communist-led Partisans and is dismayed by the violence and cruelty of the invaders of his country. A visiting chaplain, Fr Marijan Žgur, identifies with the Italians because they are fascists who stand for a type of unity and order in the world which resonate within his understanding of Christianity. The initial letters of these two men's last names (A and Ž), the first and last letters of the Slovene alphabet, serve as "book-ends" to enclose symbolically all the Slovenes, the whole people. Far more importantly, the two priests form relationships that unite the ideological extremes present in the action. This is part and parcel of Kocbek's central thesis that all Slovenes suffered during World War II and that both major political groupings (the reds and the whites, to put it roughly) genuinely believed that they were acting patriotically and had their country's best interests in mind.

In the story, the two priests, who were childhood friends in the village, jockey for position in their arguments over who is the real Christian and true patriot. The Italian army arrests a local man named Tone Turk, who has been charged with turning over important military information to the Partisans. Fr Žgur is sent by the Italian commander to hear Turk's confession the night before he is to be executed; meanwhile, in the middle of a tremendous storm, Fr Amon goes to see the Italian commander to try to dissuade him from executing Turk. The two priests in "The Fire" have very different ideas but similar crises of commitment. The story ends with a highly dramatic and intriguing battle scene.

Kocbek reaches his goal in this story, as in many other works, through the frequent use of dichotomies, or paired images of seeming opposites. Examples of these dichotomies include discussions of life and death; justice for Slovenia and treason; heavenly justice and heresy; and, most significantly, the juxtaposition of characters sympathetic to opposing political camps. Kocbek's own life embodied dynamic tensions like these, from his adherence both to socialism and Roman Catholicism, and his great patriotism which eschewed ethnocentric nationalism. This "grand old man" of Slovene letters was also, at the same time, the conscience of his country who became "emblematic of the fundamental dilemmas facing Slovenia in the twentieth century" and whose writing and politics "crystalliz[ed] the issues that have divided his society."[19] The multifaceted suffering of the Slovene nation during and just after World War II is at the heart of Kocbek's message.

Kocbek's central point about shared suffering is hammered home by similarities between the poetry of two young men who died fighting on opposite sides in the war. Karel Destovnik-Kajuh (1922–1944), a communist from the town of Šoštanj, and France Balantič (1921–1943), from Kamnik, both died in battle. Although Balantič's work tends to be more metaphysical and more stylistically complex than Destovnik-Kajuh's, it is highly telling that both of them use the same term, "črna živina," to describe themselves during the maelstrom of the war.[20] This term, meaning literally "black animal," carries the connotation of slave or beast of burden, indicating their joint realization of Slovenia's abuse by outside forces and by the contemporary war itself.

Destovnik-Kajuh's work has another nationalist aspect: his commitment to resistance and independence. Some of his poems depict poignant, sympathetic yet stark scenes of human suffering in prewar Slovenia, such as alcoholism and mental illness in the countryside. Other poems explore the motivations of young Partisans and the suffering of the loved ones of the fallen; these poems tend to be simpler than those in the first category, and somewhat clever rather than atmospheric, but at times they too deliver a strong linguistic and national punch. In one of them, a peasant joins the Partisans after he and his family are brutalized by the Axis forces. After describing the beating he took at the hands of the "devils," he cries: "Look into my blazing eyes, comrades,/ and tell me:/ do you still see the homeland there?"[21]

Perhaps the most famous of Destovnik-Kajuh's poems bears the title "Slovenska pesem," or "Slovene Song." Like the work of Cankar and Kosovel before it, and like the eloquent and voluminous journals of his contemporary Kocbek, it is an exhortation to resistance, to spurn the status of *hlapec*, or servant. The courage and the stubbornness of the small Slovene nation receives great praise. The most moving stanza is the first:

> There are only a million of us,
> a million, with our death close by among the corpses,
> a million, with the gendarmes drinking our blood,
> just one single million,
> > hard-pressed by tribulation
> > but never exterminated.
> Never, no chance of that![22]

Destovnik-Kajuh continues to exhort his fellow Slovenes to resist, stubbornly and with heads held high, and not to crouch and complain like dogs. Despite their small numbers, Slovenes are not fragile flowers and have withstood earlier "avalanches." This fierce message of self-confidence does indeed form an important subtext in much of Slovene literature, reaching back to the time of the Turks.

Introduction to Tito's Yugoslavia

This section presents a thematic analysis of Slovenia in Tito's Yugoslavia. The key features of Slovene history in this time are the enhancement of its republican status; the development of Slovene civil society and its wranglings with the central government in Belgrade; and extensive economic development.

Whatever else one focuses on in Slovene history as part of socialist Yugoslavia, the importance of the ethno-territorial administrative units known as "republics" looms very large. These units, comparable in some ways to Canadian provinces or US states, were inherited by Tito's socialist government from the previous, monarchical Yugoslavia. Their continued use was of course a federalist concession to the demographics of the Yugoslav situation; they roughly corresponded to national or historic regions. The six republics were Slovenia, Serbia, Croatia, Montenegro, Macedonia, and Bosnia–Hercegovina. Of course there was great variety in the composition and political situation of each of these units. But for Slovenes, it is of undisputed importance that after 1945 the majority of their historic territories, and all of the earlier Yugoslav ones, remained "gathered together." This allowed for the continued, if imperfect, development of a Slovene polity, consciousness, and economy. This key feature of Slovene history makes it reasonable to liken these decades to a period of national apprenticeship, in which Slovenia matured in terms of capabilities and consciousness while gradually developing its appetite for the "coming-of-age" rite of secession. That Slovenian sovereignty was firmly articulated and pushed into reality only towards the end of the twentieth century is neither a slight to the Slovenes in comparison with other states in Europe and nor was it inevitable that it would occur the way it did. These assertions also assume acceptance of another widely (but not universally) held premise: that an independent Slovene state was neither possible nor desired by a critical mass of citizens in 1918 and 1945.

The Yugoslav republics, however, were more than static administrative boundaries. They were given both privileges and responsibilities in everything from the life of the League of Communists and education to national guard units and investment policies. This situation ultimately fostered both the will to be sovereign and the ability to gain and manage independence. Indeed, it is one of the general ironies of twentieth-century multinational communist states, a category which includes the Soviet Union and Czechoslovakia, that they ultimately ran aground to large degree on nationalism – not because of the hidden shoals of "ancient ethnic hatreds," unfinished business, and other inherited incompatibilities, but because the communists' plans to use national autonomy as a "transmission belt" to legitimize the new government and promote social change ultimately created a surging centrifugal tide of secessionism.

Political and economic life

The general contours of political and economic life in the second Yugoslavia are easy enough to follow. From a loyal member of the Stalinist phalanx in 1945, Tito's state evolved into the most liberal communist (or socialist, depending on which theoretical lens one is employing) state in Europe. After 1948, the year of the famous Tito–Stalin split, the need to distinguish their ideology from that of the Soviets led the Yugoslavs to develop ever more experimental and open policies. The new policies, from a strengthened federalism through nonalignment (but not neutrality or passivity) in global politics to workers' self-management and social property (a vague but appealing concept that is in distinction to both state and private property) in the economic realm, the Yugoslav leadership, which included the very high-ranking Slovene, Edvard Kardelj, as Tito's heir apparent and the Party's chief theoretician, developed new policies. Some of them broadened and deepened existing aspects of Yugoslav political experience – such as the need to avoid too much centralism in Belgrade lest it smack of, or become, Serbian unitarism in the decisively multi-ethnic state. Some of the policy innovations were new: expanding the decentralization ultimately to the economic realm, for instance, to build on existing strengths and maximize Slovenia's and Croatia's utility (especially via tourism and industry) to the country. Others were take in direct contrast to notorious Soviet measures, such as preserving the private sector in agriculture and avoiding forced collectivization, purges against "kulaks," and, potentially, rebellion and famine. (As with the issue of the leading role or guiding role or monopoly of power by the League of Communists, the Yugoslavs settled on a sort of intellectual or political "liquidation" of most opponents, and not a physical one, at least after the early 1950s.)

Still other measures were completely new, such as when Tito helped to forge the international policy of nonalignment. He did this in conjunction with Egypt's Nasser and India's Nehru. This allowed Tito to boost legitimacy at home, in part by avoiding the divisive Cold War choice between Moscow and Washington, and by cementing links to resource-rich developing countries, many of which had significant Muslim populations, such as Yugoslavia. It also rasied Yugoslav's visibility in the world and contributed something to the resolution of several of the Cold War era's most difficult problems – apartheid, Vietnam, the nuclear arms race).

There were certainly conservative backlashes and bureaucratic retrench-ings in the face of the general Yugoslav trend of reformism. And the reforms themselves, one should note, were aimed at legitimation, viability, and governability, and much less so (except in the case of the dreamy Kardelj, for instance) at the theoretical pioneering of the true third path. It must also be remembered that, esepcially in the 1970s, some of the changes had effects opposite to those intended: by actually reducing viability through a fragmentation of economic life, just as the large dose of ethnic federalism in administration and party life seems to have provided the incubation chamber for eventual separatism.

In addition, there was another set of brakes on reform in the middle years: the League of Communists, though willing to redefine its role, would never abdicate its actual, if often indirect, monopoly on political power. It would not allow competing political parties, just as Tito would never appoint a clear and strong successor, perhaps for fear of being overshadowed either at the end of his life or in later historical appraisals. Ultimately, the desire of Slovenes and Croats for more political and economic autonomy would be joined by that of Serbs, mostly intellectuals, who thought that their state had also sacrificed too much – but not just to the central government, but to the Slovenes and Croats themselves, as well as to the Muslims of Bosnia–Hercegovina (the Bosnian Muslims or the Bosniaks), the Albanians of Kosovo, the Hungarians of the Vojvodina, and the Macedonians. Although Serbia's mounting resistance to the central government took many forms, the chief strand eventually revealed itself to be nationalist, with a conception of "greater democracy" for Yugoslavia that was strongly tinged with the idea of "greater Serbia," or territorial unity for the disparate Serbian populations and a more dominant (and, Serbs would say, a more historically and numerically appropriate) role for Serbia in the country as a whole.

Historians generally agree on the pattern that Yugoslavia's economic and constitutional reforms followed. A five-stage model, extending from the end of World War II through the secession of Slovenia and Croatia in 1991, is useful.[23]

Stalinist period

The political scene in this period was dominated by the successful efforts of the Communist Party of Yugoslavia to cement its control of the country and launch it on a new course. Horrible massacres, with victims numbering in the tens of thousands, occurred in the immediate aftermath of the war: the communists "settled accounts" in summary fashion with former collaborators, especially from Slovenia and Croatia. But they also killed people, including women and children, who were simply refugees or noncommunists, such as Serbian Chetniks; many of the victims had made contact with Allied forces in Austria and were turned over to the Partisans. The names of the massacre and burial sites, hardly ever mentioned before the late 1980s, remain heart-rending, especially Kočevski Rog for Slovenes and Bleiburg for Croats. This patent cruelty of the early communist regime was soon underscored by its use of concentration camps such as the island of Goli Otok for disposing of other domestic opponents after the break with Stalin in 1948; it heightened the sense of brutalization after World War II and also came to symbolize the degree to which the communists controlled the fate and sense of memory of Yugoslavia's various peoples. A final upshot of the war was to be the long-simmering dispute over the great port city of Trieste. Yugoslav troops captured the town on May 1, 1945, only to be forced out by the British and Americans. Tensions ran extremely high. The unwillingness of the Soviet Union to back Yugoslavia's claim to Trieste was just one sign among many that the Tito government would soon be going its own way.

The country's first constitution, promulgated in 1946, established the basic federal structure that would last until 1991. The Communist Party (CP) was interlocked with the government at all levels; other political parties were soon banned; and noncommunist politicians who had coop-erated with the Partisans, from parties such as the Slovene Christian Socialists and the Serbian Agrarians, were sidelined within a couple of years. Tito, riding a high of wartime popularity, nonetheless never stood for office; he fashioned himself Prime Minister, and then Marshal, and eventually President-for-Life. Six republics were created on a foundation of blended ethnic and historical criteria. Slovenia had the most homoge-neous population – over 95 percent Slovene; still, many Slovenes lived in Italy and Austria. While the "gathering" of Slovenia's land and people was not complete (and never would be), the postwar restoration of Istria and its hinterland meant that many more Slovenes were included in Tito's Yugoslavia than in the interwar Royal Yugoslavia. Croatia, in its historic "triune" shape including Dalmatia and most of Slavonia, had a double-digit Serbian minority. The ethnically unique Macedonia and historically distinct Montenegro were given republican status, which the main popu-lation groups there had not enjoyed before. Bosnia was an amalgam of three main ethnic groups (Bosnian Muslims, Serbs, and Croats), while two autonomous regions were created within Serbia. The regions of Kosovo (overwhelmingly Albanian) and Vojvodina (with a strong Hungarian component) were meant to provide adequate enfranchisement for these two large minority groups, or nationalities, as they were called – in distinc-tion to the country's six republican "nations." But the regions were also intended as a brake on Serbian power.

On the economic front, the period from 1945 to the early 1950s was char-acterized by central planning. As in other command economies of Eastern Europe, an all-important Five-year Plan was promulgated, industry was nationalized, and the collectivization of agriculture was set into motion. Planning seemed to the communists the logical way to achieve fast progress in industrializing and urbanizing the country; such modernization, in turn, would earn the Yugoslavs rights to the title socialist and increasing the coun-try's defense capacity, as the Soviets had done prior to World War II; it would also reduce the regional disparities which were rightly seen as a dangerous factor of potential future discord.

A number of arrests, trials, and executions mar the political record of the Stalinist period. In 1947, Črtomir Nagode, Boris Furlan, and Ljubo

Sirc were convicting of conspiring with foreign governments and other noncommunist politicians in Yugoslavia. Nagode was executed; Furlan, who had written a well-known book entitled *Fighting Yugoslavia* in 1942, to drum up support for the Slovene resistance to the Axis, and Sirc, who later became a professor and political figure in the 1990s, were imprisoned. Their aim had been to contest communist rule by forming an opposition political party; unlike some of the Croatian anticommunists returning from abroad, they had not planned an insurrection. But the government would not tolerate such dissent in this period. And the pressures for conformity were to increase before they attenuated.

Another set of infamous proceedings were called the "Dachau Trials." They took place in 1948 and 1949, just after the Soviet Union broke with Yugoslavia. Thirty-four communists who had been prisoners in Nazi concentration camps during World War II – and supposedly become collaborators – were sentenced to harsh penalties. Another thousand Slovenes were arrested in the aftermath of the Tito–Stalin split, which became public when the Soviet dictator kicked Yugoslavia out of the Cominform, a global organization of communist movements. Tito responded with a large purge of *Ibeovci* (supporters of the IB, or Informbiro, as the Cominform was called in Yugoslavia). Many Slovenes, along with even greater numbers from other republics, were sent to concentration camps, including the notorious Goli Otok in Dalmatia. The most prominent Slovene Ibeovac was long-time communist Dragotin Gustinčič, a veteran of the Spanish Civil War, who was jailed after being accused of passing information to the Soviets.[24] Yugoslavia had first reacted by trying to prove its loyalty, then by savagely attacking potential domestic supporters of the USSR, and finally, by 1950, by coming up with ideological innovations designed to rescue true socialism and brand the Soviets as deviationists. During this period, official persecution of the Catholic Church began as well. Many priests were imprisoned, some were executed, parochial schools were closed, and in general the government fostered an anti-religious atmosphere, although churches and seminaries remained open. Many of the political prisoners from this time were rehabilitated by Slovene courts in the years following Tito's death.

Administrative self-management

By 1950 a change in course was necessary as a result of the Soviet–Yugoslav rupture of 1948. This major dust-up in international relations exposed polycentrist tendencies in world communism; these would be much accentuated in the 1960s with the Soviet–Chinese split and the development of Eurocommunism. As far as Yugoslavia went, however, Tito simply refused to play the role of acquiescent viceroy in Stalin's Eastern Europe. Soviet arrogance had created major friction during World War II, and Yugoslav cockiness after their impressive victories over the Nazis and Italians had set the stage for the rupture. Ultimately, Stalin feared Tito's example, but he had to content himself with a war of words and a blockade. The reasons for this lay in the Yugoslavs' fighting ability and the potential for development of further fault lines among the Soviet satellite states if Stalin attempted an invasion. After Stalin's death, Soviet–Yugoslav relations warmed, but were very much subject to ups and downs and Yugoslavia remained a "maverick" in foreign as well as domestic policy.

The country's constitution underwent far-reaching changes in 1953. The year before, the CPY had changed its name to the League of Communists of Yugoslavia (LCY), at its sixth party congress. In 1958, meeting in Ljubljana, the LCY issued a new set of theoretical documents that really represented a recasting of official ideology; they enshrined the country's experiments with self-management, non-alignment, and *bratstvo i jedinstvo* (Serbo-Croat for "brotherhood and unity," the federalist mantra calling for ethnic cooperation); trenchant outside observers noted that the real pillars holding up the country would remain "Tito, Partija, Armija" (Tito, the Party, the Army). All of these phenomena contributed to Yugoslav stability and, ironically, one of the ways the army did so was not by the use of force but by being a relatively supra-national organization which forged at least some ties between republics. Despite the experiments and liberalization, it was still possible to fall foul of the government, as the case of the prominent Montenegrin dissenter Milovan Djilas showed. Djilas, a Partisan leader and long-time communist, was imprisoned and publication of his numerous works forbidden on account of his critiques of party hypocrisy and his calls for quicker democratization. Although public displays of nationalism were very much out of favor and censorship was always possible, socialist realism as an artistic doctrine was also passé. As a result, there were public debates about social and political issues, often in the form of cultural disputes. One of the most famous debates involved the Slovene literary historian Dušan Pirjevec, who in 1961 polemicized with the Serbian writer Dobrica Ćosić. Pirjevec stalwartly defended the value and rights of small national groups, resisting the unitarism of Ćosić, who at that time (he later became an enthusiastic Serbian nationalist) espoused assimilationist Yugoslavism, or the formation of a new, progressive, blended culture under Belgrade's direction. Earlier, the whole country had been treated to a debate on cultural policy and socialist realism between the orthodox communist Boris Ziherl and the omnipresent – and more moderate – Josip Vidmar.

This second period, which lasted until 1965, saw considerable industrial growth, but also increasing dependence on foreign loans. Obvious domestic unemployment was avoided by sending workers abroad, where they were often called *Gastarbeiter* (the German term grew popular, since most of the workers went there), who, in turn, sent home hard currency but also introduced an element of dependency into the economy. Much of the new economic system was enshrined in a new constitution in the year 1963. Federal five-year plans had far less actual effect, since local enterprises elected their management with coordination from the regional party.

Market socialism

The third period, that of "market socialism," lasted from 1965 to 1974. This period began with a palpable increase in the autonomy given, at the political level, to the six republics and, economically, to individual enterprises. A new constitution in 1963 upgraded the status of Kosovo and Vojvodina, but soon violent altercations broke out in Kosovo between the government and increasingly nationalist-minded Albanians, many of them students. Although minority questions in Croatia and especially Bosnia would later emerge as volatile, the status of Kosovo was the political issue that, more than any other, would ultimately highlight the weaknesses of Yugoslavia, fueling both a Serbian nationalist reaction and a Slovene loss of confidence. It was during this period that the Bosnian Muslims also received official recognition as a nation (ethnic group), on an equal niveau with the Serbs, Croats, and Slovenes. This meant that their identity now carried much more political weight than the old religious or regional–historical appellation had possessed. Yugoslav filmmaking and literature flourished in this period, but the government still punished overt political criticism, as the case of the neo-Marxist philosophical journal *Praxis* demonstrated. Questioning the Partisans' behavior in World War II was still taboo as well.

Although the major Serbian figure in federal politics, the secret police chief Aleksandar Ranković, died in 1966, emboldening progressive, technocratic, and nationalist elements in all republics, Tito realized by 1971 that he had to begin cooling off the national question again. He and the LCY basically took control over Croatia and shoved reform communists such as Mika Tripalo, Savka Dabčević-Kučar, and Pero Pirker out of public life. This dramatic crackdown on the Croatian League of Communists, known as the Croatian Spring, resulted in much more conformity in that republic; Croatian autonomy, with its putative connections to a fascist past or future separatism, was put on ice, but many creative and modern voices in all the republics were also silenced. With the "third-stringers" now on stage across the country, the LCY's rule was again unchallenged but vital questions were also simply ignored. The purge reached Slovenia the next year, with the summary firing of Premier Stane Kavčič, who had a reputation not only for liberalism but also for a preference – characterized as "nationalism" – for focusing on Slovene issues rather than federal ones.[25] Key reformers in Serbia and other republics also got the sack. This period showed that the League of Communists of Slovenia (LCS) had competing currents within it. Kavčič, and a later LCS leader named Milan Kučan, along with the sociologist Veljko Rus, the famous dissident Jože Pučnik, and many others, represented the reformist approach, while conservatives in the party, such as Franc Popit and Mitja Ribičič, retained considerable power. Edvard Kardelj, the country's most powerful Slovene politician and long a member of Tito's inner circle, could never allow himself to embrace political pluralism; he was also some-times chided by Slovenes for following the centralist line from Belgrade and roundly criticized for an administrative dilettantism that enshrined numerous unsuccessful economic experiments in federal constitutions. Still, by the 1970s it was apparent to many that he actually never lost sight of the importance of Slovene identity. He even promoted it by fostering industrialization and cross-border trade, supporting the new Territorial Defense Forces based in the republics, allowing limited dissent, and limiting the power of larger republics such as Croatia and Serbia.

Economically, the knotty problem of underdevelopment in the southern republics was addressed by a major new initiative, the Federal Fund for the Development of the Less Developed Regions. The source of much resentment in Slovenia and Croatia, where an increase in income taxes funded the project, this Fund charted little success due to mismanagement in the form of "political factories" (prestige projects that were often economically irrational or redundant) in the target areas and, especially in Kosovo, high birthrates. There were also an increasing number of dust-ups between republics on other economic issues; Slovenes took heat for proposing changes in social security and allocations for road construction. Even more Yugoslavs were encouraged to work abroad, and the government took pains to see to it that tourism in the country – another important source of hard currency earnings – flourished. The dinar was devalued, many price controls removed, foreign investment encouraged, and the banking system overhauled to cut down on the number of bad loans. Still, with increased borrowing from abroad and no political commitment to closing unprofitable companies or, as Kavčič had proposed, to allow private citizens to invest in and profit from individual enterprises, the economic system retained, to a significant degree, its irreality.

Self-managing socialism

The fourth period, self-managing socialism, stretched roughly from 1974 to 1988. It began with the new, bold, and ultimately infamous constitu-tion of 1974. This document set up a nearly incomprehensible degree of bargaining among companies and also between the various elements within economic enterprises, social constituencies, and the various levels of gov-ernment, possibly making some interesting statements about fairness and resistance to hegemony but resulting in a fuzzy sense of responsibility and limited freedom of action for all concerned. The size of government also ballooned at all levels. All medium-sized and large firms were broken into Basic Organizations of Associated Labor, or BOALs. (In Slovene, these where known as TOZDs, or *Temeljne organizacije združenega dela*.) The new constitution was the handiwork of Kardelj, who had long endeavored to keep Slovenia's rights and comparative advantages within Yugoslavia intact; while Kardelj was motivated partly by his own mildly anti-statist theories of property and government, he and the top leadership were also interested in limiting the volatility of traditional representative government, which, despite the government's chastising of nationalism as retrograde, was now seen as sparking ethnic conflict.[26] There was also pressure from within the League to steer a new course between the Scylla of a command economy and the Charybdis of the free market. Still, the country's foreign debt skyrocketed in an effort to keep consumers happy and unprofitable enterprises afloat. The oil shocks of the 1970s took even more wind out of Yugoslavia's sails.

For Slovenes, an important development occurred on November 11, 1975, when the Treaty of Osimo was signed. It finally put Italian–Yugoslav relations on a firm footing. It did little to change the border situation in favor of the Slovenes, who had been lamenting the exclusion of so many of their co-nationals since 1918; but it did guarantee political and linguistic rights to the Slovenes living in Italy, settle property and compensation issues from the 1940s, and provide for a fairly free and open border that would grow to be of great economic importance to Slovenia. The Treaty was also necessary because of the troubled history of the Trieste area since 1945. Tito's Partisans had liberated the city in May of that year, only to be ordered out shortly thereafter by the British and Americans. The Yugoslavs put forth as strong a claim for the city and its environs as one could imagine, based on historic, ethnic, and strategic rights. Although Italy had sided with Nazi Germany in the war, after 1943 many Italians fought against the Axis and, what is more, Italy was now a part of the emerging US-engineered West European alliance system aimed at containing communism. For nine years an uneasy cease-fire prevailed in the region, with Italians running the city proper and the Yugoslavs controlling the outskirts and hinterland. The London Agreement of 1954 was an attempt to normalize the situation; it was signed by all sides but never ratified by Italy, hence the need for the Treaty of Osimo. Over the long term, then, Osimo was a boost to the Slovene economy and it had a curious, double-edged effect on Slovene nationalism. On the one hand, the Slovene culture was, at least on paper, protected in Italy, keeping alive hopes of some eventual reunification. On the other hand, though, as Slovenia went through the rapid social changes of the Cold War years, separated by borders and emigration from communities of co-nationals all over the globe, a quiet consensus grew that the new Slovene polity (and, eventually, state) need not include all Slovenes everywhere, even in the neighboring lands. As important as Osimo was, then, its provisions, especially concerning property, again became a political football in the 1990s as Slovenia moved towards membership of the European Union. The issue was settled for the most part when Slovenia agreed to EU norms on foreigners' acquisition of property, although the evidence was mounting that Italy was ignoring its pledges to protect the Slovene minority.

By this time, the status of women in Slovene and Yugoslav society was dominated by what is called "state feminism." That is, many new rights had been secured by legal changes, many new career paths were available, and the Communist Party guaranteed women positions in government. But patriarchal attitudes within marriages and in society at large persisted, and, since Yugoslavia was a one-party state, there was little independent cultural or political space in which women's groups could operate. Furthermore, the feminization of certain jobs and professions, which occurred when large numbers of women became visible as teachers, doctors, judges, and bank workers, led to a drop in status of those careers.

More riots broke out in Kosovo in 1981. Tito, aging and retiring from the scene but refusing to endorse continued liberalization, established various collective bodies at the federal level to carry on the government after he died; the new presidency, premiership, and parliamentary presidency had membership based on the eight federal administrative units. Their leadership rotated regularly – some would say too regularly, sacrificing decisive leadership for fairness. On the international scene, Yugoslavia rose again to the challenge of confronting the Soviet Union in a war of words in the press and various international fora: this time for control of the nonaligned movement, which Moscow was trying to subvert through new members such as Cuba.

The Marković era

By 1988, it was hard to tell what was in worse shape, the Yugoslav polity or economy. The country's final prime minister, the Croat Ante Marković, put forth a very bold package designed to stop the slide. Long-term goals included privatization and a balanced budget, while short-term measures included freezing wages and controlling the exchange rate of the dinar. Whatever the prognosis was for Marković's eleventh-hour campaign, rising tensions between Serbia and the other republics drove the last nail in Yugoslavia's coffin. Riding the high from a carefully managed nationalist reaction to the situation in Kosovo, Milošević had Serbia boycott Slovene goods in 1989 because they were supposedly produced and priced in a way that was unfair to the rest of the country. A tariff war ensued, followed in 1990 by a stupendous feat of institutional legerdemain: the National Bank of Serbia appropriated about $1.5 billion for distribution to that republic's enterprises and pensioners. The result was a resounding electoral victory for Milošević's group and a death knell for the country. Although the secession of Slovenia and Croatia, which would soon follow, were of doubtful legality according to the Yugoslav constitution (which, according to most interpretations, allowed secession only with the approval of all republics), and although in important ways those first two secessions pushed Bosnia–Hercegovina into a slalom of independence drives and communitarian conflicts for which it was very ill prepared, one of the Slovene arguments for independence beckons plainly above the chaos: the Serbs were hardly a reliable partner for any type of common state. Although the Serbs had also been victims (as well as beneficiaries) of the Yugoslav experiment; although Serbs felt (perhaps understandably but not necessarily correctly) that Slovenes, Croats, and others were self-serving and ready to sell the country down the river by the 1960s; and although for many Serbs the preservation of Yugoslavia had more to do with keeping all Serbs in one country than necessarily denying anyone else their rights, the government and military under Milošević had themselves crossed the line – egregiously and concretely – into blatant disregard of the spirit and letter of Yugoslav law.

Intellectual life

Slovenia, for a nation of only two million members, has an outstanding literary tradition. Many works from the postwar period stand out for their emotional power and stylistic innovation; indeed, Slovenes were among the first in Tito's Yugoslavia to rebel against the strictures of socialist realism and to restore a healthy give-and-take with international literary trends. Here we shall mention only a few of the many writers who examined key historical or social issues or explored the role of Slovenes in the broader world. Pavel Zidar's *Sveti Pavel* (1965; St Paul) and Vitomil Zupan's *Menuet za kitaro: na petindvajset strelov* (1980; Minuet for a 25-shot Guitar) join Kocbek's work in treating the fratricidal brutality and exhaustion of World War II at a very high level of artistic achievement. Igor Torkar's *Umiranje na obroke* (Death on the Installment Plan; 1984) examines Stalinist persecutions in Slovenia, while Dominik Smole's drama *Antigone* (1959) is an indictment of the communists' postwar massacres and their continuing refusal to acknowledge them.

It is very possible, though, that Lojze Kovačič and Drago Jančar occupy the top positions in Slovene literature in terms of being prolific, socially and politically relevant, and highly artistically developed. Kovačič's *Zlatni poručnik* (1957; The Golden Lieutenant) and *Prišleki* (1984–1985; The Newcomers) treat important issues from the war years, but his numerous other works offer very wide reflection on most aspects of life in Slovenia. The unique, nearly encyclopedic, and personal perspective of these works has helped earn Kovačič the informal title the "Proust of Slovenia."

Jančar (b. 1948) is one of Slovenia's most prolific and highly regarded authors. He does not shy from controversy and his works are also fairly well represented in German and English translation. He has published many dramas, short stories, and essays, in addition to such famous novels as *Galjot* (1978), a phantasmagoric intellectual thriller set in medieval Europe. His play *Halštat* (1994) can be seen, again, as a metaphor for the unreconciled status of the victims of Stalinism. Not all of his work has political themes, of course, as in the powerful studies of the psychology of individual violence found in the stories "Violent Night" (1978) and "May, November" (1992). His work is sometimes tinged with magic realism, but it also abounds in historical conceits, dramatic endings, and various narrative idiosyncracies. Some of his main themes are outsider status, the difficulty of communication across lines of gender or culture, violence, and death. Two of his novels have appeared in English translation: *Northern Lights*, a vaguely apocalyptic and Kafkaesque tale of the Slovene city of Maribor between the world wars, and *Mocking Desire*, a combination of academic novel and rumination on melancholy set in New Orleans. Of his many fine dramas, *The Great Brilliant Waltz* stands out as truly superb and is, fortuitously, available in English. This play turns on a historian who is committed to a mental institution ominously named the Freedom Makes Free Institute. There, patients are encouraged, or forced, to act out their personal and political rebellious drives and develop "beyond them" into ostensible freedom and health. Written with a sure and erudite historical touch, the drama is also emotionally and intellectually rewarding.

Still, Jančar's richest work might well be his short stories, which are compact, psychologically sharp, gripping in terms of plot, and intellectually satisfying. But another of Jančar's great achievements across all genres is to depict Slovenes outside of Slovenia. This simple concept embodies an awakening of Slovene literature to the rest of the world and a significant expansion of possible themes for treatment.[27] Of course, many of the characters in his large *oeuvre* are Slovenes, but, significantly, many of them, are Slovenes "out there" in the world and "out there" in history: that is to say, they are individuals in locations that may or may not be Slovene and their concerns and problems are universal ones. This approach is a welcome cosmopolitan change in the world of Slovene letters, which for many decades cloaked itself consciously in questions of national identity and local traditions in what might be called the "Slovenia as history" or "Slovenes as the world" approach.

Jančar is also very important as a witness to, and critical observer of, the momentous events of Slovene, and general European, history in the second half of the twentieth century. He was imprisoned for several months in 1975 for writing newspaper articles critical of the Tito regime, and he continued to chronicle the key issues and personalities of subsequent years in both Slovenia and Yugoslavia. Deservedly earning the label "humanist," Jančar is especially adept at linking Slovene developments to ethical issues and intellectual trends in the rest of the world. He served as president of the Slovene PEN center from 1987 to 1991, worked briefly in Germany and the US, and is a member of the Slovene Academy of Science and Art. He has won both of Slovenia's most prestigious literary prizes. In

2000 and 2002, he won the Kersnik Award for the novels *Zvenenje v glavi* (Brain Buzz) and *Katarina, pav, in jezuit* (Katarina, the Peacock, and the Jesuit), respectively, while in 1993 he won the Prešeren Prize. Jančar swims against the modernist and postmodernist represented by Danilo Kiš's famous call for Yugoslavs to reject the obligatory mantle of exotic, essentially orientalized *Homo politicus* in favor of that of a modern, European *Homo poeticus*. That is to say, Jančar dares – successfully – to write in a way that is both modern and political. After all, in the final analysis, he recognizes that humans create politics and that it, in turn, helps structure human existence, so the political world is therefore a valid subject for artists. But he never whitewashes the clear link between the irrationality and unrest residing inside people with their often destructive behavior in groups.

In 1987, continuing the long tradition of Slovene scholarly periodicals (*Beseda, Revija 57, Perspektive, Naši Razgledi*) in promoting public debate on important political and cultural issues after the 1952 party congress at which liberalization was acknowledged, the journal *Nova Revija* published its now-famous fifty-seventh issue, entitled *Prispevki za slovenski nacionalni program* (Contributions to a Slovene National Program). This issue appeared in the superheated environment of late Yugoslavia, on the heels of the Serbian National Program (the "Memorandum") drafted by that republic's Academy of Science and Arts in 1986. The editors of the *Prispevki* took pains to state in a preface to the collection of sixteen scholarly essays that they were not intended as a concrete political program of any sort, much less as a new sort of "national program" in the style of *Zedinjena Slovenija* from 1848. Neither were the articles to be interpreted by outsiders as expressions of aggressiveness or of self-pity. The articles purported to have as their aims the formulation of a new concept of what it meant to be Slovene in the modern (crisis-ridden) era and the delineation of future political options. Even with these carefully applied caveats, the preface invokes the ideas of earlier conscientious and highly regarded opponents of the central government in Belgrade, such as Kocbek and Dušan Pirjevec, and it does not neglect to close with references to the "potentially sovereign" Slovene people and the "demands of a new historical epoch."

The Yugoslav authorities, who were likely unconvinced by the preface's caveats, found much more to alarm them inside. After publication they pressed for prosecution of the editors and authors, but local Slovene authorities, asserting their growing sense of independence, refused to cooperate. Indeed, in many ways, the anthology is a national program of a rather theoretical and abstract variety; it does not, for instance, examine many specific grievances or air in detail many historical, economic, or territorial disputes. But at any rate it is a snapshot of, and a forum for, the type of thinking that had spread widely in Slovenia.

Nearly all of the essays have three major features in common. The first, and most general, is the sense of all-pervading crisis in Yugoslavia at the time; one has a distinct feeling of the genuine meaning of the word crisis as something far beyond a problem or a challenge – there is an over- whelming air of the system being broken, burdened beyond its limits, discharging its passengers at a crossroads. The second common feature is an emphasis on the intertwined nature of national autonomy, on the one hand, with the all-important, modern set of values such as civil rights, individual development, and social maturity on the other. The final leit- motif is the necessity for Slovenes to overcome their historical and emotional doubts about their viability as a nation. These self-doubts have taken many forms, ranging from Hegel's damnation of "non-historical" peoples devoid of a history of statehood, to the Marxist idea that nations are temporary phenomena associated with the capitalist era, to psycho- logical manifestations of an inferiority complex. Other features shared by many of the contributions include avowals of the importance of the integrity of the language, discussions of the history and meaning of the term "self- determination," and the evaluation of earlier approaches to nationalism such as those in the works of Kocbek and Edvard Kardelj.

The specific topics of the essays include linguistics, legal studies, the historical development of Slovene nationalism, civil society, Catholicism, suicide, and exile. Some of the less controversial essays stress the necessity of the continued evolution both of socialism and of the concept of the all- important nation-state. But attacks on the Leninist nature of Yugoslav communism were volatile. The vaunted equality of nations was charged to be spurious, especially in the army; the consolidation of party power in the 1940s was nasty and bloody; and the system had retained far too many taboos despite its liberalized exterior. Perhaps most damning of all, several authors joined in a critique of the lack of political pluralism. Despite self- management and the existence of nation-based republics, the monolithic, single-party structure made national crises worse, because no one could believe that a real federation was in place while the state was subject to one-party rule. This, of course, was despite the fact that the federal party tried to rise above – and, indeed, condemned – individual nationalisms and tried to prevent conflicts among the national units and nationalities. In sum, then, this seminal collection of essays put into circulation a set of theoretical approaches for explaining what had become Yugoslavia's self- evident, and colossal, crisis; it was also a body of suggestions for paths out of the crisis. Some of the same authors and themes – reflecting the new perspectives of civil war and independent statehood – were represented in a special 1993 issue of the journal *Nationalities Papers*, edited by Peter Vodopivec and Henry R. Huttenbach.

Another venerable Slovene periodical also deserves mention here. *Mladina* (Youth) began publication in 1943; it moved through many phases in the decades of existence, alternately coming under partial party or government control and also resisting it by publishing independent-minded articles on problems facing Slovenia. In the early 1980s, *Mladina* was cut loose by the party and began functioning as an "avant-garde, oppositional weekly".[28] No taboo, including Tito's legacy and the actions of the Yugoslav People's Army, was off-limits, and in this way *Mladina* made an enormous contribution to the development of civil society in Slovenia. Its calls for political pluralism, a tolerant, modern society, and a curbing of ethnic violence made it an important player in the establishment of an independent Slovene nation-state, even if it also took aim at Slovene politicians it considered aggressive, smug, or ignorant. *Mladina* also ran frequent columns by Tomaž Mastnak. Its large, colorful cover page was usually decked out with satirical artwork or provocative photos, and they functioned as symbols, or even icons, of resistance to many. At its peak shortly before Slovenia's secession, *Mladina*'s circulation was an incredible 65,000 copies per week,[29] quite a feat in small Slovenia. The magazine was also cherished by non-Slovene Yugoslavs, too, just as much oppositional publishing in other Yugoslav languages before and after 1991 took place in Slovenia instead of in other republics.

Independent media that functioned both as fora for the concerns of their republics and as spurs to opposition of various types played important roles in the late 1980s and 1990s. In Serbia, *Vreme* ("Time") functioned in this way, as did Croatia's *Danas* ("Today"). When hard-core nationalism took over from communist authoritarianism under Milošević and Tuđman, opposition media had to fix their sights on new targets. In the 1990s, *Mladina* did not have to fight against aggressive nationalist currents in the same way, but the magazine retained its irreverent and exuberant pop-cultural appeal and its iconoclastic approach to political, social, and economic issues. Today the periodical is also available on-line (www.mladina.si) and has a vast free archive of articles and photos; it continues its function as a lightning rod and maverick information source for Slovene civil society.

Many people today think of Slovene independence as the result of some sort of full-fledged independence movement born around 1990. This view is inaccurate. The idea that Slovenia could or should become an independent state was hampered, above all, by the lack of a state tradition and by the fact that the Slovene nation (as a population group) was spread across four countries. It is also important to remember that, although centrifugal forces in the country increased after the death of Tito in 1980, Yugoslav society had long been segmented into more or less national units for administrative, party, and economic purposes; starting in the 1960s, furthermore, the country's various units and entrenched elites had begun competing and conflicting ever more publicly over resources and policies. Many other factors also contributed to the breakup of Yugoslavia from 1991 to 1995, such as inflation and strikes, the ethnic conflict in Kosovo and its manipulation by Slobodan Milošević, the Serbian domination of the military, the fears among Serbs in Croatia and Bosnia of a recrudescence of Croatian fascism, and the implosion of communist systems in

Eastern Europe and the Soviet Union after 1989. But one very important foundation of the Slovene national movement that was driven neither by history nor the headlines was the development of civil society.

The emergence of civil society, originally called "socialist civil society" or the Alternative Scene in Slovenia, can be dated to 1983.[30] Civil society, which was a widely discussed concept in Central Europe at the time and which proved to be invaluable in setting in motion the democratic transformation of the region, can be defined as the network and activities (sometimes political) of autonomous social groups; it is best thought of as horizontal, non-governmental connections between people in a given country. It is, furthermore, generally regarded to be a necessary, but not sufficient, condition for democracy; its members can be involved in anything from stamp collecting to Bible studies to gay rights movements to tourism promotion. In the early 1980s ideas about the necessity of creating civil society underneath the carapace of "real existing socialism" emerged in the writings of people like Vaclav Havel, Miklos Haraszti, György Dalos, György Konrad, Adam Michnik, and Jacek Kuron, although the consensus was that the center of gravity of civil society did not lie with dissident intellectuals; they were more important than university intellectuals or cultural figures dependent upon government sanction for their careers, but union movements like Solidarity were considered closer to the heart of civil society, because they involved large numbers of ordinary citizens.

The leading Slovene proponent of civil society was the academic and activist Tomaž Mastnak. Today, Mastnak is a sociologist and philosopher attached to the Slovene Academy of Sciences and Arts; in the 1980s he wrote and edited many important works on the theory and practice of civil society in Slovenia. This movement was so important because it demonstrated the sophisticated nature of Slovene society, both urban and rural, especially in comparison to most of the rest of Yugoslavia (parts of Croatia as well as large cities like Belgrad, Sarajevo, and Novi Sad were similarly modern and liberal). Because civil society is essentially a tolerant, voluntaristic, and pluralistic approach to modern life, it left a deep imprint on Slovene nationalism. This is true even though civil society is "pre-political" in many ways; its spokespersons, including Mastnak, expressed some unease when political movements grew out of civil society, because they were joined by all sorts of established professionals and politicians. Both civil society advocates and political oppositionists desired to end the intolerant political monopoly of the League of Communists, but this co-optation brought with it the danger of the reduction of politics to "primitive anti-communism and crude appeals to nationalism,"[31] or at least the acceptance of the necessity of "horse-trading" in the realm "politics as usual." Not being used to public compromise or competition, intellectuals and civil society advocates sometimes capitulated in the face of the mass democracy. Being born as an alternative and not opposition heightened the sense that power-holding was also alien to the movement. If legal toleration of civil society had been established by the late 1980s, there was of course the new emerging danger that economic forces and nationalism could spur a new homogenization of Slovene society. Civil society may productively be thought of as one of the main tributaries of the national independence movement in Slovenia.

A Slovene intellectual who was prominent in late Yugoslavia, and who has since become something of an international scholarly "phenomenon," is Slavoj Žižek (b. 1949). Trained in philosophy, psychology, and sociology, Žižek played an important role – mostly through his writings but also in politics – in the development of Slovene civil society in the 1980s. His 1989 book *Druga smrt Josipa Broza Tita* (The Second Death of Josip Broz Tito) is a collection of essays, most of which were published between 1986 and 1988 in *Mladina* and other Slovene media. Most of the essays are glosses and commentaries on current events in Yugoslavia, especially the trial of the "*Mladina* Four," who were accused of stealing and publicizing Yugoslav National Army documents about plans to impose martial law on the fractious Slovene republic. The thirty-five articles are arranged – in vintage, ebullient Žižek style – in three sections named after Franz Kafka's three novels, "Amerika," "The Trial," and "The Castle."

One of the main points in Žižek's reflections on the political system of late Yugoslavia and the Slovene challenge to it is that it is time for the alternative social movements in Slovenia to move into politics and leave to others (or, implicitly, to nobody) the questions of theory and the attempts to harmonize democratic principles with the League of Communists' political monopoly. This can be seen as a kind of maturation process of the Slovene body politic. The other most salient feature of the collection is to be found in the eponymous essay. The essay, not surprisingly given Žižek's maverick style and his wide-ranging and often pioneering mode of thought, embraces a contradiction by saying both that Titoism as a system, banking on "brotherhood and unity," self-management, and the adhesive effects of the party and the military, is dying due to its own logical evolution and also due to maltreatment at the hands of the country's violent, inflexible, and authoritarian leadership.

Rejecting the smear that the liberals within the party or the alternative movements outside of it are "enemies" of the state and are to blame for the chaos, Žižek asserts that in fact the very radicalization of the Slovene model of pluralism and its spread to other republics would save the part of the Tito legacy that actually has "world historical significance."[32] By this he means the legacy of having stood up to Stalin in the Cominform dispute of 1948 and then having renounced the leading role of the party in society. Although not a traditional nationalist, Žižek supported Slovene independence because of the moral and intellectual bankruptcy of Yugoslavia. Since 1991 he has continued to write on a wide variety of topics and now teaches at the University of Ljubljana. A soaring number of his works, especially on Jacques Lacan, German idealism, religion, and various political topics (including the September 11 terrorist attacks in the US) have been translated and published abroad in a variety of languages.

Other important cultural developments from the Tito era include the founding of Ljubljana's Museum of Modern Art, a television network in the 1960s, and a second university at Maribor in the 1970s. The Slovene film industry also gained international recognition for its quality. The most famous director was the prolific Franc Štiglic, who began his career with *Na svoji zemlji* (1948; On Their Own Ground). Boštjan Hladnik made a fascinating love story set in Ljubljana, *Ples v dežju* (1961; Dance in the Rain). A film version of the Vitomil Zupan novel mentioned above was made in 1980, entitled *Na svidenje v nasledni vojni* (See You in the Next War).

Conclusion

Ultimately, no matter how much the federal government scrambled to forge an economic system that would bring both general prosperity and a reduction in corrosive regional disparities, the economic situation deteriorated and tension between the center and the republics grew. With the massive bloodletting of World War II hushed up in the interest of national unity (except for the war's gory valor and an all too clear characterization of good and bad) and the perception in Serbia and Croatia that expression of their national specificities beyond the folkloric was recklessly reactionary, little pan-Yugoslav or regional civil society emerged; Slovenia by the 1980s was a notable exception to this, however. At the risk of sounding flip about what turned out to be a tragic fate, one is tempted to observe that all of the major national groups were discontented with the state of affairs in Yugoslavia by the time Tito died in 1980 – but each of them had a different diagnosis of the problem and a different prescription for treatment.

That the second Yugoslavia was a time of useful economic development for Slovenia, and even a time of indispensable political maturation, is increasingly borne out by historians; still, although most Slovenes do not feel as bitterly towards either Serbs or Yugoslavism as many Croats, Bosnians, and Albanians do, the idea of the Tito regime as a kind of useful, if not always pleasant, incubation period for Slovenia, rubs some Slovenes the wrong way. But many, many sets of figures showing Slovenia's economic situation in comparison to the rest of Yugoslavia can be adduced to demonstrate both how much Slovenia developed in this time and how the federal government in Belgrade failed to accomplish a similar modernization in most of the rest of the country.

Taking the measure of national income per capita, one sees that in 1947, Slovenia was at 175 percent of the country-wide average; in 1962 its figure was 199 percent; and by 1976 the figure had risen to 202 percent. Of the other administrative regions, Croatia and Vojvodina also often ranked as "above average" for the federation, but behind Slovenia, which retained its status as the most economically developed republic in the country. Serbia proper (or "narrow Serbia," considered apart from its two autonomous provinces), usually ranked at the top of the grouping below the federal average, followed by Bosnia, Montenegro, and Macedonia. Close to the bottom of all socioeconomic indicators was Kosovo. That Kosovo was not just a tinderbox for demographic but also for economic reasons is clear when we note that, in 1947, its percentage of national income per capita was at 53 percent, but then fell to a woeful 27 percent by 1978.[33]

One can also gauge Slovene development by looking at agriculture. In 1945, only half of Slovenes earned their living on the land; this early figure alone is amazing when compared to the rest of Yugoslavia and the Balkans. But the significance of this gauge grows when one notes that the agricultural population fell to 20 percent by 1971 and just 8 percent (on a par with Western European countries) by 1991.[34]

Yet another telling statistic is that Slovenia in the 1980s comprised 6 percent of the area of Yugoslavia and 8 percent of the population, but it produced about one quarter of the gross domestic product.[35] Especially well developed, and valuable for the whole country, were Slovenia's tourism, electronics and consumer industries, and foreign trade.

Finally, one can draw chilling contrasts between the relative levels of success of modernization in Slovenia and Kosovo, the wealthiest and poorest parts of Yugoslavia, respectively. From 1949 to 1988, for instance, the number of infant deaths per thousand declines from 81 to 11; in roughly the same period, the percentage of the Slovene labor force that was female rose from 32 to 45 percent, and illiteracy sank from 2.4 percent to less than 1 percent. Slovenia also led the country in terms of life expectancy, density of doctors, and other significant criteria.[36]

These indices of standard of living showed considerable improvement for Kosovo, as well, though generally only in terms of percentages, and that autonomous province started from a much lower level of development. Most poignantly of all, the general gap in productivity, income, and standard of living between Slovenia and Kosovo actually widened considerably over the four decades of communist rule, indicating that Slovenia continued to progress more rapidly than the south.

The regional disparities presented in these figures, again, do two things: they show the increasing, if still latent, potential for Slovenia to go its own way (or join the rest of Europe) and they also illustrate the nexus of poverty and frustration out of which political forces destructive to the Yugoslav project grew. What the regional disparities do not indicate is that Slovenia did not "belong" in a country where nearly everyone else lived in materially poorer conditions. To start with, Slovenes did not live as comfortably or produce up to the levels of Western Europe, and, in addition, they derived great benefit from the resources and markets of Yugoslavia, as well as from their forward position as a funnel for external trade to the rest of the country. In addition, many Slovenes recognized the initial advantages of security and autonomy that Yugoslavia had brought them, even since 1918; also, many were genuinely fond of the cultural and topographical diversity of the country. It is ironic, though, and a testament to the strength of Slovene civil society, that most Slovenes in and out of government took the side of the Albanians of Kosovo in the disputes of the 1980s and 1990s, regarding them as victims of failed federal policies who were now exposed to cruel and unfair treatments by increasingly radicalized Serbs. At any rate, this "comprehensive modernization of the Slovene economic space"[37] was simply one of the great facts of Slovenia's Yugoslav experience. And it was not, as we have seen, of purely economic importance.

3 Slovenia and the breakup of Yugoslavia

Introduction

One open, and important, question about the fall of Yugoslavia is: when did the country pass the point of no return? Other questions are relevant here, too. Can we determine at what point Yugoslavia's demise was assured? By what time was the will to live up to the spirit, if not the letter, of Yugoslavia's federative principles evaporated? Was it enough for loyalty to Yugoslavia to die in one key republic, or in just some elite part of one republic, or was there a system-wide failure? And, finally, did nationalism alone kill Yugoslavia, or was it, more properly, a rebellion against the political and economic control of the party that did so?

Before suggesting possible answers to this query, it behooves us to consider several of the dynamics of the country's breakdown. The first is that events and trends in Yugoslavia did not take place in a vacuum. This is especially important in the domestic sense. The image of dominos is rather too fatalistic for most historians, since it straps trends onto a track of inevitability, but the idea that individual phenomena are both causes and effects comes closer to the truth. Actions provoking reactions in other republics, and those reactions being informed by prejudice and perception as well as self-interest, ideas, and international pressure – these are crucial concepts here.

Another piece of the necessary framework relates to the relative ranking of the roots of discord in Yugoslavia. A common misrepresentation of Slovenia and Croatia is that all they wanted was a more advantageous economic system, or that the political elites in both republics were equally interested in enabling the development of the kind of democracy we all know and love: a pluralistic, tolerant, individualistic society. In fact, the motives of the anti-Titoists and reform communists in Yugoslavia were quite mixed, or at least quite varied from republic to republic.

Finally, one does well to remember that multinational states do not always have to break up. The examples of Switzerland, Belgium, Spain, and the United Kingdom demonstrate this. And when such states do break apart, they need not do so violently, as the Czechoslovak and Soviet examples show. The period after Tito's death in 1980 was fraught with danger and of course underlain by older historical realities – but history does not speak for itself. The past was recast and re-run on television screens and front pages of papers in ways that fueled the transformation of old rivalries and unresolved controversies into new conflicts that seemed to present life-or-death dilemmas.

Several popular and seductive – but reductionistic – paradigms must be resisted in order to understand Slovenia's evolution to sovereignty in a proper light. There was no magic moment in 1991 when, suddenly, Slovene national identity congealed into a nationalist political agenda and nationalism instantly produced a new country. Nor was economics the only, or even chief, motivation of the Slovene elites and ordinary citizens. Nor can we justifiably assert that perennial or primordial Slovene nationalism had been submerged in Yugoslavia and suddenly bubbled back to the surface and revived after Tito's death. As the first two chapters of this book have attempted to demonstrate, Slovene identity, based at first on very fundamental factors like common origin and language, has been a historical force for centuries, but nationalism itself is a modern phenomenon that takes a long time to spread throughout the whole society and then produce a movement for an independent state.

Two features of the Slovene national movement in late Yugoslavia seem especially important here. The first is that the breakdown of the country was *incremental*, and the second is that the pursuit of Slovene sovereignty was *embedded* in a fabric of wide-ranging political and social change. It is possible to consider the dissolution of Yugoslavia in three discrete phases. In retrospect one can assert that the country's system had become unworkable, and its economic situation untenable, as early as the mid-1970s. Younger, more liberal, and more technocratic political leaders across the country had been purged for their ostensible "nationalism" after the Croatian Spring. The world oil crisis also meant rude shocks for the Yugoslav economy and the constitutional experiments had run amok. The society was so fragmented and, some would say, distracted by consumerism, that pan-Yugoslav civic movements that might have later pushed for reform within a federal, instead of republican, framework were not emerging. In other words, by the mid-1970s, Yugoslavia's government was disabled, its culture was gradually disintegrating under the weight of nationalism, consumerism, and censorship on key historical issues, and the decks of its ship of state had been cleared of capable successors to Tito.

The years 1989 and 1990 seem to comprise the next critical phase. It was at this point that the Serbian party was coopting calls for reform by pounding the Kosovo drum and taking an increasingly heavy-handed approach to relations with the rest of the country. It is probably impossible to tell which event from these years actually represented the point of no return, but the changed atmosphere and the reasons for it are obvious. The crises of loyalty and of ends and means were bigger, for instance, than any specific event, whether it was the Serbian insistence on martial law in Kosovo, their appropriation of a massive sum of money from federal coffers, or the Slovene League of Communists walking out of a party congress and, in effect, breaking off relations with the rest of the country. A third issue is unfortunately sometimes conflated with these first two phases: the bloodiness of Yugoslavia's collapse. Although the Slovenes in many ways pushed the envelope of reforms and were organized and courageous enough effectively to jump ship when they decided Yugoslavia was unsalvageable, and although the Serbs and the Albanians have the most accumulated resentments of any of the national groups, it was the Serb–Croat rivalry that occasioned general bloodshed. Without the manipulation of this rivalry, through the actions of the camps of both Milošević and his heavy-handed Croatian counterpart Franjo Tudman, the violence in Kosovo itself might have continued but the wide-scale civil war that engulfed Bosnia–Hercegovina and Croatia would have been avoided.

It remains to discuss the matrix from which Slovenia's demands for political independence would ultimately emerge. The first, and in many ways headiest, factor is the pluralization of Slovene society in the 1980s. From new artistic movements to NGOs to self-help organizations, from calls for conscientious objector status to feminism and the promotion of equal rights for gays and lesbians, from punk rock bands to freewheeling investigative journalism to a strong environmental movement, Slovene civil society flourished. A counterculture that fed on generational differences and reacted against the communist ruling class's imposition of what had once been its own counterculture had already been in existence since the 1960s.[1] Much of it had been focused on popular music, such as jazz, rock, and eventually punk; symbols and lifestyle were more important than politics, but still the government typically saw such movements as a threat.

By the 1980s, though, there was much more activity across the spectrum of Slovene society. Independent trade unions were developed and the Slovene public sympathized with and supported strikers elsewhere in Yugoslavia. The weekly news magazine *Mladina*, the Ljubljana-based Radio Študent, the bold and raucous contemporary art-cum-philosophy collective called *Neue Slowenische Kunst*, or NSK, with its most prominent member the heavy industrial band Laibach[2] – all attracted a great deal of attention and won the Slovenes high marks for creativity and irreverence. Depending on your point of view, Slovenes either basked in their rediscovered identity or sought to fill the emotional void left by a moribund Yugoslavism by proudly sporting bumper stickers and applauding magazine ads and billboards that proclaimed "Slovenija – moja dežela" (Slovenia is my country) and "Na sončni strani Alp" (On the side of the Alps). What started as individualism, a re-connectedness to the rest of Europe, and the quest for freedom of conscience would eventually bring political pluralism, and that element of mobilization and competitiveness is, of course, a constituent element of democracy. A key topic for future study is why civil society did not take root across all of Yugoslavia and how democratization became entwined with, and confused with, nationalism in each republic.

This Slovene "alternative social scene" attracted an enormous amount of media and scholarly attention around the world, even more than the political aspects of the second trend, the "Slovene Spring." The 1980s saw the revival of simmering ideas of what was called the "liberal movement" of the 1960s. This was a gradualist reform movement within the Communist Party which, in both decades, moved quietly towards acceptance of key aspects of capitalism and of a new "asymmetric" relationship among the Yugoslav republics. Instead of an already fairly loose federation, the Slovenes envisaged an even looser confederation; the "asymmetric" ties between its sovereign members would guarantee not only language and territory but the right to experiment, or not, with alternative political, economic, and social systems.

The final factor in the mix was the defense of the Slovene language. This historically vital issue, which also caused great consternation in Croatia in the late 1960s, was raised again by the Slovene linguist Joze Toporišič in the late 1970s, who said that Slovene was endangered by the political predominance of Serbo-Croatian and by the changing demographic situation of the Slovene republic. Slovenia did have a low birthrate and the increasingly bad economic situation was occasioning more and more immigration from the other parts of Yugoslavia.[3] The journal *Nova Revija* focused attention on it again in its epochal fifty-seventh issue of 1987. The Trial of the Ljubljana Four (see below) aroused a great deal of public ire about the inequality of the Slovene language. In addition, throughout the 1980s there were major verbal battles fought inside the Yugoslav Writers' Union about language rights and cultural autonomy; they manifested themselves in heated exchanges between Slovene representatives such as the poet Ciril Zlobec and Serbs such as Miodrag Bulatović and Ćosić about a common core curriculum for schools, the abolition of "verbal offenses" (that is, restrictions on freedom of speech), and the assessment of the individual Yugoslav nations and nationalities as artificial creations or natural and authentic cultures. Naturally, the Slovenes defended their rights, and, since they saw Serbian policy in Kosovo as indicative of what could happen to smaller peoples in the new unitarist atmosphere, they defended the Albanians too.

Politics and society in Yugoslavia's final decade

Overview of a tumultuous period

Slovenia's move to independence began in the 1980s with a growing set of crises in the country at large, followed by several changes in the Yugoslav state structure and then by the legal assertion of Slovene sovereignty. As

Yugoslavia became increasingly dominated by Slobodan Milošević of Serbia, the League of Communists of Slovenia allowed the formation of noncommunist political parties. The new president of the republic was the popular reform communist Milan Kučan, who was trained as a lawyer and provided a steady hand at the helm throughout the 1990s. Specific milestones along the way included public protests over a military trial (the case of Janez Janša and three other defendants), unilateral reductions in contributions to the federal budget, Slovene support for human rights activists under Serbian pressure in Kosovo, the creation of noncommunist political parties (first the Slovene League of Social Democrats and then a number of other parties, several of which joined together in a coalition or umbrella organization called DEMOS, for Democratic Opposition of Slovenia), the exit of the League of Communists of Slovenia from the federal party, a declaration of sovereignty, the assertion of control over the Territorial Defense Force, a plebiscite with over 88 percent of the voters in favor of the declaration of independence, and finally, on June 25, 1991, that declaration itself.

A weekly news magazine, *Mladina*, kept the public mobilized and informed by publishing frequent exposés about government corruption. Slovenia also had an active civil society, with many non-governmental organizations pushing for environmental protections, women's rights, and conscientious objector status. There was also a vigorous alternative scene in the republic, involving punk rock, modern art, and gay liberation movements. After a brief war of less than two weeks, the Yugoslav People's Army retreated from Slovenia, sparing that country the massive destruction that war would soon visit on Croatia, Bosnia–Hercegovina, and Kosovo. After an EC-sponsored moratorium of three months, designed to ensure that fighting came to an end, Germany recognized the new Slovene government in December of that year; the other countries of the European Union did so in January of 1992, followed by the US the next month. The effect of Slovene secession on the rest of Yugoslavia is an important issue that warrants closer study. Certainly many Slovenes see their secession as a reaction to, and not a cause of, the final breakdown of the Yugoslav system, and especially to the ham-fisted and threatening activities of the Serbian leadership.

Various constitutions frequently referred to the right of self-determination of the Yugoslav peoples or republics, which, in Slovenia's case, at least, was clear. By 1974 the issue was murkier, involving possible interpretations including the need for the other republics to agree to secession and the proviso that international borders not be changed. Presumably, the latter qualification meant that the republic should not be split up once it split off from Yugoslavia.

Tito died in Ljubljana on May 4, 1980. Kardelj had died the year before, and the other paladins of the Partisan system such as Milovan Djilas and Aleksandar Ranković had already left politics. That Tito himself, the embodiment of the old order, should pass away in Ljubljana was highly symbolic. He had gone there to get the best medical care in the country, demonstrating his trust in Slovene accomplishments. But Slovenia would end up being the first republic to leave Yugoslavia, and in some ways its departure guaranteed the collapse of the rest of Tito's structure. Indeed, in some ways Slovenia was already looking beyond Tito. But the decade still held many surprises. And the current generation of Slovene political leaders, like their predecessors in the liberal movement of the 1960s, did not use words like "independence" or "market economy" in public. Indeed, many, or very likely most, Slovenes still believed in some reformed Yugoslavia, perhaps on a confederal basis with a de facto pluralist political system and a mixed economy. Most Slovene politicians were committed to negotiating and reforming their way to Yugoslavia based on strong territorial and cultural autonomy and built on strong social democratic political and economic principles. But the evolution of Slovene political thought was about to speed up mightily as the society diversified, matured, and, perhaps most importantly, responded to stimuli from the rest of the country.

Four country-wide trends form an indispensable backdrop for comprehending the changes in Slovenia in this decade. The first is the economic wreck that Yugoslavia had become, with high inflation and a devalued currency, a massive foreign debt of about $20 billion, and high (if hidden) unemployment. Strikes also increased in frequency and scope.

The second trend is the more or less rudderless nature of the ship of state. The 1974 Constitution and the death of Tito had obviously eroded much of the basis of Belgrade's much-maligned centralist rule. The three main political centers were now the party, the presidency, and the parliament. In the 1980s, each of them was run by a collective presidency – a committee, in essence. These presidencies, which yielded a party chief, an executive akin to a prime minister, and a speaker of the parliament, consisted of eight members. There was one from each republic, plus one each from the Serbian autonomous republics of Kosovo and Vojvodina. The chair rotated annually. Such an arrangement might of course have left all the major nationalities of the country feeling enfranchised, but it also left no one truly empowered to take decisive, long-term action as the atmosphere became ever more charged with crisis. There were, in addition, sharp conflicts over what the nationality should be of representatives from multi-ethnic areas. Should the Croatian member of a presidency sometimes be a Serb on account of the large Serbian minority in that republic? Who should represent Bosnia–Hercegovina – a Bosniak, as we would say today, or sometimes a representative of the large Serbian and Croatian populations there? What about Kosovo, where Albanians outnumbered Serbs by six to one or more by now? The political inertia was heightened by a set of scandals in the country, most prominently the Agrokomerc affair in Bosnia, and the lack of competent and popular leaders in most regions since the purges of the early 1970s.

The third trend is that the nationalism inherent in the Yugoslav federal system since 1945 had been accelerating considerably since the mid-1960s. In 1964, for instance, Tito rejected the idea of a unitary Yugoslav nation. Speaking at the Eighth Congress of the LCY in Belgrade, he stressed the continuing importance of individual nations in fighting "bureaucratic centralization" and in forging a new socialist community.[4] Then, in 1967, the distinct and, in historical terms, recent identity of the Macedonians was given a boost by the creation of a new Orthodox Church separate from the Serbian. By 1971, Kardelj could state that the "self-managing community of nations . . . [was] an essentially new category in inter-ethnic relations" that had outstripped either federalism or confederalism in both autonomy and integration.[5] Also in that year, Bosnian Muslims were given the status of a nation in a new census, after the League of Communists of Bosnia and Hercegovina had decided, in essence, to upgrade the status of that politically important group from simply a confessional or regional designation. The devolution of political and economic authority to the republican and sub-republican levels, culminating in the 1974 constitution, was officially spun as a way to avoid both etatism and ethnic conflicts. But it also hamstrung the federal government from taking action on almost anything except maintaining the military and security forces, limiting dissent, and tripping up calls for pluralism; the government had become a bankrupt monopoly, and not just in the economic sense. Some observers see the impotent state as not just incapable of controlling local nationalism but also of encouraging it. With more and more despairing Yugoslav citizens longing for decisive action to save the country, might their loyalties not have switched to republican power centers that promised a stronger hand?[6]

The final general point of background is the rising tide of specifically Serbian discontent inside Yugoslavia. Coupled with Serbia's strength, this combination of anxiety and assertiveness was potent indeed. Serbs and Montenegrins had long been preeminent in the military, and their hold on it was tightening. The Serbs were also the country's biggest national group, at 36 percent of the total population; even though parts of Serbia itself now enjoyed autonomy from Belgrade, Serbs were a powerful interest group in both Croatia and Bosnia, where they formed minorities with hundreds of thousands of members. Serbia also had traditionally strong ties to Montenegro and Macedonia, on whom it could often, but not always, count for support on key votes in the federal political bodies. Of growing concern since the 1960s was also the tendency of Serbian critics of Titoism, most prominently the famous writer Dobrica Ćosić, to equate democracy with nationalism.

One does well to recall at this point that neither the Serbian people nor the Serbian leadership wanted to deny other groups the right to live in Yugoslavia; this Serbian national assertiveness was not a conceptually genocidal phenomenon. It did not aim per se at the physical elimination of ethnic enemies. But Serbian nationalism was still highly problematic, or even sinister, to many of the country's other nationalities. There was the rough interwar historical record to consider, and the great current military and administrative power of the Serbs as well. But above all, the Serbian metamorphosis was unpopular in other quarters because of its centralizing tendencies and its insistence either that Yugoslavia's borders remain unchanged or that all historically *and* ethnically Serbian areas be allowed to detach themselves from seceding republics and rejoin to Yugoslavia. Either way, all Serbs and all previous Serbian-inhabited territory would remain in one state. In other periods, this version of state-building had offered creative possibilities for the Western Balkans. By the 1980s, it was no longer welcome among most non-Serbs.

There were three main impulses in Serbian political culture and popular understanding of history. These help to explain not only the rise and goals of Slobodan Milošević within the League of Communists of Serbia, but also the actions of other Serbian politicians and the evolution of public opinion there in the 1980s. These three factors are: a durable, passionate, and often costly attachment to Yugoslavism as a vehicle of their own national unification, even when it was interpreted differently by their neighbors; the living memory of the massive atrocities wreaked on the Serbs by Croatian fascists known as the *Ustaše* during World War II; and the recent "reactivation of the Kosovo myth" of Serbian victimization and civilizing mission.[7]

Key events of the 1980s

In 1981, just months after Tito's death the previous year, major unrest broke out in the predominantly Albanian autonomous republic of Kosovo in southern Serbia. It grew from student demonstrations to riots, at least twelve people died, and about 1,600 harsh prison sentences were meted out. The falling of taboos in Serbia and elsewhere meant that academics and journalists were free to discuss Kosovo's history and current conditions as they wished, and from this new freedom arose a veritable cottage industry of crisis reports about how vital Kosovo had been to Serbia's medieval civilization and how wickedly the Albanians there today were persecuting the remaining Serbs.

In 1982, an economic commission chaired by the Slovene Sergej Kraigher stressed the need for systematic and long-overdue reforms in the direction of a market economy. This was also the year the federal government proposed a controversial centralist common school program for all republics.

In 1984 the Writers for Peace Committee was formed in Ljubljana by Miloš Mikeln, a dramatist and satirist. Connected to the Slovene PEN Center, it is an international group that is involved in campaigns for human rights around the world, with special emphasis on contesting the misuse of language and literature for intolerant purposes and on bringing together artists from opposing camps. Writers for Peace would soon become very busy with events right in its own backyard, but even before the outbreak of war in 1991 it added to the growing international reputation of Slovenia's civil society. In this same year the Women's Section of the Sociological Society was also formed in Ljubljana. This was one of Yugoslavia's first feminist groups. The next year another and ultimately higher-profile group was formed, Lilith (Lilit in Slovene). Lilith cooperated with other alternative movements on ecological and anti-militarist demonstrations and discussions. Other concerns of these and other feminist groups included reproductive rights, counseling for victims of violence against women, and public acceptance of lesbians and gays.

The year 1985 saw the drafting of the now infamous Memorandum of the Serbian Academy of Arts and Sciences. Although never officially adopted, it was leaked to the press the next year and revealed the long list of Serbian grievances against Yugoslavia as a whole and individual peoples, especially the Croats, Albanians, and Slovenes, in particular. The Memorandum plumbed the depths of contemporary Serbian nationalism and also endorsed it. In becoming a kind of flagship text, it provided a new generation of Serbian leaders (such as Milošević) with a ready agenda for seizing power and it also spurred the growth of similar sentiments and political road maps among other groups.

In 1986, the nuclear accident at Chernobyl in the USSR sparked Slovenes' concern about their own nuclear power plant at Krško; this gave a great boost to Slovenia's Green movement, which is still a political party to this day. Beginning in 1986, and spilling over into 1987, also came a significant, if wrily amusing controversy over the celebration of Tito's birthday, called the Day of Youth. The Slovene youth organization responsible for hosting a much-fêted relay race tried to cancel or sabotage the proceedings with sarcasm, while a poster announcing the event – created by the graphics arm of the controversial NSK, New Collectivism – was soon revealed to be a copy of a Nazi propaganda poster. With the NSK's band, Laibach, playing neo-pagan music and also freely – if sardonically – invoking Nazi imagery to make points about totalitarianism, the Slovene arts scene had proven dangerous.

In April 1987, the rising Serbian communist leader Slobodan Milošević traveled to Kosovo to hitch his star to the nationalist grievances of Serbs living there. He began to outmaneuver his party bosses and to stage mass meetings of disaffected workers. Fed by economic grievances, the meetings touted the need for an "anti-bureaucratic" revolution which would address the nationalist and other demands ignored by the supposedly anti-Serbian federal government established by Tito. In this same year, the Slovene journal *Nova Revija* published its famous *Contributions to the Slovene National Program*, discussed in the last chapter. The Program was a catalog of important issues and its contributor list contained many prominent names. But the reaction of the Slovene government and party to it was also very significant: they refused to prosecute the authors or the editors as Belgrade urged.

In 1988, Milošević engineered changes of government and took control of the media in both Vojvodina and Kosovo. Resistance to the reestablishment of direct Serbian rule grew in Kosovo and serious unrest lasted until March of the next year. At least 100 people died and martial law was put back in place. Meanwhile, the Slovene news magazine *Mladina* had attracted the ire of military officials by supporting pacifism, calling for an end to Yugoslav arms sales to countries in the developing world, and exposing corruption in the Defense Ministry. The army arrested and prosecuted four men that year in connection with classified papers found in *Mladina*'s offices; the documents are believed to have detailed the military's plans to conduct a purge or impose martial law in Slovenia. The four men were Janez Janša, a former communist and military officer and now a reporter; two editors of the magazine, David Tasič and Franci Zavrl; and an army sergeant, Ivan Borštner. Even the three civilians were tried in a military court, in what became known as the trial of the Ljubljana Four. The proceedings were conducted – illegally – in Serbo-Croatian instead of Slovene. The trial caused a tremendous outrage in Slovenia. Igor Bavčar, a young politician with experience as a police officer and a university newspaper editor, played a key organizing role in the creation of the Committee for the Protection of Human Rights (CPHR) in the summer of 1988. This group collected enormous numbers of protest signatures on petitions and held large demonstrations to protest the treatment of the Ljubljana Four, and then it quickly took up other issues and played a key role in the eventual acceptance of political pluralism by the LCS. Protests were registered within the LCS, too, as Franc Šetinc resigned from the federal presidency.

In January 1989, the Serbian communists extended their control to the Montenegrin party, thereby assuring themselves of having four votes in federal bodies; now Serbia, Kosovo, Vojvodina, and Montenegro could vote together to stop any possible reform proposals supported by Slovenia, Croatia, Bosnia, and Macedonia. Over the course of this year, the CPHR took up the issue of democratic rights in Kosovo, collecting relief funds, circulating petitions, and again holding large demonstrations. Even as various proposals for a "third Yugoslavia" were floated in federal bodies, Serbia declared a boycott of Slovene products. In June, on the 600th anniversary of the important medieval battle at Kosovo Polje, Milošević held a mass rally of approximately one million Serbs to demonstrate the strength behind his nationalist program. Serbs threatened to bring one of their mass meetings to Ljubljana to show the Slovenes the errors of their ways; undaunted, the Slovenes countered by saying they would station police along their roads to turn back the buses hired out by Milošević and his cronies. As the expense of the military occupation of Kosovo grew,

Slovenes and others became more resentful of their lack of political say in the situation there. Finally, on September 27, the Slovene parliament passed fifty-four amendments to their republican constitution. These were designed to make Slovenian law take precedence over Yugoslav law. They included an unequivocal statement of their right to unilateral secession and approval of a future multi-party system. The Serbs also changed their consitution at this time to formalize control over the autonomized republics. On December 27, 1989, parliament approved new electoral legislation officially making other political parties legal. Since May, human rights groups, the Writers' Association, and groups such as the Slovene Farmers' Alliance (*Slovenska kmečka zveza*) had been calling for political pluralism and were already organizing on that basis.

The year 1990 began with the Slovene delegation to the Yugoslav League of Communists' 14th Congress being shouted down and then walking out of the meeting. They were followed by the Croats, and neither group ever returned. They also both lost power in their home republics. The year before, the leader of the Slovene communists since 1986, Milan Kučan, had already announced that Yugoslavia was a community of communities and that majority rule, much less raw power, would not be allowed to override cultural autonomy, territorial integrity, and the equality of smaller nations.[8] The LCS changed its name to the Party of Democratic Renewal and prepared for elections. In April, the reform communists lost power to a coalition of new parties called DEMOS, or the Democratic Opposition of Slovenia. This group, which picked the Prime Minister Lojze Peterle and worked with Kučan, who had been elected the new president of the republic, saw Slovenia down the rest of the road to complete independence. In May 1990, free elections in Croatia brought the HDZ (Croatian Democratic Union) of Franjo Tudman, a historian and former Partisan turned nationalist, to power; the Croatian government faced more obstacles as it prepared for secession and it proved to be considerably more authoritarian than Slovenia. By the fall of 1990, economic warfare raged within Yugoslavia, with the Slovenes refusing to make many transfers of funds and dues to the federal government and the Serbs starting a tariff war and expropriating some Slovene companies. The *coup de grâce* came in December, when the Serbian government appropriated about a billion dollars of federal funds.

For the very end of the year, Slovenia's freely elected parliament had scheduled a referendum on sovereignty and independence. It was held on December 23, and the results were exceptionally clear. Over 93 percent of registered voters turned out, and almost 95 percent of them voted yes to independence. That means that the subsequent moves by the Slovene government were supported by over 88 percent of the voting-age population.

The referendum had included a six-month moratorium on secession, both to give political solutions a final chance to work and to allow the

Slovene government to continue its preparations. There was still discussion at the federal level about ways to save the country, but Slovenia was very much going its own way and ominous, poignant armed confrontations involving Serbian rebels, the Croatian police, and the Yugoslav National Army (JNA) were wracking the neighboring republic. Shortly after the Serbian leadership committed yet another unconstitutional act, blocking the rotation of the state presidency to the Croatian candidate, Stipe Mesić, the cooling-off period was over. Slovenia promptly announced its independence on June 25, 1991. Croatia also did so that same day.

Slovenia's military confrontation with Yugoslavia

Slovenes ended up fighting Yugoslavia for their independence. In what has often been called the "Ten-day War," Slovenia's Territoral Defense units, elements of the police of its Ministry of the Interior, and ordinary citizens confronted the approximately 22,000 soldiers of the JNA stationed on Slovene territory. Because direct assistance was not forthcoming from the less well prepared Croats, politically, and to some degree militarily, Slovenes had reason to fear that additional significant JNA forces in Croatia would move into their country. The Slovene and Croatian leaderships had been in constant communication for months, about issues ranging from the referenda to possible military action, but Franjo Tudman and his political party, the Croatian Democratic Union (HDZ), had not yet assumed complete control of the Croatian government; in addition, the JNA had already succeeded in clipping the wings of the Croatian Territorial Defense forces and they were not able to act independently yet.

To put the quick success of Slovenia's military and political forces into proper context, one should recall that the Yugoslav leadership was in many ways unprepared and unwilling to fight a major war in that republic; also, the totals of fewer than 100 dead and 300 wounded on both sides, although tragic, contrasts sharply with the numbers of deaths from other wars of Yugoslav succession: 10,000 people of various nationalities in Croatia and over 200,000 in Bosnia. One should also not neglect to mention the massive waves of refugees in those two states and Kosovo, and further casualties from various types of conflict in Kosovo, Serbia, and Macedonia. The ability to act as subject rather than object and challenge authority in order to have more control over one's own fate can certainly be demonstrated in ways other than military action. Indeed, non-violent contestation of injustice and civil disobedience to authoritarianism had often been used in Slovenia, as in other Yugoslav republics, and elsewhere around the world in the twentieth century, including India, the US, and South Africa. Nonetheless, it is no exaggeration to stress that the 1991 military performance was an important rite of passage for the Slovene nation; careful examination of the military events reveals as well that the fighting was so well prepared for and managed by political forces that the war was actually, to a significant degree, a political event.

The Territorial Defense Forces (TDF) in Yugoslavia were instituted in 1968 after the Soviet invasion of Czechoslovakia. Tito and the leadership of the LCY had sympathized with the Czech and Slovak reform communists of the Prague Spring, and, as so often in the past, they were put on notice by the Warsaw Pact crackdown that their own brand of socialism might be in peril from Moscow. Theoretically, the TDF were meant as a kind of "national guard" to supplement the JNA in the event of any outside invasion of the country, including one sponsored by NATO. Since the first pluralist elections in Slovenia in April 1990, however, the republic's 22-year-old TDF, called the *Teritorijalna obramba* (TO) in Slovene, had – with the help of some constitutional amendments – begun to function as an embryonic independent military force. The Yugoslav government quickly realized this and moved to reassert direct control over the TDF in Slovenia and in the non-Serbian regions of Croatia and Bosnia–Hercegovina. The JNA was successful everywhere but Slovenia. The Slovene government and party officials at both the federal and republican levels coordinated their efforts to stop the JNA seizures. Even though 70 percent of the TO's equipment was confiscated,[9] the Slovenes considered their resistance a success because a fair amount of equipment remained in their hands; their efforts at planning a quick, effective course of action had paid off; and they were soon able to find semi-legal ways to re-arm over the next year. Eventually, the Slovene TO was capable of mobilizing as many as 60,000 lightly armed recruits and reservists. A secret alternative command structure was created.[10] The Slovene government replaced General Ivan Hočevar as commander of the TO; Major Janez Slapar was loyal to the local government. Short of an early, draconian intervention, events in Slovenia were once again slipping out of control of Belgrade. The government there, with its three rotating presidencies, was often too gridlocked for decisive action; the military leadership was, at this point, still unwilling to act on its own, without the government's directive.

Further Slovene preparations for war were political. Its representatives abroad sounded out key European countries on independence. Part of making their case abroad was also presenting Slovenia as a responsible and productive country that would not cause unnecessary violence and would honor its financial obligations. Slovenia began managing its own borders and customs facilities and pledged to prevent any new JNA deployments into its territory. Finally, in May 1991, Slovenia started keeping its draftees within its own borders and incorporating them into the TO instead of sending them off for service in the JNA. The knowledge and energy of many in the Slovene government at this time is admittedly fascinating. Most often singled out for praise for their management of the run-up to the decisive break are President Kučan, Interior Minister Bavčar, Information Minister Jelko Kacin, Defense Minister Janša, and Foreign

Minister Rupel. The sober preparations and heady success of this era for Slovenes must be contrasted with the anxiety and frustration ordinary people felt in other republics. For them, even if many of Slovenia's grievances were justified and even if the rising tides of Serbian and Croatian nationalism were unpalatable, the Slovene maneuvers often seemed selfish. Leaving Yugoslavia, especially if Croatia left too, would mean leaving reformist forces in the rest of the country – in particular Bosnia – in a drastically weakened state. Now the Albanians of Kosovo would, in addition, have no allies. So in republics where democratization was not as advanced as in Slovenia, the sense of powerlessness of ordinary individuals made the price tag of Slovene independence seem very high. Slovenia seemed to many to be pushing the country towards an abyss that would engulf the other republics once Ljubljana was independent and waltzing its way back into Central Europe.

The declaration of independence came, as we have seen, on June 25, 1991. On June 26, the JNA initiated its efforts to take control of Slovenia's border crossings. This was both a symbol act of reassertion of federal control and an attempt to cut Slovenia off from the outside world. The second phase was supposed to be a march on Ljubljana and the arrest of the rebellious government officials. When stiff resistance was encountered at some border stations, and with the TO and other Slovenes blocking many roads and trying to blockade many barracks, the JNA bombed television and radio stations and the Brnik airport outside Ljubljana. About 2,000 Yugoslav troops left Slovenia during the ten-day period of conflict, while about 8,000 were captured and later released by the Slovenes. It has been noted that the Slovenes took great pains to publicize their defense to boost their image abroad. But the fighting was also real, with the effectiveness of portable road barricades and both anti-aircraft and anti-tank rockets enhanced by the rugged terrain of the country. The nature of the Slovene resistance, emphasizing in effect mass civil disobedience and sabotage, was also very difficult to neutralize – indeed, this was as it should have been, in terms of the original purpose of the TDF.

The federal Prime Minister Marković and the Yugoslav Defense Minister, General Veljko Kadijević, saw themselves as defending the Yugoslav idea from a dangerous example of secession. But back in Belgrade the power shift to the camp of Slobodan Milošević was under way; his great concern was that territories inhabited by Serbs be "allowed" to remain in Yugoslavia, even if the republics that housed them split away; this entailed a horrible carving up of Croatia and Bosnia. But it meant that Slovenia did not really figure in Milošević's plans; Serbs have no historical or ethnic claims to Slovenia. Meanwhile, the army, stunned by the resistance with which it met, soon realized that a much bigger fight was about to commence behind it in Croatia, so a cease-fire was arranged in Slovenia. Between mid-July and the end of October, the JNA withdrew its troops from Slovene territory. International alarm at the fighting resulted in an important meeting on the Istrian island of Brioni; on July 7, 1991, officals from the European Community met with officials from Slovenia, Croatia, and Serbia. The upshot of the negotiations, accepted by the Slovene Parliament three days later, was that Slovene independence would be put on hold for a three-month cooling off period. The outcome for Slovenia was not much in doubt, especially since, by October, the war in Croatia was raging and the JNA was very much involved there. Wide-scale international recognition of Slovenia began in January 2002; on the 15th of that month, Slovenes across the country greeted news of the EC's decision to recognize them with champagne toasts and queries of "When will the United States do the same?" Finally, in April, both China and the US recognized Slovenia and the next month Slovenia became the 176th member of the United Nations.

A number of factors account for the JNA's inability to hold Slovenia. First is simply the element of surprise, or, more accurately put, inexperience and lack of preparation: Slovenia was the site of the first secessionist war in Yugoslavia, and the Yugoslav commanders still had green, multi-national forces, as well as a long-standing orientation towards defending the country from outside attack. This means the JNA had de facto limitations on its ability to act in pursuit of its vaguely defined domestic mission (as opposed to later, when the JNA became a Serbian military organ operating for Milošević). Second, the JNA seems to have egregiously misunderstood the true tenor of Slovene politics at the time, believing that a show of force would be enough to induce loyal elements in the republic to jettison their mutinous leaders and that, in any event, Slovenes were not prepared for actual bloodshed. Third, the JNA stayed its hand because it assumed the international community was against the secession. Fourth, as already discussed, the Croatian secession, following quickly behind the Slovene, proved a tremendous distraction. Finally, it is possible that some remaining Slovene officers in the JNA slowed down an effective Yugoslav response. Plans for a much harsher military reaction to Slovene secession did exist. Had enough of these factors been differently disposed to allow a more aggressive JNA response to Slovenia's declaration of independence, the level of bloodshed on both sides would have been much greater but the ultimate result would, in all probability, have been the same.

Reactions to the end of Yugoslavia

General criticisms of Western support of the breakaway republics

Nowadays, Slovenia is obviously an integral member of the world diplomatic community. Indeed, at the time of independence it was welcomed as a new state by many individuals and governments across the world. Today, even the shards of the former Yugoslavia have recognized the fait accompli of each others' sovereignty. But approval of Slovenia's split from Yugoslavia was not universal at first. The West was definitely caught by surprise by Yugoslavia's rapid spin towards dissolution. Today, observers continue to differ sharply in their judgments over whether or not the West (that is, the European Union, the US, and NATO) ended up making the situation worse by rushing precipitously to the diplomatic assistance of Slovenia, Croatia, and Bosnia, thereby emboldening ethnic separatists, or whether the timidity of the Western response gave the Serbs and Montenegrins, acting in the name of a non-existent federation with a very real military, time to maul the other republics. In other words, did the West move too fast to help the breakaway republics, or too slowly? Indeed, how much of the blame for the chaos in the successor states to Yugoslavia does the West need to bear?

Some commentators, mostly but not exclusively Serbs, see US support of Slovenia as the beginning of a post-Cold War global grab at hegemony, with the projection of military power through NATO as a key compo-nent; these critics also tend to doubt the motives of countries like Germany, long suspected of aims to revive a Habsburg-style opening to the Adriatic and of anti-Serbianism, for helping the supposedly pro-Teutonic or even inherently fascist Croats and Slovenes. Actually, a much stronger case can be made that the West hesitated a very long time before recognizing Slovenia and the other breakaway republics, and Western support for them was not decisive until 1995. The Yugoslav drama of destruction unfolded largely according to the nature of its own construction. The wars and atrocities against civilians were not inevitable, but the breakup, as we have seen, had become increasingly likely. But, just as the West could neither have caused nor prevented the breakup by itself, it still could have made it much less bloody by a unified and decisive intervention after the Slovene and Croatian declarations of independence in June of 1991.

Why this intervention did not take place is worth analyzing, because it informs us of stereotypes that are still powerful in West European and North American society and because it shows the difficulties – certainly not yet overcome – in collective international action of the sort that is increasingly in demand today, as the "vacuum" of the post-Cold War world is being at least partially filled by a global campaign against terrorism. Even after it became apparent that no amount of cold-shouldering or scolding was going to keep the Slovenes and Croats "in line," and even after reliable reports of mass atrocities against civilians began to circulate and evoke unpleasant, if partial, comparisons to the Holocaust or the Spanish Civil War, little decisive action was taken.

Of course, there are major underlying factors in the West's indecisive-ness such as ignorance of the Balkans (and the assumptions that Slovenes and "the others" are all just alike and that they are all violent and intractable), inertia, and distraction (by the first Gulf War, for instance). In the Bosnian case, the fact that the beleaguered national group was

Muslim might have had a braking effect on government interest in, or public support for, intervention, though this would now be hard to demonstrate. From the American point of view, the lingering effects of the non-intervention "Vietnam syndrome" and a foreign policy calculus centered on industrial and consumer resources like oil might well have been in play.

But specific factors influencing the Western approach to Slovene secession and the whole dissolution of Yugoslavia also include the following:

- Serbs, who presented themselves as the aggrieved party hurt by Slovene secession, had a good reputation in the West, at least based on their alliances with the US, France, and Great Britain in the two world wars;
- Yugoslavia had been a useful bulwark against Soviet expansion in southern Europe, and Cold War-vintage policy experts in Western capitals were reluctant to see it splinter;
- Yugoslavia, because of its prominence in the Nonaligned Movement and its economic experimentation under the aegis of a socialist "third path," was popular among leftists who continued to defend it as a sort of "pet project" even after its essential nature had changed with Slobodan Milošević's rise to power;
- the United States was starting to retreat from some international commitments just at the time that Europe was moving closer together politically, but the "division of labor" between the two pillars of the Western "international community" had not yet been (and still has not been) worked out. Europeans, alas, were not used to being leaders in foreign policy since 1945;
- as many observers have pointed out, the "outbreak of war ran against the spirit of integration and cooperation which prevailed in the international community following the fall of the Berlin Wall in 1989."[11]

The various international organizations, of which NATO and the EU were just the most visible, were not tooled up to meet a crisis, either in intellectual or in practical terms. Yugoslavia was, once again, a paradigm-buster, just as it had been in the 1960s when it became the most liberal, open, and independent communist country in the world.

NATO and the US came in for even more pointed and heated criticism in 1995 and 1999. Many people both in the NATO member states and across Europe opposed President Clinton's efforts to create a settlement in Bosnia and, to a greater extent, the Alliance's intervention in Kosovo. There were many reasons for this opposition, most of them, frankly, having nothing to do with pro-Serbian feelings. Many outsiders believed, erroneously, that the history of the Balkans and the motives of its peoples are too complex to understand. Another set of reasons given for non-involvement claims that all Balkan peoples are equally guilty for the war, that they are all similarly murderous and unreliable, that the Bosnian nightmare was a civil war and thus off-limits to the international community, and that the (supposedly) "ancient ethnic hatreds" in the region would make choosing sides or reaching a peaceful settlement impossible.

Sometimes the proposition that the US has no material or even moral interest in the region is advanced. Many more Americans fear military involvement abroad, because of the lingering humiliation, divisiveness, and frustration of the Vietnam War. They set preconditions for US involvement such as the necessity of a "clear exit strategy," "no US losses," and the use of "overwhelming force." While these phrases spring from sensible political and military considerations, they also can induce a kind of self-imposed isolationism that is at odds with America's traditions of human rights and some of its key strategic interests. Divisive partisan politics in the US also led many people to state, in advance, that President Clinton's plans were doomed to fail. Bi-partisan support for foreign policy initiatives was once the standard in the US House and Senate, but many Republicans abandoned it during the last four years of Clinton's administration. This intrusion of short-sighted partisanship into foreign policy tends to create a cycle of self-fulfilling pessimism. Indeed, policies are more likely to fail when they are invariably labelled as failures from the start.

Many pacifist voices have also been heard, reminding the world of a perennial and important issue of ethics: what is the relationship between ends and means? Can people really use war to make peace? Can violence effectively stop violence, or does it perpetuate itself against our best intentions? Is the greater good ever served by taking human life? These objections, it should be noted, do not stem in any way from the specifics of Balkan history. They are the same objections, for instance, raised by Quakers throughout American and British history about the moral justification of any war. The pacifist doctrine of "turning the other cheek" saves the would-be rescuer from committing violence, but its adherents usually still believe in getting involved in the issues; the avoidance of bloodshed must also be accompanied by constructive and concrete steps towards reconciliation. Most religious traditions today include some pacifist thinking. These concerns are, of course, important to many non-religious people too, on ethical or rational grounds.

NATO's right to attack a sovereign state, Serbia, because of its behavior within its own province of Kosovo and without a United Nations mandate has been often – and understandably – called into question since the bombing campaign of 1999. Other criticisms of the recent NATO interventions continue to mount. Some observers object to what they perceive as US imperialism. Since the Cold War is over, the Soviet Union is gone, and the American economy is booming, the US is now cocky and aggressive. Washington is seen as "globalizing" its political reach in the same way American corporations are extending their reach into the world economy. Bossing around the Europeans and crushing independent-minded Serbia are seen as parts of this plan.

Germany's participation in the recent actions in the Balkans initially upset some Europeans – not least among them many Germans. They fear a reawakening of aggressiveness and militarism in the prosperous and newly reunified Germany which, since 1990, is once again the largest country in Europe west of Russia. Some critics – Michael Ignatieff and Zbigniew Brzezinski among them – have even focused on the nature of military technology. The sophisticated electronic hardware used by NATO forces – which let the destruction shower down on Serbia from ships safely offshore and from planes flying at 15,000 feet – shows that it is possible for the rich countries of the world to destroy more people and infrastructure than ever before. The fact that countries can be so massively assaulted with ever fewer NATO lives being put at risk adds another concern: that such force is more likely to be used than in the past. In recent history, as long as countries had to attack each other using ground troops, tanks, ships at close range, or low-level bombing raids, the anticipation of losses tended to have a certain deterrent effect. Electronic warfare, which includes global financial battles and propaganda as well as cruise missiles, gives the attacker greater immunity. This, in turn, can help governments overcome the reservations that a jumpy or sensitive public might have about losses or entanglement, as in America's Vietnam syndrome.

Peter Handke

The writings of Peter Handke will now be examined as an example of emotional opposition to Slovene independence as well as intellectual opposition to the eventual NATO interventions in Bosnia–Hercegovina and Kosovo. Handke is a person with deep ties to, and a deep understanding of, Slovenia but he would have preferred it to remain within Yugoslavia and he would rather have not seen so much of the world blame the Serbs for the Balkan conflicts in the 1990s.

A world-renowned avantgardist in prose and drama, Handke (b. 1942) is half-Slovene. He grew up in the southern Austrian province of Kärnten (Koroško), and he has long personally identified and sympathized with Slovenes. Many of his works portray his tender regard for the Slovene language, landscape, and culture. Growing out of the context of the post-World War II collection of socially conscious and politically engaged literary heavyweights in the Gruppe 47 (Group of 47), which included Heinrich Böll, Günter Grass, Ingeborg Bachmann, Hans Magnus Enzensberger, and Alfred Andersch, Handke made major waves in the late 1960s when he renounced both realistic art and political engagement. He set out on a prolific career that has been stubbornly experimental; his goal has been characterized as a personal, esthetic emancipation.[12] His most famous works have been the plays *Kaspar* (1968) and *Publikumsbeschimpfung* (1966; Offending the Audience); the novella *Die Angst des Tormanns beim Elfmeter*

(1970; in English as *The Goalie's Anxiety at the Penalty Kick*), and the novel *Die Wiederholung* (1986; in English as *Repetition*). Handke is important in the context at hand because he contested Slovenia's desire and right to become independent. Yet there is also, as we shall see, more to this story, because Handke has a deep understanding and appreciation for the emotional and physical texture of twentieth-century Slovene life and his earlier fiction, beautifully written and extremely popular in Slovenia, did a great deal to popularize and even memorialize Slovene distinctiveness.

Let us begin with Handke's earlier fictional works on Slovene themes. Slovenia plays a major role in three of his novels: *Die Hornissen* (1966; The Hornets), *Die Wiederholung* (1986), and *Mein Jahr in der Niemandsbucht: Ein Märchen aus den neuen Zeiten* (1994; My Year in the No-Man's-Bay), as well as in the reflections in *Noch einmal für Thukydides* (1990; Once Again for Thucydides) and the compendium *Ein Wortland: Eine Reise durch Kärnten, Slowenien, Friaul, Istrien und Dalmatien* (1998; Word Country: A Trip Through Carinthia, Slovenia, Friulia, Istria and Dalmatia), co-authored with Lisl Ponger. The most renowned of these works is *Die Wiederholung*, which was released in English translation as *Repetition* in 1988. This novel is the second installment of Handke's repeatedly and experimentally revisited family history. It is the beautiful story of a young Austrian's hike across Slovenia around 1960. The young man, of mixed Slovene-Austrian parentage (more or less an autobiographical parallel to the author), is looking for his brother Gregor who deserted from the Nazi army during World War II and disappeared in the rural areas of northern Slovenia. The journey begins in the grimy, mountainous industrial town of Jesenice and proceeds through the Alps, across the Mediterranean karst region, to Maribor, Slovenia's second city.

Handke's prose is lustrous throughout and, in establishing why the young Filip Kobal feels so totally at home in Slovenia, he catalogs many of the unique and beautiful aspects of Slovene culture, landscape, architecture, and language. It is easy to see why this book met with such joyful praise from Slovenes. The pointedly fond and vivid descriptions of Slovene *realia* are undergirded by an equally heartening message of common humanity, of something universal that goes under and over borders to link all people. The novel is also a crucible of Handke's authorial proclivities: micro-description, philosophical digressions, the inescapable primacy of language above everything else human and natural, and – somewhat ominously, perhaps, for his later political views on Slovenia – epistemological anxiety and skepticism bordering on relativism. The book celebrates "appearances" and initiation over "laws" and conclusions, while the reader gets the distinct impression that Slovenia's association with Yugoslavia is a fortuitous one.

In general, Handke maintains that the nature of human socialization and the limitations of language are the real causes of individuals feeling oppressed or, perhaps better, repressed. Freedom comes through the unmediated reporting of perceptions; attention to forgotten details and overlooked coincidences as well as poetic innovation in language are the keys to this kind of expression, whereas meaning (as in political ideologies, historical causes and effects, or symbolic interpretations) is just a "rationalistic construction that robs the individual of the immediacy of experience."[13] Some critics find Handke's works plotless and repetitive. But many others, such as the American novelist William H. Gass, have found great value in his "unaimed writing, unaimed in order that something fundamental may be struck"; Handke deserves praise because "[i]f one is to see the world in a grain of sand, one must first see the sand."[14] At any rate an objective label for Handke's approach might be "post-modern romanticism": a critique of reason and a fired-up poetic imagination are yoked together to help individuals escape cultural preprogramming and find personal liberation and fulfillment.

Nationalists might argue that his work is "denaturalized" because it pays so little attention to the web of loyalties and emotions underlying nationalism. But Handke would probably say in his own defense that political loyalties like nationalism cloud one's perception and impinge upon individuality in unacceptable ways. And although he has spent his whole career fighting against these and many other inherited distortions of individual sensitivities, he nonetheless understands the concept of home very well indeed, in terms of a local nexus of family life and geographical affinity; after all, much of his prose is autobiographical and recounts and reworks the experiences of his youth in the mixed German–Slovene region of southern Austria.

Let us now turn to Handke's political statements. In the 1990s, Handke was engaged in a colorful running polemic with many other intellectuals about the breakup of Yugoslavia. To him, the secessions of both Slovenia and Croatia were frivolous and destructive acts; in 1991, Handke began, by his own admission and to considerable public outcry, intervening "for Yugoslavia." He has stuck to a subjective position – based on nostalgia and emotions – that Yugoslavia should not have split apart. He took several trips to Serbia and then published his impressions of that country and its people. Handke stated that these trips – which others regarded either as feints too short to allow much intellectual probing, or courageous acts of defiance and solidarity with suffering, much-maligned Serbs – were undertaken in pursuit of "aesthetic veracity,"[15] not as political or historical investigations; this seems to mean that he wants to see Serbia for himself and to see it in human, not political, terms, in the hope of understanding it better and eventually promoting reconciliation. He objects vigorously to the "multiple prepunched peepholes"[16] through which the world is forced to view the Serbs. The main target of Handke's anger is the Western media, which had a feeding frenzy on the images and details of the wars. Their one-sided reporting, blaming the Serbs for everything and transmitting almost exclusively the suffering of non-Serbs, has sold well in the West. But, he continues, it also amounts to scapegoating and has provided the impetus and rationalization for the embargo and the bombings which, in turn, have brought a great deal of new and unjustified misery to Serbs.

Later, in a controversial 1991 work entitled *Abschied des Träumers vom Neunten Land: Eine Wirklichkeit, die vergangen ist: Erinnerung an Slowenien* (The Departure of the Dreamer from the Ninth Country. A Reality That Has Passed: A Memoir of Slovenia), Handke stated bluntly: "I see no reason, not a single one – not even the so-called 'Great Serbian Panzer Communism' – for the [existence of] the state of Slovenia; nothing but a fait accompli."[17] Building on his well-known personal connections with, and fondness for, Slovenia, Handke argues along three routes that the formation of an independent Slovene state was both unnecessary and wrong. First is his self-described "fairy-tale like" state of enchantment with Slovenia; one can only assume that Handke feared that any change in Slovenia's political status would ruin his private land of milk and honey. Second, Handke courageously rejects nationalism as an essential category of human description, and he also spurns such shopworn – but nonetheless, in the eyes of many, useful – cultural concepts like "Central Europe" (Slovenes actually belong there) and "the Balkans" (Slovenes were stuck there for over seventy years against their will). Third, it would seem that Handke had great affection for Yugoslavia as a whole and what it stood for: its independence between the superpower blocs; its stunningly attractive diversity of peoples, religions, cuisines, and landscapes; its leftist or progressive politics; and, perhaps most controversially, the safety and equality it afforded the Slovene people who (Handke asserts) joined Yugoslavia both wisely and voluntarily in 1918.

Handke consistently opposed the secessions of the Yugoslav republics of Slovenia, Croatia, Bosnia–Hercegovina, and Macedonia in 1991 and 1992. He also strongly condemned NATO's intervention against Serbia in the Kosovo conflict of 1999. It should be noted that there have been many crticis of the NATO and US policies in these events. And Handke performs a valuable service in eschewing the demonization of the Serbian people and reminding the world of Serbian civilian casualties, especially during the 1995 expulsions from the Krajina and then during the NATO air campaign. Nonetheless, the reaction to Handke's opinions has been important too. Despite their beautiful style, his writings have been considered by many to be too flip and cavalier, or at least hopelessly naive, and thus inappropriate to the very grave subject matter of the wars of Yugoslav succession.

Handke's texts, full of neologisms and beautifully written in a deceptively simple style, bring up other issues of interpretation which lie beyond the scope of this history book. He asks thought-provoking hypothetical questions about what he himself would have done as a Serb in Croatia in 1991, but his narrative often seems one-sided in its own way (although this might be deliberate on his part). He is, in these books, not concerned with the causes or the total extent of the bloodshed. Readers are tantalized with an unresolved dilemma: should intellectuals be above hate-mongering and calls for retribution (as he views NATO's involvement), or does such a supposedly principled stand actually amount to indifference in the face of verifiable evil?

These kinds of debates, again, involve far more than Balkan history; they range into media criticism, ethics, and even epistemology. But Handke does make some concrete contributions that interest students of history directly. His writing works against the demonization of the Serbian people. It is certainly true that there has not yet been a great deal of media attention on how average Serbs have fared in the 1990s. If victims are usually silent, then Serbian victims – of the wars and of their own government – have been invisible too. Handke works to correct this phenomenon by describing his everyday encounters with people there and by questioning the media stereotypes of individual Serbs as frenzied, hyper-politicized nationalists.

And Handke performs another valuable service in reminding the world of Serbian civilian casualties, especially during the 1995 expulsions from the Krajina and then during the war over Kosovo. In his writings from 1999, Handke describes the effects of the bombing of non-military targets like factories, bridges, civilian airports, neighborhoods, and passenger trains. Serbia has become "the zone of fiery and fickle chance explosions."[18] Handke comes to the conclusion that the NATO raids were far more than just a military action but constituted a diabolical attempt to paralyze and subdue an entire country.[19] Others have, of course, speculated further from such conclusions and arrived at a general critique of the United States' ostensible humanitarian interventions as camouflaged attempts to construct a new world order with hegemonic economic and political intentions.

Reasonable people may still disagree over the moral and political effects of Slovenia's secession, although the nationhood of the Slovene people is beyond doubt. Open-minded observers who reject demonization to present the Serbs to the outside world as a nation of real, diverse, and now often suffering individuals are carrying out an important act of intellectual and moral honesty. Still, Handke's admonitions about not rushing to judgment are not exactly what most people would consider informed political engagement. Many expected that he might show greater appreciation of the gravity of the conflicts in Yugoslavia in the 1980s and 1990s and the suffering or anxiety of many of that country's national groups. For Handke, art comes first, and he asserts the primacy of individual perception and emotion.

Alain Finkielkraut

The work of another prominent West European intellectual stands in stark contrast to Handke. The writings of the French essayist and philosopher Alain Finkielkraut are an excellent guide to understanding Western reaction to the assertion of sovereignty by both Slovenia and Croatia. Adam Michnik and Milan Kundera, two major Central European intellectual figures, also quickly spoke out in support of Slovene independence. In the 1990s Finkielkraut quickly emerged as an impassioned and erudite supporter of the right to national self-determination in the Balkans, a harsh critic of Serbian aggression under Milošević, and a relentless gadfly interrogating the European Union (EU) on its hypocrisy and lack of resolve. He praised the Slovenes for their tradition of peaceful resistance to authoritarian rule and reassured the West that Slovenes were not "Jacobins." Rather, they had legal and historical justification for their declaration of independence of June 25, 1991.[20]

Finkielkraut successfully lays bare many of the misunderstandings and double standards in American and European – especially French – thinking that generated the inability to intervene effectively for years in Europe's biggest war since 1945. First, plain ignorance of Central European and Balkan peoples fostered the idea that Croats and Slovenes were really just "tribes." The thousand-year history of the Croatian state, the linguistic distinctiveness of the Slovenes, and the artificiality of the Yugoslav "nationality" were ignored. This ignorance allows Balkan peoples to be blended together in popular understanding and at the same time labelled as "barbarians," due to orientalist stereotypes about their societies.

Second, the new states of Eastern Europe were accused of chauvinism, of smugly turning their gaze inward and erecting new borders between their neighbors and themselves, in an era when the rest of Europe is engaged in wholesale economic and even political integration.

Third, Europe's high-sounding but superficial obsession with the Holocaust and "Nie wieder!" ("Never again!") allowed it to be seduced by Serbian misinformation about the fascist nature of the newly independent Croatian government and, by extension, the Slovene one too. The bloody and idiotic policies of the World War II-era Independent State of Croatia, led by the dictator Ante Pavelic and his fascist Ustaša party, are of course a major stain on Croatian history, just as the eras of Hitler and Stalin present huge and somber issues for Germans and Russians. Unfortunately, the garbled historical writings of Croatia's first president, Franjo Tudman, and his intolerance and aggressiveness made Croatia susceptible to essentialist and reductionistic labelling. In fairness to the Serbs of the Krajina and Slavonia, one should note that the new state egregiously ignored its obligation to set their historical fears at ease, even though fascism per se never had deep roots in Croatia. Still, the specter of its revival was used to justify massive "pre-emptive" atrocities and to deny the right of self-determination to the Croatian and Slovene peoples. (If Finkielkraut's argument has a weak spot, it is his whitewashing of Tudman's political and scholarly record.)

Fourth, for a varied set of reasons, Yugoslavia was still considered highly worthwhile and viable as an integral state. Since Slovene and Croatian separatism threatened that state, they were regarded as undesirable or illicit. Among leftists, Yugoslavia was the proud anti-Stalinist bastion of workers' self-management and the Nonaligned Movement. In general, Marxists tend to view nationalism as just a temporary phenomenon, one occasioned by socioeconomic changes and then discarded by further changes onto the scrap-heap of history. Specifically, Marx and Engels also inveighed against the national aspirations of small or weak peoples in Eastern Europe (and elsewhere); they considered them primitive, anachronistic, and non-historical.[21] In this view, the Slovenes and Croats are "tattered remnants" and "historically absolutely non-existent." For rightists, Yugoslavia had been the proud and useful anti-Soviet bulwark shielding NATO's southern flank and checking some of Moscow's manipulation of developing countries. So, for many groups, if Yugoslavia was good, Slovenia and Croatia were a priori bad.

Fifth, West European isolationism was increased by an important social trend, consumerism. Whereas nineteenth-century liberalism exulted in the nation-state as a safeguard of individual rights, today's liberalism "conceives of no other freedom than that of a consumer and entrepreneurial society"[22] and so "any national aspirations appear pathological." This individualistic proclivity might be heightened by the evolution of both democracy and secularism – away from any kind of "transcendent powers to deliberate and decide."[23]

Sixth, Europe, in its well-intentioned zeal to check the great-power nationalism which injected so much imperialism, war, and genocide into earlier epochs, has lost the ability to appreciate the difference between small- and large-state nationalism and between civic and ethnic nationalism.

Two further, perhaps mostly French, reasons for Slovenia's and Croatia's lukewarm reception into the family of nations were resentment at the death of Yugoslavia, a state which France had an important historical role in creating in the aftermath of the Great War; and fear of a powerful Germany, which would profit from the re-emergence of its traditional allies in Mitteleuropa.

In conclusion, since Slovenia and Croatia were determined to be democracies, Finkielkraut asserts that the Western animus against their nationalism was as unjust as its ignorance. One of the results of this potent cocktail of factors is an astounding snobbery. Slovenes are told by West Europeans: "You are obviously different from us, but you are wrong to try to assert your differences from the Serbs." The other side of this coin is member states' insistence on the maintenance of linguistic and cultural diversity within the EU and also their cultivation of racial and social diversity within their own countries – and yet diversity abroad is scoffed at as "retrograde."[24] The upshot is that Slovenes, Croats, and Serbs are "like the 'Negroes' in colonial discourse" – and they are all interchangeable.[25] Because the "secession of the non-Serb republics is not the cause of Milošević's imperialist politics but its inexorable consequence."[26] When

Serbs present themselves, in political and strategic terms, as the victims of the breakup of Yugoslavia, it is as if, according to Finkielkraut, "the Nazis of this story have wanted to pass themselves off as Jews."[27] He thus observes that the Berlin Wall has come down, "but Yalta remains." The idea of Munich-style appeasement is inadequate to account for Western indifference in the face of so much suffering, however, because Milošević presented no threat even to Yugoslavia's immediate neighbors. The trenchant conclusion to this sad state of affairs is Finkielkraut's remark that if Seville, Venice, Vienna, or Brussels were being brutalized, the EU and US would be mobilized for instant military action on the basis of "common values [and] fundamental interests." What is happening to Šibenik, Zadar, and Cerska, on the other hand, is nothing short of the sacrifice of "universalist and humanitarian principles" to *sacro egoismo*.[28]

A parting look at official Slovenia: Edvard Kardelj

There was always more than one official Slovenia. In the nineteenth century, for instance, the clericals and the liberals differed on many key points. After 1945, and especially by the late 1960s, there were many Slovene communists espousing significant modifications to Titoism (which was already a significant modification of Stalinism) from inside the LCY and the LCS. Slovenes were among the first to reject the new Yugoslav orthodoxy, which the country's leaders such as Kardelj saw as a home-grown "separate road" to socialist utopia. So much attention is paid today to the Slovene challengers to the system that it is worthwhile to recall how relatively flexible, conducive to national identity, and innovative Titoism could sometimes be.

Edvard Kardelj (1910–1979) was a leading politician and communist theoretician in the former Yugoslavia. Although he was a Slovene by birth, he is associated primarily with the main federal (or supranational) party in South Slav history, the League of Communists of Yugoslavia (LCY). Kardelj, who befriended LCY leader Josip Broz Tito in the interwar years, held many high-profile positions in socialist Yugoslavia – so many, in fact, that he was often considered to be Tito's heir apparent. He chaired the committees that wrote the country's various constitutions and published many works on issues of nationality and the limits of dissent. He also designed the ideological underpinnings for Yugoslavia's systems of economic and foreign policy, known respectively as workers' self-management and nonalignment. Many of his voluminous writings on political and economic issues have been translated into English and other languages.

Public perceptions of Kardelj in the 1990s

There are several dangers inherent in the pursuit of information on a figure like Edvard Kardelj. One of them is that, in a small country such as Slovenia today, or even yesterday's Yugoslavia, there are many people who can still vividly recall the abuses of power perpetrated by certain leaders in the immediate past. Wrongs done to family members understandably make people angry. It is especially the experiences during and right after World War II that embittered many Slovenes to Kardelj, both at home and in the diaspora.

Another tricky issue is that many important politicians and cultural figures of today were communists until recently, or else are friends with them, or realize that they must live and work with such people in a very small country. Thus, they are very often inclined to speak guardedly about the past, even that of the discredited communist regime.

Nonetheless, many people today have a negative opinion of Kardelj. Many of these opinions are strongly negative; some are neutral and show that Kardelj's influence is still felt today through a large portion of Slovene public life. Few, if any, are unabashedly positive. Even close former associates of Kardelj have made remarks to the effect that Kardelj's ideas, whether or not they have been ultimately proven unworthy, belong to a specific time and place. Whether their validity has been permanently annihilated is an issue that many of them have left open, although they have said that Kardelj's ideas certainly do not fit today's social or political climate. Such views are typical of communist "old believers."

Commonly voiced negative views on Kardelj cluster around three topics. Regarding his status as a theoretician, many people see him just as an intellectual tinkerer; they say, for instance, that "he experimented and people paid." He was the "quintessential dilettante." A young reporter from *Mladina* (the alternative political and cultural magazine) excoriated Kardelj's foreign policy of nonalignment, which he and Tito worked so hard to establish; he said this collection of leaders from the decolonizing world was simply the "biggest group of the most lunatic people in history." A Slovene professor told me that I was wasting my time studying the movement of "Negroes and thieves" that cost Slovenia so much money in foreign aid.

Another locus of popular criticism is very personal. Cries of "what a huge swine!" (*svinja velika!*) are not uncommon at the mention of Kardelj's name. He was "complex-ridden" (*zakompleksan*) and attempted to ameliorate his inferiority complex by playing the role of bossy, omnipresent ideological watchdog. This purported inferiority complex was due in large part to the physical disabilities with which Kardelj was burdened. He had back, muscular, and digestive problems. One interlocutor even crudely expressed contempt for Kardelj because he was physically kaputt (*pokvarjen*).

Most accounts of Kardelj's career emphasize the fact that he was once a schoolteacher. For instance, two American scholars have described the Partisan leadership in the following terms:

> They included Edvard Kardelj, a former schoolteacher from Slovenia; Aleksandar Ranković, once a tailor in Serbia; Milovan Djilas, a young

and fiery Montenegrin; Koča Popović, poet son of a Belgrade million-
aire; Vladimir Bakarić, son of a Croat judge; and Moša Pijade, the
oldest of the group, a Jewish intellectual who had shared a prison cell
with Tito.[29]

The goal of the authors of this passage was simply to provide a small
amount of background material on the chief Yugoslav leaders other than
Tito. But often the inclusion of the term "schoolteacher" occurs out of
the context of Kardelj's other activities, or at least its significance goes
unexplained, as it did when British intelligence officer Fitroy Maclean
mentioned Kardelj "looking like a provincial schoolmaster, which, as it
happened, he was."[30]

   One of the most biting critiques of Kardelj's ideas came from another
Slovene politician who knew him well, Stane Kavčič. Kavčič was removed
in the purges of the early 1970s, which followed the national unrest in
Croatia and other regions. Kavčič wrote in his memoirs that evidently
Kardelj

> was to some extent trapped in his calling as a teacher. Teachers in
> Slovenia – especially left-oriented ones – operated in the intermediate
> realm between physical and intellectual work. They were too far
> removed from the physical side, too schooled to identify with their plebe-
> ian blood. And what is more, they felt that the doors into the scientific
> and intellectual elite were pretty much closed to them. Therefore, they
> created their own world, in which pedagogy and social-revolutionary
> reveries occupied positions of importance.[31]

   It is as if the ineffectiveness of his ideas were related to some innate
pedantry in the minds of schoolteachers (and professors?); being a communist and a pedant, then, were supposedly the chief hallmarks of Kardelj's
career, making him doubly misguided and his ideas doubly foul.[32]

Kardelj's legacy and contradictions

On the basis of Kardelj's long tenure as LCY administrator and theoretician, I have drawn four basic conclusions on the impact of his career.
First of all, Kardelj worked out the most complete view of the Nonaligned
Movement of any of its Yugoslav observers. It was during the debates
between the Yugoslav and Chinese leaderships in the 1950s and 1960s
that Kardelj first put forward his fully developed theory of international
relations. Although his theoretical work *Socialism and War* was published
before the first nonaligned conference in 1961, its principles were those
already at work in the Nonaligned Movement. Two of the most important
of these were Kardelj's insistence that no socialist state exercise hege-
monistic power (even in terms of criticism) over another, and his conviction

that the global "balance of forces" was favoring progressive (or socialist, or at least anti-imperialist) causes and thus cooperation between almost all states was ultimately possible and desirable.

In the 1970s Kardelj linked Yugoslavia's domestic and foreign policies in a way that seemed to embrace both workers' self-management (which he had designed) and nonalignment (which he had helped design). Yugoslavia's orientation in foreign policy was a "consistent reflection" of its orientation in domestic policy, or the "flip side" of the same coin, so to speak.

The second legacy of Kardelj turns on the nature of Yugoslavia's relationship with the USSR. Many observers have noted with suspicion that Yugoslavia tended to vote against the US and with the Soviet Union on many issues during the era of nonalignment, especially in crises in the Middle East and Vietnam. The documentary record gives no indication that Kardelj had any loyalty to the USSR after the Tito–Stalin rupture other than that lingering natural admiration due to a powerful and pioneering potential ally. Obviously Kardelj felt that Yugoslavia could derive benefits, especially economic ones, from some sort of relationship with the Soviet Union, though he worried that too much trade with any one part of the world would compromise Yugoslavia's political independence. The problem, then, of his early affection for the USSR is actually an issue of his inability to wean himself away from a conspiratorial brand of authoritarianism which effectively ruled out the possibility of sharing power with noncommunist groups. One could say this was the legacy of Leninist leadership in Kardelj, or one could say it was the Soviet example of one-party rule.

On a number of counts, then, there is indeed similarity between the system Kardelj helped design and maintain and the system in the USSR. One-party rule, cooperation on numerous international issues (especially in the 1940s and later those of an "anti-imperialist" nature), and a belief that socialism in some form or another would triumph in human history link the two regimes. But observers should not lose sight of Kardelj's anger at Soviet hubris in 1948, at the USSR's lingering inability to divest itself of the residual deleterious effects of Stalinism, and at the Soviets' attempt to usurp the independence of the Nonaligned Movement by manipulating members such as Cuba, Vietnam, and Afghanistan.

The third aspect of Kardelj's legacy is the broadest and most troubling. The tension between authoritarianism and creativity in Kardelj's thinking manifested itself in the way in which he drew the line on certain types of social criticism that he considered destructive or counterproductive. A case in point here would be that of the famous dissident Milovan Djilas in the 1950s. A decade before that time, Kardelj had committed his most serious human rights violations by agreeing to bloody reprisals against monarchist and "white guard" forces which had survived the war in Yugoslavia. Later, by virtue of his position in the ruling elite, Kardelj enjoyed the luxury of preaching self-management for others while deciding on the definition of that autonomy. In addition, his refusal to relinquish the power his party exercised in a one-party state limited the creativity of other elements in Yugoslav society. It was a hopeless venture to try to recognize competing "social forces" without allowing them their "politicized" expressions. In other words, Kardelj and his colleagues wanted to allow the debate of ideas but not the competition of parties.

All of Kardelj's many attempts to democratize Yugoslavia by allowing greater participation of its citizens in public affairs were ultimately undercut by his parallel insistence that democratization be safeguarded by excluding "unhealthy" and "anti-socialist" forces from the scene. In effect this meant a refusal to acquiesce in any loss of power for the League of Communists. Like Tito, Kardelj sensed that the tensions among the Yugoslav nationalities would fracture the federation if the party relinquished too much control. It is also possible, as some interviewees suggest, that Kardelj's chief concern was for his own power. At any rate, he died before his system collapsed. His country had, indeed, changed radically during his lifetime, but Kardelj's incessant theorizing and experimentation eventually helped to choke the creativity out of the Yugoslav experiment and to produce the sea of bureaucracy which considerably worsened the economic conditions in the country.

The final aspect of Kardelj's legacy is also negative. A tension between liberal socialism and Leninist centralism resided in Kardelj. This tension was, unfortunately for Yugoslavia but perhaps fortunately for Slovenia, never fully resolved. Where Kardelj attempted to liberalize the system partially he usually left as much confusion as progress. Nonetheless, wavering somewhere between social democracy and communist orthodoxy, Kardelj left behind a Slovenia which today has become independent and has embraced most of the principles of a market economy but retains a high percentage of population in favor of a broad social safety net and caps on maximum income.

At first appearances his work might seem, on balance, to be positive. He tinkered constantly with the legal apparatus of the country, urged that Yugoslavia move in a more "liberal"[33] direction, and he contributed to the republics' (and especially Slovenia's) self-confidence by investing them with a mission[34] and providing for economic differentiation. Ultimately, though, Kardelj's ideas proved incapable of keeping the country together. Furthermore, one can easily argue that some of his policies made the breakup of Yugoslavia bloodier and added oil to the flames of the civil wars that raged in the Balkans in the 1990s.

For instance, the cluttered and eccentric economic system of workers' self-management, which he had the guiding hand in designing, was largely responsible for ensuring that Yugoslavia would not recover from the oil-price shocks of the 1970s. Furthermore, Kardelj's concern with national party units and then with increasingly small sub-national economic units helped fragment the country's sense of common identity. His support of Tito's purges of reform forces who were more liberal – and in all likelihood more capable – than he, sidelined dozens of young, intelligent, less ideologically hidebound politicians, economists, and publicists who could have influenced the eventual dissolution of the country in a positive way. The creation of the Territorial Defense Forces in the late 1960s, another move that Kardelj supported strongly, formed the basis for today's armies in Bosnia–Hercegovina, Slovenia, and Croatia. Kardelj supported a Yugoslavia that was in every way highly militarized and had an enormous military bureaucracy. This enormous officer corps feared that a breakup of the country would deprive them of their *raison d'être* as well as their pensions and social status. Thus, in the early 1990s they agitated – by force in the final instance – against a breakup of the country, something that had become virtually inevitable due to a loss of faith in the federal leadership.

These observations implicate Kardelj in the dissolution of Yugoslavia. One can also point to Kardelj's life-long defense of the value of nations as a contributing factor in a more positive event: Slovenia's secession from Yugoslavia in 1991. His defense of Slovene nationhood, which began with the publication of *The Development of the Slovene National Question* before World War II, and his propagation of Slovenia's relatively privileged economic position within the Yugoslav federation kept the possibility alive that Slovenia could successfully secede from the rest of the country. Also, the fact that Kardelj was not a Stalinist – at least, not after the 1940s – in terms of domestic policy meant that some sort of critical political dialog did stay alive in the country.

The issue of secession, however, reminds us once again of one of the salient failures in Kardelj's life and work: his inability to foster durable faith in a federal, socialist Yugoslavia. Even if his interest in the progressive possibilities of nationhood and his support for a relative degree of decentralization ended up benefiting Slovenia in its drive to gain independence, these very principles contain the seeds of what is perhaps a greater tragedy. Kardelj went half-way in fulfilling two fundamental human desires: economic independence and national self-determination. His need to maintain order in and around the LCY prevented him from letting either of these trends develop fully. One of the results of this failure was the collapse of the country and the outbreak of today's heart-rending nationalist wars; this is the squandered dream of "Bratstvo i Jedinstvo" ("Brotherhood and Unity") among the South Slavs.

When Yugoslavia first broke up, Slovenes had occasion to miss the raw materials and markets to which they had had access for decades; there were initially also some fears of what it would be like to be exposed to pressure from much bigger neighbors like Italy and Austria. Yugo-nostalgia also involves an appreciation of the culture, food, music, and landscapes of the old Balkan state, as well as, for many, pride in the struggle against the Axis in World War II and at least a grudging recognition that Tito brought a great deal of international attention to the country. More long-lasting and historically important, though, an increasing number of Slovenes realize that, perhaps to a limited degree and perhaps inadvertently and inconsistently, Kardelj proved to be a guarantor of the survival of the Slovene nation by means of his insistence on economic and political federalism and his search for a progressive role for nations in socioeconomic development and in international relations.

Perspectives on the other Slovenia: Bučar and Kocbek

Official Slovenia existed alongside many alternative Slovenias, and it gave way to them in 1991. Slovene politics, literature, art, scholarship, and civil society today are diverse and complex. This section could easily include analysis of any number of other thinkers or movements, from the NSK to the Christian Democratic movement. But Bučar and Kocbek have been chosen. First, because they evolved out of the same socialist movement which, at its broadest, also included Kardelj. Second, they represent what might be considered uniquely or characteristically Slovene ways of meeting the challenges and demands for change that faced Slovenia in the twentieth century. Their hallmarks are persistence and conscientiousness, not a jettisoning of the past or slavish imitation of outside models.

France Bučar (1923–)

Bučar is an important scholar who has maintained a fairly high public profile both in Tito's Yugoslavia and in newly independent Slovenia. He was born in 1923 in Bohinjska Bistrica and joined the Partisans during World War II. Trained as a lawyer, he held several government positions after the war and took up a university position in public administration. Bučar evolved into a major critic of Titoism, a development that cost him his university position in the late 1970s. In 1990 he was elected as president of the first democratic Slovene parliament. Two of his major works were *Podjetje in družba* (The Enterprise and Society) and *Resničnost in utvara* (The Reality and the Myth). In the latter study, published in Slovenia in 1986 and in Canada three years later, he combined reflections from the fields of philosophy, economics, history, and sociology to mount a frontal assault on "real existing socialism" in Eastern Europe, including its oft-heralded, "liberal" Yugoslav variant. In terms of being a critic from "inside," that is, not primarily a nationalist and not necessarily hostile to socialism, Bučar is similar in some ways to the Serbian and Croatian philosophers of the Praxis movement of the 1970s. But Bučar went further than they did in enumerating the troubles with Leninism itself, not just with Stalinism (which the Yugoslav leadership as a whole had renounced and tried to replace). He was a leading member of the DEMOS coalition and was president of the Slovene parliament from 1990 to 1992; during that time of great turmoil he was one of the members of the Slovene negotiating team (which also included Kučan, Lojze Peterle, Janez Drnovšek, and Dimitrij Rupel) which met on the island of Brioni with negotiators from the European Community and the Serb-dominated federal Yugoslav government in an effort to end the fighting in Slovenia and create a mutually acceptable timetable for Slovene independence. He remained a public figure throughout the mid-1990s, serving in parliament again, running for the mayoralty of Ljubljana, and announcing publicly that the government's control over media in post-independence Slovenia threatens to lead to a new form of dictatorship.

In straightforward language and thought-provoking fashion, *Resničnost in utvara* discusses everything from broad philosphical and theoretical concepts such as democracy, freedom, equality, economic efficiency, sovereignty, and human rights to concrete issues within the Slovene experience such as consumerism, environmentalism, nationalism, and the historical role of the Catholic Church.

The foundations of the book's argument are a thorough-going and convincing refutation of the principles of Leninism, or democratic centralism, a set of policies that continued to be embraced by the Yugoslav communist leadership throughout their entire existence, long after the break with Stalinism in 1948. Despite the LCY's averral that it wanted to exercise only a "leading role" in society (rather than brutalizing it or dominating it directly), Bučar argues that its mechanisms of control nonetheless stifled true freedom, which is the meeting of basic needs and the proliferation of choices for more and more people or, alternatively, the removal of limitations on things and statuses. Thus the entire system of self-management was really just a façade; it was designed to make the people feel empowered but, in reality, it retained the political monopoly of the party. Socially owned property was also a travesty, because it amounted to a "privatization of all nationalized wealth ... by the political party which has secured, for itself, a monopoly over the general and individual management of this property."[35] At best, one might add, socially owned property and the system of self-management were unworkable; at worst, they constituted "state capitalism," a term usually hurled by the Yugoslavs with indignation at the Stalinist system. Furthermore, managerial professionals and technical experts, not politicians, need to be in position to run a modern economy. Like the Praxis dissidents and other well-known Yugoslav dissidents such as Milovan Djilas, Bučar criticized and fell foul of Yugoslav dogma; although the LCY had broken with Stalinist orthodoxy, it established a new one, and independent thinkers continued to be punished.

In more general terms, Leninism as a system became focused on short-term strategies for perpetuating itself; the communists had become an elite and had lost their connection to the society around them which had evolved and grown more sophisticated and diverse and was becoming even more so. In Bučar's words, the "difference between the social system and its social environment" became ever greater, requiring the social system (Leninist party rule) to exert ever more energy or force to preserve its dominant position.[36] Fostering consumerism was one important way of distracting people from politics; the constant struggle to make ends meet held down public consciousness and prevented the creation of too many dissidents. (One might add here that another famous Yugoslav critic, the Croatian essayist and novelist Slavenka Drakulić, condemned consumerism for different reasons – precisely because it was too easy to satisfy wants in Yugoslavia rather than too difficult.) Bučar even denies that Lenin was Marx's legitimate heir, since Leninism's "voluntarism" meant that communism came to power in under-industrialized countries; this represents a historical discontinuity since Marx foresaw communism springing up organically in highly developed countries where the social system was ready for a natural transition. Despite the attack on Leninism, Bučar defended the historical role of socialism. He saw much good in its extension of democracy into the economic (rather than just the political) realm and in its humanistic appreciation of the equal value of all human beings. Early capitalism limited the freedom of many in order to boost the freedom and wealth of a few; late capitalism threatens to drown creativity and ethical concerns in a sea of materialism. This greed, inequality, and spiritual malaise bothered him, and this skepticism about capitalism's level of social justice – even while recognizing its productivity – is a hallmark of Slovene society in general to this day.

Some of Bučar's most interesting writing concerns the national question. His proposed solutions to Yugoslavia's problems focused on political pluralism, and not the splitting off of the national republics, but he does believe that secession can be a transmission belt for sparking all sorts of other positive human-rights changes. But what separates his ideas from those of typical Slovene nationalists is his assertion that the real Slovene national problem lies in the Slovenes' relationship with the country-wide Leninist ruling party, not with other national groups! He soft-pedals popular Slovene concerns about living with "Balkan-type" peoples such as the Serbs; likewise he mentions, but is little concerned with, the reconstitution of a greater Slovenia that would include their co-nationals in Italy and Austria. For Bučar, it is natural that the Yugoslav communists think in pan-Yugoslav, federal terms, because that is the society in which the movement was founded and those are the borders in which the bloody, long war against the fascists was fought; territory means power, for parties as for governments. The bigger the country, the better also for Yugoslavia's position in international relations, not least of all because of Tito's policy of balancing between the superpowers and forging the Nonaligned Movement in the developing world. Thus, he denotes Yugoslavism simply as a

Leninist nationality policy. A definitive break with the Yugoslav system became necessary after the attempts at recentralization by means of the (Serbian-instigated) constitutional changes of 1988; more than a matter of pride or profit, Slovenes at that point – as in 1941, one might add – began to feel that their very survival was at stake.

The book also depicts world socialism in a deep crisis, because capitalist values dominate the international order; the limitations on traditional sovereignty imposed by today's interconnected economies means that "the individual state can no longer determine, on the basis of its own will, the level of the standard of living of its own citizens."[37] Thus, the needs and wants of society evolve beyond static Leninist ideology.

Bučar also discusses two other historial issues that deserve consideration here. First is the assertion that Slovene communist leaders were pressured into pursuing somewhat "nationalistic" policies vis-à-vis the federal government during the Yugoslav decades by pressure from below. This was necessary "in order to retain at least some contact with the nation and, thus, at least some semblance of legitimacy."[38] The channels through which this grass-roots pressure was funnelled (elements of civil society such as farmers' groups and human rights organizations) and the mechanisms by which the Slovene sense of distinctness was preserved or even nurtured, promise to be a fruitful topic of study for future generations of historians.

The second issue concerns Slovene domestic politics during World War II. While the well-organized communist Partisans made very clever use of the Axis powers' horrendous invasion and occupation to gain legitimacy and greatly increase their strength and the scope of their activities, the Catholic Church backed itself into a corner. Although the Church had played a key role in the preservation of the Slovene language and culture under Habsburg rule, and although its clericalist and anti-modernist impulses (popularized by the bishop and editor Anton Mahnič, a late nineteenth-century devotee of the philosophy of Thomas Aquinas) were shared by much of the population, the Church ended up condoning or siding with the occupiers and with local right-wing and anticommunist forces collectively called the *Bela garda*, or White Guard. Conservatism and unwillingness to work with the communists lay at the root of this Church policy, but another influence was a belief that the Slovenes were too small and vulnerable as a people to be anything other than neutral (and let the great powers duke it out over their heads and settle the war without significant Slovene participation). There is also the policy of the Church's leaders in the Vatican to consider – and no unequivocal and wholesale condemnation of fascism came from that quarter. At all events, the reputation of the Church suffered mightily in Slovenia during and after World War II. One should note here that the Christian Socialist movement of men like the poet Edvard Kocbek are an exception to these criticisms of the Catholic Church. Their story ends up as a critique of the communist postwar government, which hounded them from public life.

Edvard Kocbek (1904–1981)

Edvard Kocbek was a Slovene writer, political figure, and Christian Socialist activist who left an important impression on Slovene culture and society through both his life and his works. His essays, short stories, and especially his poetry are still both popular and highly regarded by critics; his principled commentary on politics, both in Slovenia and abroad, galvanized and polarized Slovene society even while he won a place as one of the most enduring and popular public intellectuals. Some of Kocbek's writings on World War II are discussed in Chapter 2 of this book, while his famous essay on Central Europe is considered in the Conclusion.

Even Kocbek's political opponents respected his artistic production, and his dogged and brave dedication to his beliefs has resonated far outside the Catholic tradition. As a socialist, Kocbek wanted to transform the society in which he lived to reflect left-of-center ideals of social justice and economic democracy; as a Christian, Kocbek eschewed violence, condemned authoritarianism and human rights abuses by governments on the left and the right, and viewed the natural world as a repository of symbols of divine truths and the human world as a nexus of relationships and possibilities for individual redemption. His humanism is present in both of these facets of his thinking – so much so, one might argue, that Kocbek's ideas and concerns are essentially internationalist rather than nationalist. Although he was deeply patriotic and became the "grand old man" of Slovene letters, his message challenges the chauvinism and smugness of many nationalist thinkers. Tension in his world views (between his Catholic faith and European socialism, traditionally dominated by secular activists) and contradictions in his reputation (his patriotism which was not ethnic, separatist, or jingoistic nationalism) are hallmarks of Kocbek; they, along with the high quality of his writing, make him an intriguing subject for study across disciplinary lines.

There are two images from Kocbek's poetry that can give us a sense of how this man acted, thought, and felt. One image, from the poem "Who Am I?", is of "a generous rose/ready to erupt." This flower is a representation of truth and beauty that is not contingent upon human acceptance or understanding; "[o]ne day," the poet writes, "it will look/ this arrogant century in the face/ and the century will blush."[39] Kocbek always had confidence that history would vindicate his ideas and his activities, even when current political trends ran – often painfully – against him. The other image is of a visitor to a war-ravaged village; as he watches, life gradually begins returning to the ashes and scorched stones. This provides an epiphany to the observer. When Kocbek writes "I grow larger,/ become a giant,/ now I see over/ the shoulder of all horror,"[40] he has triumphed over the pain of witnessing the destruction around him and risen above the political squabbles that occasioned the atrocity. He does not identify the perpetrators, but he knows what motivates them and what is greater than they are.

When Edvard Kocbek was born on September 27, 1904, in Sveti Jurij ob Ščavnici (today known as Videm ob Ščavnici), a village in Prekmurje, Slovenia was still part of the Habsburg Empire. His father was an organist and church sexton. Kocbek himself was a voracious reader as a boy, sailed through elementary school, and was sent to the large nearby city of Maribor to study at the classical *gimnazija* (lycée). His high school studies there and elsewhere lasted for a total of six years, and then from 1925 to 1927 he studied theology at the Roman Catholic seminary in Maribor. At this point Kocbek intended to become a priest, but in 1927 he suddenly broke off his studies and returned home. Apparently, he "had realized he could serve his fellow man better from outside the church than from within," but there may have been personal reasons for leaving, too.[41]

Kocbek then moved to Ljubljana, the capital of Slovenia, and enrolled in the University there as a student of Romance languages and literatures. It was at this time that he also began his activism in the intellectual circles of the liberal Catholic youth movement; he became editor of the journal *Križ* (The Cross). Between 1928 and 1932, Kocbek studied abroad, for brief periods, in Berlin, Lyons, and Paris. He met, and subsequently maintained correspondence with, numerous West European writers and philosophers. During this time his essays and translations were published back home in Yugoslavia, many of them in the Catholic journal *Dom in svet* (Home and the World); they introduced Slovenes to the ideas of Christian existentialism and also to the works of Catholic writers such as England's G.K. Chesterton (1874–1936) and France's Paul Claudel (1868–1955).[42]

Kocbek graduated from university in Ljubljana in 1930 and then went to teach French in next-door Croatia. For six years, the Yugoslav authorities sought to keep him "on ice" by posting him at schools in Croatia, outside of his home republic, in order to sever his ties to other Slovene intellectuals and activists. In this period he published his first collection of verse, the highly acclaimed *Zemlja* (The Land). By turns Dionysian, psalm-like, and bucolic,[43] this collection made an enormous splash. Most critics, across the political spectrum, were enchanted by the collection. Even commentators to Kocbek's left, who called (unfavorable) attention to his overly "abstract" religious concerns and to his "artizem" (a stylistic attitude of "art-for-art's sake"), joined in the praise that this poetry represented a new synthesis of form and philosophy and as such was a milestone in Slovene art; Kocbek's mixture of existentialist, expressionist, and personalist poetry was called "metaphysical" (*bistvogledni*) realism.[44]

After returning to Ljubljana to teach in 1936, he met many prominent Slovene communists (including Tito's close associate, Edvard Kardelj, and the economist Boris Kidrič) and published articles on Marxist–Christian relations; Kocbek consistently stated throughout his whole life that he agreed with the goals of the Yugoslav communists but not their methods.[45] It was then that one of his essays ignited a major controversy, resulting in the authoritarian and very conservative Yugoslav government shut-ting down *Dom in svet* for a year. This article, "Thoughts about Spain" ("Premišljevanje o Španiji") published in 1937, condemned General Francisco Franco's rebellion in Spain; it also condemned fascism in general, criti-cized the smugness and self-interest of bourgeois (middle-class) Christians, and called upon Slovene Catholics to support the beleaguered government of the Spanish Republic. Catholics and conservatives around Europe and the world supported Franco because of his anti-communism and his ties to the Church and landed aristocracy. Kocbek then continued publishing in a new journal he founded, *Dejanje* (Action), from 1938 to 1941.

When the Germans and Italians invaded and carved up Yugoslavia in April 1941, many Slovenes went into hiding in cities or in the country-side, where they eventually formed armed units to fight the Axis forces and also their Slovene collaborators, called Whites or *Domobranci* (Defenders of the homeland). This phenomenon was repeated across Yugoslavia, with many groups of varying political stripes taking up arms against the invaders and, ultimately, each other. In 1942 Kocbek went into the underground himself. Most of the Slovene rebels had grouped together into an organ-ization called the *Osvobodilna Fronta* (Liberation Front, or OF), which included several different leftist and centrist organizations, including Catholic ones. The OF was ostensibly a coalition, but the communists, linked to the Partisans of Josip Broz Tito throughout the rest of Yugoslavia, were dominant. These groups, however, were united by their common anger over the Nazi and Italian invasions, and by the subsequent gross mistreatment of Slovenes at the occupiers' hands; it should be remem-bered here that both the Italians and the Germans were calling for the assimilation, expulsion, or extermination of Slovenes as a national group, at least in large areas of the occupied territories. Kocbek described his decision to join the OF as a decision to bleed willfully and consciously, since the decision that we should bleed has already been made by others; military resistance (and the cooperation of Christians with communists) was the only thing that could save Slovenia at this point, and at least he and his fellow partisans were not going to "bleed passively [but rather] bleed incomparably more honorably and usefully."[46]

The communists obviously had the goal of carrying out a successful resistance war (or war of national liberation) and then transforming the socioeconomic foundations and political system of the country (social revo-lution). Many of the members of the OF shared only the first goal. Although Kocbek had reservations about Tito's Partisans, he also desired a rebirth of Slovene culture and society and he thought that the war might consti-tute a radical break with the past. Nevertheless, Kocbek reported that "something strange, and dangerous, was seething in the atmosphere" on March 1, 1943; on that day, his Christian Socialists, the Communist Party, and the Slovene "Sokols" (a nationalist youth movement) signed the Dolomite Declaration. Upon thus agreeing that the Slovene communists, led by Edvard Kardelj, would have the leading role in the OF and that the Socialists and the Sokols would not establish separate organizations, Kocbek "sensed non-Slovene and non-democratic intentions" in the air.[47]

During the three years Kocbek was a part of the Yugoslav resistance, he negotiated on the Partisans' behalf with local bishops and the Vatican; kept voluminous notes on daily life and politics; accompanied Tito's high command through Bosnia, to the Adriatic island of Vis, and at the liberation of Belgrade; maintained links to other Slovene writers, intellectuals such as the historian Fran Zwitter, and artists such as the famous painter Božidar Jakac who hoped to reinvigorate the cultural scene after liberation; finally, and perhaps most significantly, he played a leading role in the October 1943 Kočevski Congress which decided that Slovenia would rejoin a reconstructed Yugoslavia after the war, provided that national equality was guaranteed and that all Slovene regions (presumably even those traditionally in Italy and Austria) were incorporated into one major administrative unit.

Immediately after the war, friction between Kocbek and the Communist Party (soon to rename itself the League of Communists, or LC) started. He held two important government positions, one in Slovenia and one in the federal government in Belgrade, and he made an enthusiastic tour of the Soviet Union in 1950. The first set of his wartime journals, under the title *Tovarišija* (Comrades), came out in 1949. Kocbek was getting a reputation for asking tough, touchy questions; his personal combination of naivety and zeal for change was also coming into conflict with his understanding of political ethics and procedural democracy, especially as they applied to his native Slovenia. In 1945 Kocbek essentially asked the Communist Party who had given it the right to introduce a "party state";[48] indeed, although Tito was very popular, no elections were ever held confirming the CP's mandate to rule. Then, two years later, he asked the CP leadership what became of the tens of thousands of collaborators (Slovene Whites, Croatian fascists known as Ustaše, and Serbian Chetniks) who fled towards the advancing British and American armies in the spring of 1945.[49] Kocbek was told that these people were being detained for "re-education"; in reality, they had been executed by the Partisans and Kocbek soon found this out.

In 1951 Kocbek's relationship with the Yugoslav government was ruptured irreparably. He published a volume of short stories entitled *Strah in pogum*. These war tales were immediately banned because the protagonists worked through their moral dilemmas regarding loyalty and the use of violence in ways the Party found unacceptable. The stories (see below) contained too much Christian theology, albeit of a very progressive and humanistic sort, and there was too much "equation" of the motives, personalities, and suffering of Slovene partisans and their enemies, the local collaborators and Italian occupiers. Kocbek was forced out of all his public offices in 1952 and excoriated in the press. Ironically, the 1950s is the decade in which Yugoslav socialism actually began to move away from its Stalinist roots; by the early 1960s, Tito and Kardelj had developed a much more liberal variant of communism than prevailed in the rest of Eastern Europe. But Kocbek, like the Montenegrin communist, Partisan, and writer Milovan Djilas, fell foul of the authorities just when outside threats (coming from the Soviets and their allies after Stalin and Tito severed ties and "excommunicated" each other in 1948) seemed greatest, when relations with the Vatican had reached their nadir, and before domestic hard-liners in power had been reined in.

Kocbek was absent from public life until 1963, when his second volume of poetry was issued. By then, the Yugoslav – and especially Slovene – political scene was much liberalized; in 1964, Kocbek even received the Prešeren Prize, Slovenia's highest literary award. Three years later his other volume of war memoirs, *Listina* (Documents), was published; his other autobiographical observations on the 1940s and 1950s would appear gradually after his death in 1981. Some of his writings are missing, but eventually four more volumes of his poetry were also published.

Kocbek's sixtieth birthday in 1974 proved to be the main milestone in his later life. Back in the good graces of his fellow Yugoslavs, at least in writers' circles, Kocbek's works were being reprinted. The large Slovene population across the border in Italy, centered on the important city of Trieste, was, like other Slovenes in Austria and Argentina, interested in Kocbek and his work. The editors of the Triestine journal *Zaliv* (The Bay), decided to issue a commemorative study of Kocbek. One of them, Boris Pahor, interviewed Kocbek for the monograph – and Kocbek decided to "tell all." He spoke publicly for the first time about what he had learned in the 1940s and early 1950s about Tito's postwar massacres of Yugoslav collaborators and civilians, many of which not only involved Slovenes (on both sides) but also took place on Slovene soil. The interview was eventually reprinted in Slovenia, and the journal, issued in March 1975 and promptly banned by the Yugoslav government, naturally made its way into the country too. Once again Kocbek was bombarded in the media and party fora with accusations of disloyalty, spitefulness, obscurantism, and even senility. His artistic reputation was secure at home, however, and though his political views did not receive much airtime again until after the death of Tito in 1980, his ideas were nonetheless kept alive by many other editors, writers, professors, and students.

Since 1990, four slender volumes of Kocbek's graceful, often metaphysical poetry have appeared in English. One may characterize Kocbek's poetry as being, on the one hand, deceptively simple, and, on the other, original and unique without being especially innovative. He did not develop new poetic (or prose) techniques but, within the basically realistic style in which he operated, he was able to develop metaphysical themes that provoke considerable thought in the reader. All of his works, especially the earlier ones, have delightful lyrical passages. His chief topics are nature, politics, religion, and the eternal and archetypal labors and desires of ordinary people, often peasants. These themes are often intermingled, and what I term his political poems also contain more general historical thoughts and a number of very poignant reflections on his own place in history, as a dissident and an activist in a small country in a bloody century. These particular poems have no ring of egotism or self-justification; they are humble but at the same time confident, steeped in a faith in human progress and a mixture of unfolding revelation and belief in immutable moral principle.

Space here permits only mention of one additional poem from one of the categories above. The poem "Smuggling" expresses Kocbek's confidence that religion still has a place in the twentieth century. Although people profess to prefer physical, intellectual, and psychological distractions ("a hygienic conscience-dusting") to religion, they cannot shake God out of their system or out of the world. Kocbek notes that although "the rest" (everything beyond science and distraction) has been pushed away, it still

> furtively sticks to his fingers
> gets under his nails, in his pubic hair,
> collects in his eyes and eardrums,
> slowly it crawls up his back
> as he sleeps, slips into his dreams,
> smuggles into his blood and heart
> and vengefully digs into
> his right big toe.[50]

Readers will note that the imagery used to depict religion are not flattering; the tone is one of inevitability and challenge, something that people simply have to deal with whether they want to or not. This characterization of religion is one that crops up in various kinds of literature with religious sensibilities from different genres and different countries; for instance, the novels of Graham Greene have many characters who treat religion as a kind of primordial given which has claims on them they would rather ignore, but cannot, and who do not feel worthy of salvation but, through grace, may have it.

None of Kocbek's diaries or his short stories have yet been translated into English, but there is growing scholarly interest in his oeuvre. Most critics find his poetry to be a greater artistic achievement than his prose, although the lyrical power and thorough analysis of his journals sets them apart from most other Yugoslav war writing. The Croatian literary scholar Ivan Cesar has noted that "[a]s a prose writer, he [Kocbek] is some kind of ideologist, a Christian, an anti-Christian, a politician, but as a poet he is a lyricist, an artist."[51] Nonetheless, his several volumes of memoirs are a treasure trove of information and perspectives for historians.

Yugoslav evaluations of Kocbek's work changed over time. Josip Vidmar was one of the leading Slovene literary critics of the post-World War II era. He was, as we have seen in earlier chapters, an important Slovene intellectual from the 1930s on. His views on art were in many ways traditional or conservative in a socialist sense; that is to say, although he was certainly not an advocate of socialist realism, he frowned on works that were too emphatically religious or avantgardist. He also criticized works that were too critical of Tito, the League of Communists, the Partisan movement, or the Yugoslav idea.

Vidmar and Kocbek spent time together in the Partisan forces during the war, and they shared an appreciation for the three great Slovene writers, the commonly accepted national triumvirate of France Prešeren (a Romantic poet) and Ivan Cankar and Oton Župančič (a modernist prose writer and modernist poet, respectively). Vidmar also reports in his memoirs that he, Kocbek, and several other writers, painters, and critics who were "in the forest" (a phrase meaning they had joined the Partisan movement against the Nazis and their allies) felt bound "to the whole of our torched, tormented, and thrashed Slovenia."[52]

Despite these common experiences and feelings, Kocbek and Vidmar parted ways when Kocbek was pushed out of public life in the early 1950s. Vidmar was not Kocbek's harshest detractor (that dubious distinction would be more likely to fall to a critic such as Boris Ziherl or Miško Kranjec), but his views are representative of the rather strong and abiding negative evaluation of the mainstream Yugoslav communists. Vidmar's substantive critiques of Kocbek's work focused on the way his journals "teem with ideological [i.e. spiritual or religious] excursions," which Vidmar finds "banal";[53] on alleged inaccuracies regarding the portrayal of the Partisan leadership's inner circle in Kocbek's historical writings; and on Kocbek's incapacity to chart ideological growth (i.e. become a card-carrying communist) because, as the devout son of devout parents, "[a]ll the gods, the church, and all of that got into his brain and blood and he never moved beyond it."[54] On the technical level, Vidmar finds Kocbek's writing to be too beholden to "foreign models" and to suffer from diction and conversation passages that are "exaggerated and somehow strange."[55]

Despite these criticisms, however, Vidmar has high praise for certain aspects of Kocbek's writing. He does not have comparable praise, one should note, for Kocbek's individualistic and conscience-driven Christian Socialist political engagement. Sheerly in terms of their literary quality, Kocbek's memoirs are high on Vidmar's list (if not at its absolute top) of all Slovene wartime writings about the Partisans; they are also said to be historically valuable as a resource for understanding the daily lives of the anti-Nazi fighters, as well as the events and many of the (non-political) personalities associated with the guerrilla movement.[56] Last, Vidmar even states that Kocbek was the greatest Slovene poet of the first generation of the twentieth century and, further, that, despite his deceptively simple style, he was "the most complex and probably most interesting" Slovene poet of the century.[57]

Another very positive note about Kocbek's legacy is sounded by France Bernik and Marjan Dolgan. They wrote that Kocbek's short stories about World War II put "an end to the apologetic, ideological and psychological simplification of war prose and its dogmatic differentiation between positive and negative heroes."[58] Not surprisingly, Slovenes were in the vanguard of such modern war writing in Yugoslavia, as were Serbs such as Oskar Davičo with his 1952 novel about the German occupation of Belgrade, *The Poem*.

Much of the abiding political relevance of Kocbek today lies in his writing on the Spanish Civil War (1936–1939) and on nationalism. In his controversial essay "Thoughts on Spain," Kocbek was writing to a Catholic audience in Yugoslavia with whose basic political loyalties he vehemently disagreed. Most Catholic public opinion in Europe sided with Francisco Franco and the anti-Republican rebels in Spain; to be sure, the Royal Yugoslav government did as well. Kocbek was writing to remind his fellow Slovenes that the Republic was a legitimately elected and moderate government and that Franco's forces were intimately tied to fascist movements within Spain and, most ominously, in Nazi Germany and Italy. Kocbek's critique of short-sighted, misinformed, and manipulated middle-class Slovene Catholics who had fallen prey to fears of a "red terror" (Bolshevik attacks on the Church and the privileges of the landed aristocracy) in Spain were meant as a general wake-up call on how fascism operates across the continent. In addition, Kocbek took pains to point out that the anti-Catholic excesses and atrocities sometimes caused by the Republic's supporters had their roots in Spain's great and enduring poverty, the ignorance of most of its citizens, and the long history of exploitative rule by the dynasty, the military, the landowners, and the Church. Certainly, the history of the Spanish Civil War is a complicated and hotly debated topic. But Kocbek urges his readers to work towards clarity on two sets of questions. The first involves sources of information and representations of a given conflict. Do we really understand the problem? From whom do we have our information and impressions? Are they accurate? How can we gain access to other information that might provide a clearer picture of a problem?

The second set of questions deals with making difficult ethical choices. Kocbek begins his essay on Spain with the sentences:

> The world today is no longer easily understandable; instead of clarity on the issues, a deliberate and equivocating vagueness is widespread. Indecisiveness and inarticulateness are not actually our natural companions in life; they are, however, the basic and self-serving yardsticks of a humanity which has lost its sense of heroism.[59]

In fact, Spain was a distant and confusing land to most Slovenes, who knew little about it other than that it was a deeply Catholic society. The war had also grown complex, especially given the complex diplomatic relationships that the Republicans and the Francoists had with Great Britain, France, the US, the Soviet Union, Italy, and Germany. The Republican side itself consisted of a welter of groups of different political orientations: traditional democrats and liberals, anarchists, communists, socialists, and ethnic separatists. Kocbek also argues that bourgeois Christians were fond of hypocrisy, which was a form of deceit used to conceal and justify their own self-interest in a "conscious and shameful exchange of higher values for lower ones."[60] Kocbek advocates the use of discernment in picking the more or essentially right course of action in confusing situations. He militates against the passivity produced by lack of understanding or the unwillingness to opt for the lesser evil.

Kocbek also illustrates the concept of "civic," as opposed to "ethnic" nationalism. Civic nationalism is based on a people, or nation, representing a political population, united by common ideas and values, rather than an extended kinship group united by bloodline or race. Kocbek, whose first volume of poetry, *The Land*, demonstrated his intense emotional attachment to Slovenia, and whose political patriotism was repeatedly manifested during World War II, can certainly be called a "nationalist" in the way that nearly every European or North American could be since 1800 or 1850; that is to say he manifested self-identification with a group of people linked by common language, culture, and ideas, and he felt protectiveness and a desire for positive change for that group as his fundamental political loyalty.

But Kocbek's nationalism is of the distinctly civic variety, unlike that manifested by many nations in the twentieth century around Slovenia. He has no common ground with German or Austrian Nazism, Italian Fascism, the Croatian Ustaša movement, or the various aggressive and intolerant Serbian ethnic nationalist movements such as the Chetniks or Slobodan Milošević's postcommunist paramilitaries and bureaucrats. What follows is a small sample of the ways Kocbek treats nationalism in his writings.

First of all, Kocbek expresses, with great tenderness, his love of the Slovene countryside and people. There are numerous poems on this theme, but one of the most interesting for a historian is "The Lippizzaners," about the impressive white horses, long bred in Slovenia, which were the mainstay of the famous Imperial Riding School in Vienna. Kocbek writes that Slovenes picked the most beautiful of animals as their national symbol – far prettier than double-headed eagles or whatnot chosen by most other countries – and that it anchors the identity and status of their small country in the bigger world. In the days of the Habsburg Empire, for instance,

> the emperors of Vienna spoke
> French with skillful diplomats,
> Italian with charming actresses,

Spanish with the infinite God,
and German with uneducated servants:
but with the horses they talked Slovene.[61]

A rather more emotional and individual rendering of the same idea is found in "Slovene Hymn," where he sings in praise of his homeland:

You are the ark of our covenant, which we guard, we must be watchful each night and sing the songs we are pledged to.
O fearsome ripening of the ageless secret, unspeakably strong wine,
We sense in you our blood, we are drunk like young fathers.[62]

This national feeling, however, is not limited to Slovenes. Kocbek in various other poems mourns for the flag-wrapped dead of all nations, and he stresses that all nations have elements of genius. He does this and acknowledges common humanity even while lamenting, in "Black Sea," that "all of our waters/ tend toward you," referring to the political allegiances that focused Slovenia eastwards in the twentieth century.

Appreciation for other nations within the human family had echoes in Kocbek's poems on the gulf between Slovenes that emerged during the Axis occupation. He urged publicly that Slovenes should reconcile and admit that all who died during the war, whether aligned with the Partisans or with the Whites (not to mention the civilians who aligned with neither), suffered equally as individuals and even that they all died for Slovenia. When the great Serbian novelist (and Kocbek's fellow Yugoslav) Danilo Kiš wrote that "Nationalism thrives on relativism; it has no universal values, aesthetic or ethical,"[63] he was referring to ethnic nationalism; Kocbek and he saw eye-to-eye on the dangers of that concept.

In conclusion, it is perhaps useful to liken Kocbek to a Slovene amalgam of Aleksandr Solzhenitsyn and Graham Greene. Of course, Solzhenitsyn is an Orthodox Christian of a very different political persuasion from Kocbek, but the two share the same fate of being highly respected writers who identified with Christianity and also underwent considerable persecution under communist rule. The comparison to Greene presents itself on the basis of the fine line between sin and holiness in Kocbek's stories; it is also supported by a sense of a morally divided self and a politically divided Slovenia, both of which eventually move towards reconciliation across landscapes strewn with violence and misery.

As a poet, Kocbek helped push Slovene literature into new territory in the 1930s, although after that time he can no longer be considered a technically innovative or avant garde writer. Readers of our day might find his poems refreshingly straightforward and concrete; still, his work is highly original because of the power of his language and images. His work is also important because, even though much of it is very personal, it treats of politics and history and theology – big, universal questions with big implications.

Kocbek's political critics judged him, above all, to be too individualistic. In the parlance of more moderate East European communist systems, that label was often used to mark independent thinkers whose thinking was leftist enough to save them from being painted as saboteurs or foreign agents but who, for reasons of personality or conscience, refused to join the party and play within its rules. According to the League of Communist stalwart and his fellow Slovene Josip Vidmar, Kocbek's work "shows us how this religious adept and seeker in the middle of our war of homeland defense is trying above all, to find himself and reach personal fulfillment." Vidmar feigns pity for Kocbek, claiming the poet must feel anxiety at being "incarcerated in himself" and a "stranger" to events of great national and historical significance.[64] Blithely equating a lifelong spiritual quest with simple-minded navel-gazing underscores the philosophical gulf between Kocbek and his former fellow revolutionaries.

A leading scholar of Kocbek, Michael Biggins, has written eloquently that "Edvard Kocbek lived an eventful, controversial life that in recent years has become emblematic of the fundamental dilemmas facing Slovenia in the twentieth century."[65] He is thus a kind of "spiritual father"[66] of the newly independent Slovene state whose writing and politics "crystalliz[ed] the issues that have divided his society."[67] This is an important and fully justified conclusion. Other scholars have noted that he was the first (and perhaps the only) Slovene of the twentieth century to be widely known in Europe. He also, over the long term, helped give the numerically small Slovene people (about 2 million compared to 22 million other Yugoslavs in the 1980s) an articulate voice and a sense of self-confidence; they were already a distinct nation, of course, but one with no state traditions and one much outnumbered by all of their neighbors, whether Italians, Austrians, or Croatians.

But Edvard Kocbek was more than just a witness to a great deal of tumultuous and significant history; his poetry, short stories, and essays do more than reflect and chronicle war and the ideological battles between fascism and communism and everything in between. While proclaiming his personal beliefs, Kocbek also produced literary works of high quality and provided us with significant eyewitness commentary on politics and history. Today his life and work symbolize for many a very specific type of courage and hope; for Kocbek, these very words "hope" and "courage" were never vague or hackneyed platitudes. Rather, he demonstrated both the courage to stand by one's beliefs in times of upheaval and the hope that engaged and informed people can improve this world.

4 Independent Slovenia

Politics, culture, and society

Government and administration

Structure

When most Slovenes think geographically, they think of their country in terms of its nine traditional regions. These do not correspond to any level of government administrative units (see below), but they are rooted in people's minds because of types of landscape, historical experiences, and dialects. Ljubljana, far and away the largest Slovene city at 270,000 residents, sits almost in the middle of the country, more or less at a kind of continental crossroads for Central European, Mediterranean, and Western Balkan cultures. Maribor has over 100,000 people, and other important cities include Celje, Kranj, Koper, and Novo Mesto. Naturally enough, Ljubljana also has a predominance of – but not a monopoly on – the country's government offices, cultural institutions, and businesses. The city is famous for its beautiful river running through the Old Town; for its historic skyscraper, the Nebotičnik; for its castle, parks, and views north to the often snow-covered Alps; for its major brewery, Union; and for the nearby mountain of Šmarna Gora, a favorite spot for hikers and paragliders. One of the smallest regions is Prekmurje, the "land beyond the Mura River," in the eastern corner of the country, bordered by Austria, Croatia, and Hungary; its capital is Murska Sobota. Other small regions include Koroško (or Koroška), the bottom part of the historic province that now lies mostly in Austria, and Bela Krajina, one of the most remote and unique parts of the country. The coastal area, Primorska, includes the major port at Koper but also most of the mountainous border with Italy, including the famous World War I battle sites around Kobarid (Caporetto); the town of Hrastovlje is also world famous for its Romanesque frescoes of a "Dance of Death." Notranjska and Dolenjska account for much of the hilly interior of the country, laced with castles and caves, while famous Gorenjska extends west and north from Ljubljana. It contains the national park around the famous Mt Triglav, the highest peak in Slovenia at 2,864 meters. It also includes the beautiful small towns of Kamnik and Škofja Loka as well as many ski areas and the breathtakingly beautiful lakes of Bohinj and Bled. Last, but not least, Štajersko is home to the major cities of Maribor and Celje and also the medieval castle town of Ptuj and Slovenia's other much-loved brewing giant, Laško. Altogether, Slovenia is about the size of New Jersey in terms of territory. Its population of just under two million (1,964,036) is roughly equal to that of Utah or West Virginia.

The government itself – again, as opposed to the electoral system, described below – is broken down into 193 local units, called *občine*. This word translates as municipality or township, although it is also similar to, if smaller, than a county in the US; what is most important here, though, is that Slovenia does not have an equivalent of states or provinces.

Legislative authority in Slovenia is vested in a parliament. In communist times the legislature was tri-cameral, but the new configuration has two houses. The more powerful house is called the National (or State) Assembly, called the *Državni zbor* in Slovene.[1] It has ninety members, elected for a maximum term of four years via a variety of direct and indirect mandates. The indirect mandates are dispensed by a complicated system that blends local and national results in the eight electoral units and eighty-eight electoral districts. One seat each is guaranteed to the Italian and Hungarian minority groups, and these sole delegates have veto power over legislation specifically affecting their groups. In 2000, the percentage of votes necessary for a party to win a seat in Parliament was raised from 3.2 percent to 4 percent, similar to the level in many other countries; other changes to make the system more similar to majority voting have also occurred, but the proportional electoral system is still strong. In general, of course, this National Assembly is the body that passes legislation and confirms, upon the President's nomination, the Prime Minister. Indirect mandates make it easy for leaders of small parties to obtain seats in Parliament. The voting age is eighteen, and permanent residents have the right to vote in some local elections.

The other house, known as the National Council or *Državni svet*, advises the Assembly and can initiate legislation in the Assembly, plebiscites, and inquiries. It has forty members who are not picked by direct election but by various "interest groups" or electoral colleges – often regional or professional bodies or socioeconomic groups – from around the country. The Council also possesses a kind of veto which can delay, but seldom stop, legislation from the Assembly. Its members are elected for five-year terms. Due to its supporting role, the *Državni svet* is not often a headline-grabber, but it serves an important function, since it can prolong and help direct discussion on important issues, even amid flash-floods of populist sentiment or on controversial issues that vex the directly elected lawmakers. It has been noted that this body shores up the state of civil society in Slovenia, which is by many indications in decline.

The President is directly elected by the population every five years. He or she may serve only two consecutive terms. The President has, of course, the ceremonial role of head of state but also real powers. Chief among these other functions are the role of commander-in-chief of the armed forces, the responsibility for calling elections of the National Assembly, and the appointment of many officials including ambassadors. The President of Slovenia lacks many of the executive powers of the presidency in the US or, especially, the Croatian model of Franjo Tuđman, but he or she can dismiss the National Assembly and call for new elections if that body is unable to decide on a Prime Minister.

The Slovene constitution was passed in December 1991. Adapting the country to the standards of the European Union required some changes in the document; for instance, restrictions on the right of foreigners to purchase land in Slovenia had to be loosened and extradition matters clarified. The constitution also specifies the flag, coat of arms, and national anthem. The current criminal code came into effect in 1995. Slovenia, like nearly every democratic and industrialized country in the world, does not have the death penalty.

The court system is topped by a Constitutional Court; its members are nominated by the President and approved for a nine-year, nonrenewable term by the National Assembly. In addition to checking the constitutionality of laws and executive acts, the Court can be invoked to rule on whether treaties are constitutional and also on whether Slovene laws fit with the country's treaty obligations. There is also a regional and appellate court system. The President, the Parliament, and the existing body of judges all have a hand in the appointment of new judges, who serve life terms. Slovenia's judicial system is considered to be impartial and independent. There is also a governmental ombudsman for human rights.

The legal and socioeconomic situation of women in Slovenia is in many ways comparable to Western Europe, and it is better than the situation in many other former communist countries. The typical and pernicious wage differential (also known as the "glass ceiling" of less pay for equal work) between men and women exists in Slovenia, but it stands at 86 percent there, higher than in either Italy or Austria. Despite requirements such as a 40 percent female quota for candidates in the 2004 European parliamentary elections, the proportion of female politicians and officials is far below the percentage of women in the general population, 51 percent; at many levels of government and political life, around one-tenth of the positions are held by women. Female representation at the highest levels of government – in cabinets and Parliament – tends to be higher than overall trends in the administration, most professions, and the business world. The one-year allowance for maternity leave is far more generous than, for example, in the US, and women are well represented in many professional fields. Significant, if underreported, problems remain with violence against women and human trafficking in and through Slovenia.[2] In addition, there is little doubt that the discourse of nationalism which gained momentum in the 1980s had a chilling effect on the movement for women's emancipation and social and cultural equality in Slovenia. Nationalist movements tend to have this effect in most countries, because popular culture and elite political circles tend to begin linking women's child-bearing ability to the biological survival of the reviving nation. Instead of individual fulfillment and empowerment, military and political struggles tend to lead a society to emphasize heroic, macho roles for men and supportive, domestic roles for women.

In terms of nearly all major human rights indicators, democracy is functioning well in Slovenia. The country regularly receives praise for its free and fair elections, rule of law, independent judiciary, press freedom (especially in print media), judicial independence, nonpartisan educational system, and low rate of corruption. The country also holds frequent referenda, which are governed by a complicated set of procedures. Parliament can initiate one, or 40,000 voters signing a petition can do the same. If it is a binding rather than just consultative referendum, then the result is valid regardless of the level of turnout. Many public issues have been "settled" in this majoritarian fashion – so many that Slovenes have begun to worry about the cost of so many days of voting and about what it means when up to 49 percent of the population are losers on an either-or proposition. A very complicated referendum, with three options, in the late 1990s sought to clarify the system of proportional representation in the National Assembly, but the results were unclear.

The Slovene military consists mostly of land forces, though there are a few naval and air units. The government ended the draft in October 2003, although obligatory enlistment in the reserves will continue for a few more years. Accession to NATO made both a professional army and a more specialized one important, so Slovene military reforms will continue for some time. The country participates in a variety of training and aid programs with the US and other NATO members. Currently there are about 7,000 people in the armed forces and about 12,000 in the reserves. The projected force level once Slovenia is fully integrated into NATO is around 14,000.

Political parties

Today there are thirty-four registered political parties in Slovenia, although in any given country-wide election only half of that number might actually field candidates. Independent candidates are not unusual. The evolution of today's political parties in Slovenia began in 1989, although the first multi-party elections were those held for Parliament in April 1990. The League of Socialist Youth, an organization controlled by the LCS, transformed itself into a political party in that year. This soon became the Liberal Democratic Party, and it remains to this day the most successful political group in the country. As is the case in many European countries, however, it does not rule alone but in coalitions, since it is possible, but unlikely, that any one party could win over 50 percent of the votes in the crowded field.

In 1986, Milan Kučan became the head of the League of Socialists of Slovenia (LCS). This generational change was similar to other parties in Eastern Europe, but the Slovenes also had, as we saw in Chapters 2 and 3, a long tradition of opposition to centralism: over the course of 1989, the LCS and its associated organizations made various programmatic statements about both representative government and nationalism that cast it in the same mold as the much more prominent communist parties of Poland and Hungary.

Janez Drnovšek, the long-time Prime Minister and current President of the country, is a member of this party. Two former mayors of Ljubljana, Viktorija Potočnik and Dimitrij Rupel, who has also been Ambassador to the US and is currently the high-profile Foreign Minister, are two of its other leading lights. The platform of the Liberal Democrats today is centrist or somewhat left of center by European standards; their main goals include preserving social justice and social harmony in Slovenia while also, like most of the other parties, securing the new sovereign state, promoting the growth of both democracy and market-based economic restructuring, and pursuing integration into Euro-Atlantic institutions such as the EU and NATO. They have been called the inheritors of the updated legacy of Slovenia's nineteenth-century Liberals: "serving the national cause through integration in a wider framework which *inter alia* allows the development of business."[3]

A similarity to other Central and East European countries is that the Liberal Democrats also have proven to be a better organized party than most of their competition, since many of its members were political figures in the communist era before 1991. Many of its leaders are also popular as individuals, because of their earlier reputation as moderate but efficient representatives of Slovene interests in the federal government and the LCY. Nonetheless, the LDS was not part of the seven-member DEMOS coalition that won the April 1990 elections although, with 16 percent of the vote, it was the second most popular party and, through the vagaries of the election system, won the most deputies to Parliament. In the 1992 elections, however, they were the biggest vote-getters with over 23 percent of the vote. Then, in 1994, the party merged with three others: the Green Party of Dušan Plut and Leo Šešerko; the Democratic Party of Slovenia, a small group but one with many luminaries such as Igor Bavčar, France Bučar, and Dimitrij Rupel; and the Socialist Party of Slovenia, with Ciril Zlobec. This new groups is now known, technically, as the Liberal *Democracy* of Slovenia, although the acronym remains the same.

Another descendant of the former LCS was the Party of Democratic Renewal (sometimes translated as Reform), which in 1990 was almost as successful as the LDS. Leading lights in this movement were Ciril Ribičič, Milan Kučan, and Matjaž Kmecl. This party soon merged with other left-of-center groups to form an enduring party with an unusual name: the United List of Social Democrats, often called simply the *Združena lista* in Slovene. One of these new partners, the Democratic Party of Pensioners, later left the combined party to become independent again; the other two parties are the Social Democratic Union and the Workers' Party. Some of the leading figures in the United List have been Janez Kocijančič and the current speaker of the Parliament, Borut Pahor, as well as the most recent mayor of Ljubljana elected in 2002, Danica Šimšič.

Two parties on the center-right of the political spectrum embrace in many ways the legacy of the old clericals. One of these even bears the same name, the Slovene People's Party (SLS). The brothers Marjan and Janez Podobnik, as well as Franci Demšar and Franc Zagožen, have been four of its most prominent leaders. There is not a great deal separating this group from the Slovene Christian Democrats, except that the latter were more enthusiastic about Slovenia's accession to Euro-Atlantic institutions. The Christian Democrats' leader, Lojze Peterle, had led the first noncommunist government in 1990 as part of DEMOS; his place in the history books was thus assured, since he was at the helm when Slovenia gained its independence. The Christian Democrats absorbed the Peasant Party in mid-1992. The SLS and the Christian Democrats formed a joint party in the late 1990s called SLS+SKD. Peterle left about that time to join the conservative New Slovenia Party, founded by Andrej Bajuk, who was Prime Minister for a few months in 2000.

Two other parties defy easy classification. One of these is the Slovene National Party, founded in 1991, somewhat later than many other parties, and composed partly of ex-communists, but decidedly on the right of the political spectrum. Its leader is Zmago Jelinčič, though a branch under Sašo Lap split off in 1994 to form the Slovene National Right. Jelinčič has raised concerns about the number of immigrants and refugees in Slovenia, among other things. The social and economic changes of the past thirteen years have provided fertile ground for self-styled protectors of Slovenia's cultural patrimony. Although Slovenia will always have an active political right, the relative electoral success of some of its representatives thus far may have been a case of "forbidden fruit" – that is, of embracing a taboo from the communist era – and of the inexperience of their political opponents, especially in the center.[4] That said, European politics, like American, have shifted noticeably towards the right in the past generation.

The other hard-to-define group was originally known as the Social Democratic Party of Slovenia (SDSS), not to be confused with the United List of Social Democrats referred to above. Under its two original leaders, Jože Pučnik and France Tomšič, the SDSS was slightly left of center, as befits its name. Today, however, this party tends to attract populist support and protest votes. It became known simply as the SDS (Social Democratic Party) under its next leader, Janez Janša. He was a famous dissident in the 1980s; after serving as Defense Minister early on in the independent Slovenia, he became embroiled in a number of controversies. In 2000, Janša was reappointed Defense Minister in the conservative government of Andrej Bajuk, and in 2004 he decried the government's plans to restore citizenship to the stateless persons known as the "erased." The party changed its name to the Slovene Democratic Party early in 2004, managing, like the LDS, to keep its initials the same in doing so. Janša remains the leader of the SDS and its vice-president is Miha Brejc.

There are quite a number of other parties, such as the Slovenian Youth Party and New Slovenia. Many of Slovenia's thirty-four registered parties are rather small and regularly do not clear the threshold to take seats in the national Parliament. When a smaller party does make it to this level, however, it can still have an effect on policy and administration by joining a coalition. Although, in most cases, the ideological divisions between the major parties, as opposed to personal ones, have not been rancorous, the large number of parties pretty much guarantees that even the biggest parties will need coalitions in order to form a government. It then relies on coalition partners, big and small, to pass its legislation, including its proposed cabinet; in turn it picks its fifteen cabinet members from the ranks of its allies.

Electoral history

Slovenia has had nine major sets of country-wide elections; these have determined the President and the membership of the National Assembly. There have also, of course, been numerous nation-wide plebiscites and votes for the National Council. The nine most important elections, however, together with parliamentary coalition shifts between elections, have resulted in Slovenia's having had two different presidents and four different prime ministers since independence. Presidential elections took place in 1990, 1992, 1997, and 2002. Parliamentary elections were held in 1990, 1992, 1996, and 2000, while elections to the European Parliament occurred in June 2004, just after Slovenia joined the European Union.

In April 1990, elections in the modified Yugoslav system were held. The six-party DEMOS coalition, which had been established in December 1989, in the wave of newly legalized parties, won majorities in all three houses of the Parliament of that time. It was a diverse coalition, which would soon break apart, but it helped mobilize the citizenry and pilot the country towards independence. Nine other parties took part in the election. Lojze Peterle, a Christian Democrat, became Prime Minister. In the other major election held at the same time, the reform communist Milan Kučan defeated the DEMOS candidate, Jože Pučnik. Kučan's substantial margins of victory in all three of his presidential campaigns show that most Slovenes agree with his reputation for moderation, open-minded-ness, and pragmatism, even though conservatives, especially in the émigré community, have at times been uneasy with his past ties to the League of Communists. Peterle stepped down in April 1992; although he lost a vote of no-confidence on economic issues, there are indications that his conservative social policies may have contributed to his defeat as well.

The elections to the National Assembly from 1992 on would establish the primacy of the Liberal Democrats. Their leader has been Janez Drnovšek. In December 2002, Drnovšek was elected President; after two terms, Kučan was constitutionally ineligible to run again. Despite health problems, Drnovšek is widely appreciated in Slovenia as an honest and competent steward of the country's resources and values in a time of change. The Prime Minister's portfolio was assumed by Finance Minister Anton Rop in 2002, who received broad support in Parliament. A well-known professor of economics, Dušan Mramor, moved into the position of Finance Minister. The Liberal Democrats and their coalition partners currently control fifty-eight of the Parliament's ninety seats.

The LDS, as we have seen, was formed in 1994 from a merger of the Liberal Democratic Party with three other center-left parties. From 1992 to 1997, Drnovšek's party – usually the biggest single vote-getter but lacking a majority – ruled in a "red–black" coalition with the Christian Democrats, the United List of Social Democrats (*Združena lista*, consisting mostly of former reform communists), the Greens, and the Social Democrats (SDSS). Since 1997, except for a few months in 2000, the LDS has ruled with the Slovene People's Party of the center-right, and the small Democratic Party of Pensioners of Slovenia. The current coalition also includes the United List. The October 2000 elections would have allowed the LDS to rule without the People's Party, but Drnovšek opted for a stronger coalition that included them. The results from that election for coalition members were: LDS, 36 percent; United List, 12 percent; Pensioners' Party, 5 percent; People's Party, 10 percent. Janša's Social Democrats received 16 percent and the National Party got 4 percent. The new Slovene Youth Party received 4 percent, possibly heralding a resurgence of civil society and activism.

The year 2000 brought important new currents into the Slovene polity. Drnovšek's government received a vote of no-confidence in April that year, and then two months later, after numerous attempts and shortly before President Kučan was going to call for new elections, the prominent economist Andrej Bajuk finally was able to put together a government. This was the first Slovene government in which reform communists did not play an important part; furthermore, Bajuk is from Argentina, where his family emigrated from Slovenia in 1945, and he is widely seen to be the representative of a reinvigorated right wing in Slovene politics. In August 2000, during his time in office, Bajuk formed his own political party, New Slovenia (NSI); the well-known former Prime Minister Peterle later left the Christian Democrats in order to join it.

Bajuk was not brought into office by popular vote, but he had won a parliamentary seat in 1996 as a member of the SLS. His approval ratings dipped very low during his premiership from June to October 2000, and in the autumn elections the NSI fared poorly, winning just 9 percent of the vote; they are not currently in the governing coalition. Still, Bajuk's four months in office made quite an impression. His supporters praise him for opening the door to a long-overdue changing of the guard, for trying to eliminate the proportional electoral system, and for trying to speed up privatization. His critics charge that he made inefficient use of his time and slowed Slovenia's accession to the EU;[5] that he insisted on too much personnel change among officials in order to punish the LDS and reward his own followers; and that he needlessly divided the country by reappointing the mercurial Janša to the post of Defense Minister.

The second presidential election took place in 1992, after just two years, because a new constitution had been adopted the year before. Kučan won a five-year term with a hefty 64 percent of the vote. Two other candidates also stood out in this race, however. The populist Ivan Kramberger was assassinated, and Ljubo Sirc, a victim of the Stalinist persecutions of the 1940s who had escaped to England to become a successful economist, represented the LDS, albeit unsuccessfully; although he was nominated by the LDS, he received little support from them, and his supporters questioned the fairness of media coverage and public financing of campaigns as well as business donation practices, all of which they claimed continued to favor candidates of the old nomenklatura. Nonetheless, in 1997, Kučan won another five-year term, this time defeating his closest opponent, Janez Podobnik of the People's Party, 56 percent to 18 percent. The fourth presidential race was much closer. Prime Minister Drnovšek took 45 percent of the vote in November 2002, followed by Barbara Brežigar, an independent candidate supported by the SDS and NSI; she had served as Justice Minister in the Bajuk government and had a reputation for being tough on corruption and eager to press for faster economic reform. In the first round, Jelinčič of the National Party finished third with 10 percent, and there were six other candidates, including France Bučar, the venerable dissident who had presided over Slovenia's first independent Parliament after 1990 and then also run for President in 1992. The second round was held on December 1, and Drnovšek prevailed with 56 percent.

In June 2004, Slovenia and the other twenty-four EU members all voted for representatives to the European Parliament. The turnout in Slovenia was a dismal 28 percent; it was also low in many other countries. The old Parliament had had 625 delegates; the new one, representing twenty-five members instead of fifteen, has 732. Slovenia disposes over seven seats, two of which went to the New Slovenia Party, which led the local race with 24 percent. A mini-coalition of the LDS and Pensioners' Party finished second with 22 percent, also garnering two seats. Janša's Social Democrats, now renamed the Slovene Democratic Party, also won two seats by finishing with 18 percent. The final seat went to the United List, with 14 percent of the vote. Other parties ran, including a women's party, Jelinčič's National

Party, and a coalition of the Greens and the Slovenian Youth Party, but they did not receive enough votes to get a delegate. The biggest surprise from the election, beyond the low turnout, was the fact that the People's Party (SLS) finished fifth, with 8 percent, and won no seat. Even though the European Parliament has only an indirect impact on individual countries, elections such as this are widely seen as a barometer of public opinion and satisfaction with a country's own government. The more conservative elements in the Slovene polity would seem to be on an upswing at the moment, with the center-right undergoing something of a deflation.

Political trends

Since gaining independence, Slovene political life has been characterized by relative stability, despite the presence of a large number of political parties and coalition governments. The administration, state, and society as such are extremely stable. There have been many mergers of political parties, and a few secessions.

As in most of the other former communist countries of Europe, former members of the nomenklatura played a prominent role in Slovenia in the 1990s. In places like Poland, Hungary, and the Czech Republic, these people returned to political life, whereas in Slovenia they had never left it. The vast majority of these former communist leaders and parties now function as moderate (and generally pro-EU and pro-NATO) social democrats who are seen by many as a humane and competent counterweight to the neo-liberals who held sway after 1989.

Another major theme common to Central Europe at the start of the new millennium is a renewed struggle to come to terms with the legacy of World War II in the region. Compensation for Nazi slave laborers across the region, as well as the Jedwabne controversy in Poland, the renewed international discussion of the expulsion of Germans from the Czech Republic and Slovenia after 1945, and the selection of a Holocaust novelist, Imre Kertész, as the winner of the 2002 Nobel Prize in Literature, are all evidence of historical controversies that need to be faced, either by reconciliation or at least further public airing and broadened scholarly consensus.

Unlike the rest of Eastern Europe, lustration has played little role in Slovene politics, although much has been made of Kučan's communist past and Jelinčič's associations with Yugoslav military intelligence. This process involves the declassification of government files from the communist era to show people's connections to the Communist Party and, especially, to the political or secret police. Yugoslavia's socialist system was relatively liberal by the 1980s, although, as we have seen, it was possible to fall foul of the military. Only a few surprises from the archives have been verified, but many documents remain missing or have not yet been published. But more than anything the key to this issue is the fact that it was the LCS itself that spurred reform in Slovenia and many of its veterans are still prominent politicians, so there was not a large class of dissidents – within the country, at least – who could be compromised by such revelations.

Except for issues relating to World War II-era killings and to Church–state relations, there tend to be few political litmus tests; maintaining a large degree of social harmony through safety-net features and acceding to an expanded EU and NATO are quite popular across much of the spectrum. Many parties have shown their willingness to compromise, a trend especially evident in the cooperation between the Liberal Democrats and the People's Party.

Economic restructuring has moved along at a careful pace, while Slovenia attempts to prove it is a good neighbor to the rest of Europe by properly managing its nuclear power industry and fighting organized crime, illegal immigration, prostitution, and, potentially, terrorism.

As in Poland, there has also been some controversy over the political role of the Catholic Church. Slovenes are sharply divided over the merits of banning abortion and returning religious education to the school system. Much of the Catholic Church's property, mostly land and buildings, like other property confiscated by the Tito government after World War II, has been returned or compensation paid; the process of "denationalization" began with new legislation in 1991. St Joseph's Church and other buildings were given back to the Jesuits and reopened in 1996. Furthermore, in 1993, ecclesiastical registries of births, deaths, and marriages dating from before 1900 were also returned; these had been seized by the government in 1946. There have, however, been disputes over some key Church-related items. The government decided not to return the island in Lake Bled and, in May 2002, a court reversed the Ministry of Agriculture's decision to restore 8,000 hectares of land in Triglav National Park to the Church. Nonetheless, in 1998 modifications to the denationalization legislation were passed by Parliament allowing restitution or compensation to the Church to continue, despite earlier criticism that the property was a vestige of feudalism. Critics of the Church's claims have asserted that the controversies they have unleashed have tied up secular denationalization as well, although at the time of writing most claims have, indeed, been addressed.

Other observers have noted that close ties between the Church and some of the parties in the original DEMOS coalition may have led to tensions that broke up that grouping, although one of the issues sometimes mentioned, the memorialization of Slovenes in the World War II era who died on the collaborationist side or simply as victims of the Partisans, is considered to be of moral significance by many Slovenes. At any rate there seems to be little point in blaming the DEMOS breakup on religion, since the evolution (and eventual mergers) of Slovene parties seems in many ways natural, and most coalitions in transition countries tend to be united more by what they oppose than what they support.

After considerable persecution in the early communist years, and growing secularism for decades, the Roman Catholic Church in Slovenia has logically regained considerable prominence since 1991. The Church in Slovenia consists of the dioceses of Koper and Maribor and the archdiocese of Ljubljana. The Archbishop at the time of the breakup of Yugoslavia was Alojzij Šuštar, known in some circles as a moderate but who was nonetheless intent upon returning the Church to the public life of the country. He presided over the reintroduction of the public cele-bration of Christmas in 1991 and also some of the first memorial services for the victims of the massacres at Kočevski Rog. Other goals of the Catholic leadership have also been met: some parochial schools have been reopened, *in vitro* fertilization has been restricted to married women, chap-lains (both Catholic and Protestant) have been reinstated in the armed forces, and future censuses will ask an optional question about religious preference. Finally, in 2004, a Slovene–Vatican agreement regulating the legal status of the Church was ratified by Parliament. This "Agreement Between the Republic of Slovenia and the Holy See on Juridical Questions" defines the legal status of the two independent parties, commits them to follow certain procedures for resolving issues and disputes, and guaran-tees the status of Catholic schools, charitable institutions, mass media, and pastoral presence as equal to other privately sponsored initiatives. Opponents of this agreement said it was unnecessary, gave undue consid-eration to the Catholic Church, and infringed on Slovenia's sovereignty. Due to the considerable historical significance of Catholicism in Slovenia, and the persecution of the Church after 1945, such opposition would seem exaggerated. The Church's moves to restore religious instruction to public schools and to place a pro-life (anti-abortion) article in the Constitution were defeated.

Society

One of the basic facts of Slovene society is the make-up of the popula-tion. Slovenia is often touted as "ethnically homogeneous" and, by comparison with other former Yugoslav republics, it is. But in fact Slovenes form only about 88 percent of their republic today, far behind the posi-tion of the eponymous population groups in, say, Albania, Poland, and Hungary, at 98 percent. In 1948, Slovenia was 97 percent Slovene, and then natural mixing with the other Yugoslav groups began. Censuses were conducted most recently in 1991 and 2001. It is estimated that Slovenia's population will reach the two million mark in 2010. Currently, counting cross-border and diaspora Slovene populations, and subtracting Slovenian citizens who speak primarily other languages, there are about 2.2 million Slovene-speakers in the world.

The current population mix is also 3 percent Croatian, 2 percent Serbian, 1 percent Bosnian (technically, Bosniaks, formerly called Bosnian

Muslims), and 6 percent other nationalities. The Croats live mostly in mixed areas along the border between the two countries, and some Serbs have lived in southeastern Slovenia for centuries. Most of the other minorities are either people who moved into Slovenia for employment or family reasons in Yugoslav times or who came there after 1991 as refugees; some of the post-1991 arrivals were people with Slovene roots. Somewhere between 2,000 and 10,000 Roma (Gypsies) also live in Slovenia. As in other European countries, especially former communist lands such as the Czech Republic, Hungary, and Romania, the Roma must deal with a higher incidence of discrimination, poverty, and lack of representation than other population groups. The tiny German-speaking population, some of whom identify themselves as Austrians and some as Germans, consists of fewer than 800 people. It is scattered across the country, although most of its members have some connection to the Kočevlje/Gottschee area. This group is recognized only as a cultural and not legal entity, despite the Austrian government's interest. In Habsburg times, and indeed up through the end of World War II, there was a much larger German-speaking population in Slovenia, especially in urban areas and especially in the north.

An important cultural and legal niche in the country is occupied by the small Italian and Hungarian minorities; these groups, as "autochthonous" (naturally occurring) minority groups, enjoy close relations with their cross-border co-nationals and a special status within Slovenia that guarantees rights for local official language use, including in schools; radio programming; and one seat each in the National Assembly, held by a representative they choose in a special electoral process.

Considering the fact that there are only 8,499 officially registered Hungarians in the country, in the areas around Lendava and Murska Sobota, and even fewer Italians – 3,063 along the coast – this can be seen as a substantial set of privileges. These rights were important even in the Yugoslav time. They were then part-and-parcel of Tito's federalist system, which was itself designed both to enfranchise and mobilize all national groups and to limit the power of bigger ones; at the international level, these rights were also meant as goodwill gestures, or, one might say, confidence-building measures or bargaining chips: protecting the rights of Hungarians and Italians in Slovenia (and in Vojvodina and Dalmatia, as well) was meant to encourage Hungary and Italy to protect the rights of *their* Yugoslav minorities.

Today, there are only a few thousand Slovenes located in a few villages in Hungary, but of course the minorities in Austria and Hungary are much larger. At least 100,000 Slovenes live in Italy, in three different provinces in the northeastern part of that country. Slovenes comprise 17 percent of the Trieste (Trst in Slovene) province, 12 percent of Gorizia (Gorica), and 5 percent of Udine (Videm).[6] These three provinces plus the province of Pordenone to the west make up a bigger administrative division of Italy, the Autonomous Region of Friuli-Veneza Giulia (Furlanija-Julijska krajina), which contains other minorities such as Croats and several hundred thousand speakers of languages from a small group of Romance languages including Friulian and Ladin. (Croatia contains another small Romance-language population, the Istro-Romanians, while the Swiss canton of Graubünden is home to the best known such group, the Romansh or Rhaeto-Romansh, with about 65,000 speakers.) The status of Slovene communities varies from area to area in Italy, with generally the fewest rights and least cultural presence in Udine and the most of both in Trieste. The turbulence in Italian politics over the past decade, with the rise of new right-wing parties and regional (not Slovene) separatist movements, has led to less tolerance of the Slavic minorities there. Slovenes watch conditions across the border in Italy with considerable attention and concern, but it is hoped that common membership in the European Union will provide an effective forum for insuring minority rights in Italy.

In contemporary Austria there are at least 30,000 Slovenes. They live mostly in the southern reaches of the *Bundesland* (state or province) of Kärnten (Carinthia in English, Koroško in Slovene), with a few thousand next door in Steiermark (Styria or Štajersko). As we have seen, the interwar period was rough for this minority group, as it was for Slovenes in Italy. But since the 1950s, the status of Slovenes in Austria has gradually improved. Dual-language roadsigns and schools are common, and there are Slovene cultural organizations for religious, theater, sports, and other activities; student aid societies; periodicals; folkore groups; and major publishing firms. Austria has another significant Slavic minority, and most human rights activists see the fate of the two groups as linked and as indicative of the state of civil rights in the country. This other autochthonous minority in the nearby *Bundesland* of Burgenland is Croatian. They are known as the *Gradišćanski hrvati*. There are at least 50,000 of these "Burgenländische Kroaten," as the Austrians call them; in some ways they have a higher public profile in Austria than the Slovenes, because of their number, their proximity to Vienna, and the fact that in the turbulence after the two world wars there were no border disputes with Croatia involving this group, which actually lives somewhat farther north and is related to smaller communities in Slovakia and Hungary. Both groups have been subjected to massive assimilationist pressure over the decades, however. Another problem in guaranteeing their cultural survival is that accurate measurements of their very numbers are hard to establish. In Austria, for instance, controversies rage over whether mother tongue, language of daily communication, or cultural self-identification should be used in the censuses.

Slovenia's history and culture have been greatly influenced by Roman Catholicism. Today, a strong majority of the country still actively identifies itself as Catholic, though that number has fallen since 1991 from 70 percent to 58 percent. Archbishop Alojzij Šuštar retired in 1997 after seventeen years in office and was replaced by Franc Rode, whose family was part of the anticommunist emigration to Argentina after World War II. He, along with the auxiliary bishop of Maribor, the theologian Anton Stres, is sometimes considered a conservative. During Rode's tenure, Pope John Paul II made his second visit to Slovenia in September 1999 and beatified Bishop Slomšek of Maribor, the important nineteenth-century cultural figure. Archbishop Rode was promoted in 2004 to a position in the Roman curia, where he has the rank of cardinal. The provisional heads of the Slovene Church today are the Auxiliary Bishops of Ljubljana, Monsignor Andrej Glavan and Monsignor Alojz Uran; the former serves currently as arch-diocesan administrator. The only other Slovene cardinal today is Aloysius Ambrožič of Toronto, who gained international recognition as the host of World Youth Day in 2002, which was attended by 200,000 people and the Pope.

The country's small Protestant religious minority has its historic center in the eastern region of Prekmurje; in 2001 this Lutheran community, which has both Slovene and Hungarian members, received its first bishop, Geza Ernisa. There is a very small Jewish community of about 150 persons as well. Slovenia's Muslim population has grown to include at least 50,000 people. Osman Djogić was named Slovenia's first mufti, also in 2001. Then, in 2003, a controversy developed about whether or not to allow the construction of Ljubljana's first mosque. Many specious arguments have been raised against its construction, while human rights groups at home and abroad insist that the issue is a test of Slovenes' tolerance and the maturity of their much-vaunted democracy. Although Jelinčič and other politicians have called for a local referendum on the issue, Mayor Danica Simšič has said the right to build the mosque is already guaran-teed by the constitution. Serbs and other former Yugoslavs make up the country's Orthodox community. There are small groups of Hare Krishnas, Mormons, and other groups, all of which are allowed to practice freely.

Connections between Slovenes and Slovene-Americans have increased in intensity since 1991, with more tourism and initiatives such as the Indianapolis–Piran Sister City Committee, which involves five different Indiana-based organizations.[7] An important scholarly organization in Ljubljana, the Institute for Slovenian Emigration Studies (*Inštitut za slovensko izseljenstvo*), is part of the Slovene Academy of Arts and Sciences and publishes a major journal with contributions in English, Slovene, and other languages, *Dve domovini/Two Homelands*. Another organization, the Institute for Ethnic Studies (*Inštitut za narodnostna vprašanja*), founded in 1925 as the Minority Institute, focuses on minorities within Slovenia and theoretical questions of nationalism as well as emigration issues; its main journal is *Razprave in gradivo/Treatises and Documents*, with articles in Slovene and English. In the 1990s Paul Parin, who was born in 1916 into an Austrian family living in Slovenia, published his memoirs and a volume of stories based on his experiences in Slovenia, especially during his time as a volunteer in Tito's Partisans. Irene Portis-Winner has continued her studies of the village of Žerovnica and its connections to Cleveland, Ohio. Occasionally, Slovene emigrants will hold large meetings when they return to the country, and an increasing number are applying for citizenship and work permits in the country. Some controversy has arisen over the language, education, and residency requirements for repatriation.[8] Politically, the Slovene diaspora is split, with many, but not all, post-World War II emigrants tending to be more conservative than earlier ones.

Slovenes now have a national holiday on June 25, the date they declared themselves an independent country in 1991; December 26 is a related holiday called Independence Day. It commemorates the Slovene declaration of sovereignty from Yugoslavia in 1990. Other official holidays include Christmas, New Year's, Whitsunday, Reformation Day (October 31), and All Soul's Day. A unique aspect of Slovene folklore that is still celebrated is the old spring fertility rite known as *kurentovanje*. People dressed in bizarre costumes of sheepskin and leather masks, complete with trunks, horns, cowbells, and clubs, parade through towns to ward off evil spirits. The processions are often linked to pre-Lenten, Mardi Gras-like celebrations, known in Slovene as *Pust*.[9] Slovene Christmas traditions are also unique. The traditional Central European St Nicholas (Miklavž) comes on December 6. But after Christmas observances were removed, pushed from public life after World War II, the figure of Father Frost (Dedek Mraz) became popular as a sort of general Slavic deep-winter character associated also with New Year's. The American-inspired Santa Claus (Božiček) has also increased in popularity of late.[10] The Feast of St Martin, or Martinmas, is considered to be the day that new wine is ready, and Slovenes are very proud of their famous wines, with many excellent white and red varieties. Especially in Dolenjsko, Michaelmas is celebrated by a mass hike and feasts of traditional food.

Since 1999 there has also been a government-sponsored Joyful Day of Culture on December 3, the birthday of the founder of modern Slovene poetry and a Romantic national hero, France Prešeren, in 1800. The anniversary of Prešeren's death in 1849, February 8, is a special day. It is the Day of Slovene Culture and is marked by special exhibits, awards ceremonies, and presentations. Another national holiday is Resistance Day, on April 27, which commemorates the founding of the Osvobodilna Fronta, the mixed communist and noncommunist resistance movement after the Axis invasion of 1941; this is followed on the calendar by May Day which Slovenia, like nearly all industrialized countries save the US, celebrates as Labor Day.

In 2003 the Slovenes went to the polls for a referendum on another type of calendar issue: whether or not the government should allow most retail operations to be open only ten Sundays a year. Slovene voters approved the restriction, from a combination of motives including protecting workers' rights, promoting family life, and observing the traditional Christian day of rest. The issue is also instructive because it was the fifth national referendum of 2003, causing some observers of the Slovene political scene to wonder if the cost per referendum (almost $3 million) makes the procedure worthwhile, especially given the traditionally low turnout.[11] Issues of this nature that gather 40,000 signatures can be brought to a plebiscite, a characteristic advantage, many would say, of life in a small democracy; whether all types of political issues are equally well served by this procedure, and whether politicians seek to "hide" on controversial issues behind referenda in countries like Slovenia – as they might also do behind the phrase "let's let the states or counties decide" in the US – are open questions, but certainly the idea of consultation with the citizenry is an appealing one.

Over the decade of the 1990s, Slovenia, along with Poland, Hungary, and the Czech Republic, were widely viewed as the "not-if-but-when" countries as far as membership in NATO and the European Union were concerned. This helped occasion a shift in the sources and allegiances of common attitudes and pop culture. A new generation of young Slovenes has now grown up for whom communist rule is not even a memory; this can mean even greater political stability but it seems to be bringing an increase in political complacency and passivity as well. The former bonds that held the Yugoslav peoples together have weakened considerably: Slovenes tend now to know much more about Italian and Austrian politics and literature (not to mention American pop culture) than about trends in Serbia or even next-door Croatia. This trend is even affecting mutual perceptions in Serbia, Croatia, and Bosnia–Hercegovina, the languages of which have often been considered variants of a common tongue. Since 1991 there has been a politically driven separation of the three historically attested variants. The attempts to standardize them once and for all into Serbian, Croatian, and Bosniak, which have encountered political and dialectal obstacles in all three cases, have indeed redirected the younger generations' attention inward, to the culture of the new nation-states. In a similar fashion, elsewhere in Central Europe many young Czechs view Slovaks not as "cousins" with whom they share many historical commonalities and linguistic similarities, but as total strangers. There is not much nostalgia, of course, for the days of communist rule, but the recent artistic and cultural exhibitions and museums on themes from the communist decades in Poland, the Czech Republic, and Hungary are reminders that the past neither can, nor should, be completely forgotten. Meanwhile, in Slovenia, many streets still bear the names of communist-era leaders, though an increasing number have been changed. Debates over renaming are often lively and reflect both political and religious allegiances and citizens' perspectives on the post-World War II history of the country.

Slovene life expectancy has risen steadily since 1991. It now stands at 80 years for women and 72 for men. Not all postcommunist countries have met with such success; in Russia, for example, a deterioration of social services and an increase in alcoholism has led recently to a steep drop in life expectancy. But Slovenes continue to be concerned about their suicide rate, which is the sixth highest in the world. Investigators around the world concerned with high incidences of suicide in countries like Slovenia, Estonia, Latvia, Lithuania, and Hungary, are pursuing possible causal connections to alcoholism, genetic structure, literacy rates, and economic conditions.

Culture

Intellectual life and the arts continue to overlap with politics in Slovenia to a considerable degree. This has often been the case in the past, although the influence of culture on long-term issues of national identity is probably even greater. Some of the leading authors in Slovenia as the twentieth century drew to a close were Berta Bojetu, Andrej Blatnik, Mate Dolenc, Evald Flisar, Brane Gradišnik, Drago Jančar, Milan Jesih, Kajetan Kovič, Nedeljka Pirjevec, and Rudi Šeligo. Dolenc, whose works often deal with maritime themes, has been a prolific writer since the 1960s. Jesih won the 2002 Prešeren Prize, Slovenia's highest literary award, for his poetry and plays. Andrej Blatnik, a much-heralded short story writer, has even had a collection of his stories brought out in English, *Skinswaps*. Maja Novak and Feri Lainšček are other young prose writers attracting considerable attention. More and more works by Edvard Kocbek continue to appear in English translation, but Drago Jančar remains the most internationally recognized of Slovene writers. As discussed in the previous chapter, his novels and short stories, mostly on rather weighty intellectual and historical themes, are starting to appear in English, and even more have appeared in German. Jančar defends Slovenia's secession while encouraging both continued cultural contact with the Balkans and a coming to terms with political crimes of the past.

Slovenia boasts a large number of well-known poets, many of whose works are available in English translation; they include Aleš Debeljak, Niko Grafenauer, Alojz Ihan, Boris Novak, Tomaž Šalamun, Veno Taufer, and Dane Zajc. Some of them, such as Šalamun and Taufer, are decidedly avant-garde, while Debeljak's oeuvre is complemented by an intriguing set of memoirs entitled *Twilight of the Idols*. Novak is also famous for his human rights activism: during the early 1990s he spearheaded the effort of the Slovene PEN Center and the Writers for Peace Committee to assist a large number of writers and their families in war-torn Bosnia. Grafenauer was the prominent editor of the famous journal *Nova Revija* which galvanized Slovene and, later, international public opinion during Yugoslavia's breakdown. Two young Slovene poets from Austria, Cvetka Lipuš and Maja Haderlap, are also highly regarded. Boris Pahor, a novelist from Trieste, has written important memoirs, as have some Slovene-Americans, such as Metod Milač. Ela Peroci, Slovenia's most famous children's author who was comparable in renown to America's Dr Seuss, died in late 2001.

Recently, three novels by the young Slovene sensation Miha Mazzini have been translated for the US market.

In the twelve years since independence, Slovenia has produced quite a few important books that reflect current national consciousness. Two landmark historical works are the double-volume historical sets entitled *Slovenska kronika XIX stoletja* (Slovene Chronicle of the Nineteenth Century) and *Slovenska kronika XX stoletja* (Slovene Chronicle of the Twentieth Century). This lavishly produced and illustrated, large-format collection (of which three of the planned volumes have already appeared) bridges the gap between scholarly and popular history. It contains chronological entries on events, individuals, publications, and trends written by a large team of scholars and is illustrated with photographs of people and places as well as reproductions of important documents. Also of note is the *Ilustrirovana Zgodovina Slovencev*, a similar work on a smaller scale. Historical research in Slovenia is progressing steadily, partly because scholars can now ask questions that earlier could not be asked, or at least could not be answered due to the unavailability of communist-held archives. The publishing of these and many other important historical works has been paralleled by the completion of the sixteen-volume *Enciklopedija Slovenije*, a massive and attractive scholarly publication that was begun in 1987 and completed in 2002.

An important recent novel is *Zadnja Sergijeva skušnjava* (The Last Temptation of Sergij) by a talented young writer, Jani Virk (b. 1962). This satirical treatment of contemporary Slovene politics and society takes independence as a given and focuses on the familiar (and sometimes hilarious) set of ills, misunderstandings, and shortcomings of a modern or postmodern society. The rest of (former) Yugoslavia seems light-years away, while Western Europe and the rest of the electronic, globalized, capitalist, democratic world seems so close as to be nothing but a blur – that is, a confusing set of cultural options. Slovenes are beset by an appetite for all of these new options combined with a lot of their old hang-ups, and democracy is satirized as a mediocre system – yet, somehow, still exhilarating and worthwhile – upheld by greedy and ignorant politicians. The contrast between aging, intellectual dissidents and the country's new yuppie political class is fertile ground for satire, while the premises of the book reflect Slovenia's place among "normal" modern countries (i.e. countries with market economies and representative government), with all of their attendant social and political conflicts.

Indeed, Slovene novelists are producing many fine works these days, too few of which ever see translation into English. But it would be fitting at this point to mention the work of a somewhat older Slovene writer from Austria. Florjan Lipuš (b. 1937) is renowned as a writer of both essays and fairly experimental prose pieces dealing with the skepticism and loneliness of alienated individuals.[12] Lipuš has long been famous as the leading light among Slovene writers "north of the border," that is, in the Austrian state of Carinthia; his 1972 novel *Zmote dijaka Tjaža* (The Mistakes of the Student

Tjaž) has long been considered the first great Slovene novel from Austria, helping gain much-deserved critical acclaim for Slovene literature outside Slovene borders. But, now that Slovenia has become an independent state, the implicit linguistic and political agenda in Lipuš's writing bears re-examination.

It is possible to read Lipuš, as the Austrian critic Karl-Markus Gauß has observed, and note primarily his "avant-garde art of language and socially critical sensibility."[13] But Gauß adds that there are two political assumptions underpinning his work as well: the insecurity of Slovenes' existence in Austria and the wrongs done to the Carinthian Slovenes at the hands of the Nazis and the Deutsch-Kärntner, as the local Austrians sometimes – in an ultimately rather sinister fashion – call themselves. In what may be his most important work, *Jalov Pelin* (Sterile Wormwood), written in 1985, Lipuš created a novel that at first seems simply rather surreal and grim. It concerns a young man who has returned to his native village in southern Austria to attend his father's funeral. But what we are witnessing is the passing of an agricultural old society, the venerable Slovene way of life in southern Austria, with many evocations of its poverty, violence, pain, and isolation. The book contains some key autobiographical elements; Nazi racism and World War II inflicted much suffering on Lipuš and his family. Lipuš's works are unsentimental and do not endorse typical programs for encouragement of Slovene nationalism or survival, either in the Catholic or socialist and Yugoslav vein. But, in addition to a bittersweet sense of loss in *Jalov Pelin*, the important and ultimately optimistic relevance of the work to a study of Slovene nationalism is the style of the language in which it is written. Lipuš writes in a mixture of the exuberant and grotesque, using neologisms and stretching the standards and expressive capacity of Slovene. He has noted elsewhere that it is the Slovenes' sense of self, their self-consciousness, that has enabled them to survive their centuries of political powerlessness; and this self-awareness is based on their language. In turn, this language must not be treated like a museum exhibition and allowed to atrophy. It must evolve and be "unique, directed forwards and upwards."[14] It remains an open question if this plea for linguistic openness and appreciation for historical consciousness will be heeded in the future by Slovene writers, many of whose works are starting to show a preoccupation with increasingly personal, albeit very up-to-date, themes.

An important academic publication, a normative dictionary, was also published in late 2001. This type of dictionary encompasses "an extensive overview of rules of spelling, punctuation, pronunciation, and various other elements of grammar and style."[15] A massive joint scholarly endeavor, headed by veteran linguist Jože Toporišič, this is the first undertaking of this type in Slovenia since 1962. Such works, which undergird small countries' sense of identity and unity, tend to be very popular in Eastern and Central Europe, where many nations and nation-states reached full development only in the twentieth century.

Since 2002, issues of language and literacy have again come to the fore in Slovenia. Studies have revealed that Slovenes read far less than was assumed, although the literacy rate has, of course, been extremely high for decades; there is a growing public perception as well that the increasing influence of businesses geared for international markets and of pop culture from other countries is putting Slovene at a real disadvantage compared to German and, especially, English. The Academy of Sciences and Arts, the Slovene Writers' Association, and the National Assembly have all issued strong calls for increased use of Slovene in domestic advertising and business and among cultural and diplomatic elites.

Mladina, the key periodical from the democratization movement of the 1980s, remains the country's premier news weekly. The main newspapers today include the dailies *Delo*, *Dnevnik*, and the tabloid *Slovenske novice*, along with *Dnevnik*'s major Sunday edition, *Nedeljski dnevnik*, from Ljubljana. Other important papers include *Večer* from Maribor, *Primorski dnevnik* from Trieste, another news weekly called *Mag*, the business daily *Finance*, and the Catholic weekly *Družina*. *Ognjišče* is a well known Catholic monthly. Two other post-communist papers, the conservative *Slovenec* and the liberal *Republika*, were founded and then discontinued in the 1990s. Because of Slovenia's successful transitions of late, the Voice of America ceased its Slovene-language radio broadcasts in 2004, while Radio Free Europe greatly reduced its news coverage of the country. *Pavliha* is a biweekly satire magazine, *Ekipa* covers the world of sport, and *Ciciban* is for children.[16] The government-run Radio-Televizija Slovenija (RTVS) has two television and three radio channels, and there are many other private channels for both, some of which are regional and some national.

Important historical journals include *Zgodovinski časopis* (The Historical Review), *Glasnik Slovenske matice* (The Herald of the Slovenska Matica, or national literary society), *Borec* (Fighter), and *Zgodovina za vse* (History for Everyone). The leading fora for literature and literary criticism are *Nova revija*, *Literatura*, and *Sodobnost*. The Slovene Writers' Association (Društvo slovenskih pisateljev), a prominent group since 1968, publishes the eminent series *Litterae Slovenicae*, which features translations of important prose, poetry, drama, and essays into various world languages; the Association also awards an annual international prize at the Vilenica Festival. The SAZU also puts out a *Letopis*, or annual, among its many publications. The Society for Slovene Studies, an international academic organization, has published *Slovene Studies* since 1979. An important bi-monthly journal on politics, economics, and literature is *Razgledi* (Views). The chief academic journal for the social sciences is *Teorija in praksa* (Theory and Practice).

The main publishing houses, as in the time of Yugoslavia, are DZS (Državna založba Slovenije), Mladinska knjiga, Cankarjeva založba, and the Maribor-based Obzorja. In Austria, the publishing houses of Drava, Mohorjeva/Hermagoras, and Wieser produce many high-quality books on Slovenia in both German and Slovene. Of the many new publishing firms begun since the fall of communism, Mihelač is the best known. There is a major book fair every autumn in Ljubljana.

Slovenes, long known as avid hikers, mountain climbers, soccer players, and skiers, have established an international profile, winning gold medals in the double sculls and fifty-meter rifle shooting at the Sydney Olympics in 2000 and a bronze in ski jumping at the Salt Lake City Olympics in 2002. Their soccer team was also one of only thirty-two teams to qualify for the 2002 World Cup soccer competition. Slovenes have, in addition, begun breaking into the National Basketball Association with players such as Boštjan Nachbar and Marko Milič. Earlier Slovene sports heroes include the skier Jure Franko from the 1984 Sarajevo Olympics, and Leon Štukelj, who won six Olympic medals in gymnastics in the interwar period. In less traditional sporting news, starting in 1997, Benka Pulko set two Guinness world records in her 2,000-day motorcycle journey around the world, driving on all seven continents and charting the longest solo ride ever by a woman. Last, but not least, Davo Karničar became the first person to ski down Mount Everest in 2000. The other most famous incident in Slovene skiing history, of course, occurred in 1970 when ski jumper Vinko Bogataj suffered a dramatic crash that was played for years as the introduction to an American sports show on television, accompanied by the words "the thrill of victory . . . and the agony of defeat." Bogataj later became an official at the Sarajevo games and then worked as a coach in Slovenia.

Slovenia's film industry flourished in the 1990s. Few of its films have been international hits, except for several by Maja Weiss, as well as *When I Close My Eyes* (dir. Franci Slak, 1993), *Idle Running* (Janez Burger, 1998), and *Bread and Milk* (Jan Cvitkovič, 2001). Many others have been well received at international gatherings. A new film festival is now held every spring in Portorož, and it is there that "Vesna" Awards, the Slovene equivalent of Academy Awards, are given out. Some of the recent hits there have included works by Vince Anžlovar and Sašo Podgoršek, and older favorites include the children's series *Kekec*, about a brave little boy in the Alps, by Jože Gale.

Besides the omnipresent Slavoj Žižek,[17] other Slovene scholars have begun publishing in the English-speaking world; notable recent works in the fields of sociology, philosophy, and history include some by Tomaz Mastnak, Renata Salecl, Slavko Splichal, Mitja Velikonja, and Alenka Župančič. So far, autobiographies by several leading Slovene political and cultural figures from the 1980s and 1990s, such as Janez Drnovšek, Janez Janša, Jože Javoršek, Lojze Peterle, Dimitrij Rupel, and Ciril Zlobec have been published, and several exist in German translation, though not in English. It is to be hoped that more works of this type will appear. Former President Kučan's memoirs could indeed be a valuable and enlightening historical document, in the same way that the 1988 autobiography of an earlier reform communist, Stane Kavčič, are so useful.

Slovenes now generally look to the US, Germany, Austria, and Italy more than ever for their pop culture models. Some observers already lament the fact that today's Slovene students know little about the language and culture of the Croats, Serbs, and Bosnians, Slovenia's political bedfellows for seventy years. But certain echoes of the past can still be heard, some of which reflect a certain "Jugo-nostalgija." For instance, a film festival dedicated to the works of the Bosnian director Emir Kusturica (*When Father Was Away on Business*; *Do You Remember Dolly Bell?*; *Underground*) was held in 2000. Not necessarily nostalgic, but rather demonstrating moral concern for the vast human suffering in Yugoslavia's political cataclysm, have been anthologies of poetry, fiction, and essays about the wars to the south, such as a special edition of the journal *Sodobnost* from April 2001, entitled *Pisatelji za mir/ Writers for Peace/Književnici za mir*. In 1996, Drago Jančar published a book on the brutal war in Bosnia entitled *Short Report about a Long-besieged City: Justice for Sarajevo*. While Croatia was still gripped by postwar trauma (and the effects of President Tuđman's authoritarian rule), Serbian newspapers were being sold in Slovenia and Serbian bands, remembered from the common Yugoslav days, could still draw crowds in Slovenia – and were free to do so. In 2001 there even came the establishment of an Adriatic Basketball League, because markets in Slovenia, Croatia, Bosnia–Hercegovina, and Montenegro are too small to be profitable; the League might try to expand to include Serbia, Hungary, and other nearby countries.[18]

Currently the most popular rock band in Slovenia is probably Siddharta, which was formed in 1995, has released four albums, and is starting to be known internationally. They are popular with both fans and critics not only for their music, but also for their lyrics, videos, and their collaboration on various projects with Laibach and with respected pop mainstay Vlado Kreslin. The presence of the great punk band Pankrti (The Bastards, working from 1977 to 1987) is still felt; they produced eight albums and were influenced or admired by such famous international bands as The Clash, Jello Biafra, the Sex Pistols, and the Dead Kennedys.[19] As a mainstay of the alternative scene, there were political implications to some of their numbers, especially hits such as "Lublana je bulana" (Ljubljana is Sick) and "Bandiera rossa" (The Red Banner, a reference to anarchy). Laibach itself, founded in 1980, is still very active at home and abroad. It continues its commentary on modern society by manipulating ideologies and images of power. The band frequently sings in German and blends fascist imagery with audio clips of Tito and other Yugoslav realia; it constructs entire albums on such exemplars of power as Opus Dei, Pope John Paul II, Jesus, and Karl Marx. A 1988 release consisted of nothing but eight different cover versions of the Rolling Stones' "Sympathy for the Devil." Ironically, it also has a 1994 album called NATO, although the parody is a bit murky compared to some of the bawdy illustrations of Slovene "grovelling" run by the news magazine *Mladina* in recent years.

Contemporary pop stars include Natalija Verboten, Nuša Derenda, Fraj Kinclari, Irena Vrčkovnik, Adi Smolar, and Magnifico. Jazz is well represented by Mia Žnidarič and others. The Kvintet Avsenik and many other bands playing the brassy, festive folk sounds of *narodna zabava* music remain popular; the music is also called *Oberkrainer*, reflecting its connections to German and Austrian musical traditions. Just as the films of Kusturica dealing with the common era of Yugoslav history are very popular, so is the eclectic, modern music of Serbian composer Goran Bregović; a band from Austria known as the Wiener Tschuschenkapelle, which specializes in lively, multicultural renditions of Balkan folk music, has received an enthusiastic welcome in Slovenia. Popular venues for musical offerings include the Križanke Hall and also Cankarjev Dom, which is also a popular exhibition spot. In 2002 a transvestite singing group called Sestre (Sisters) won a contest sponsored by RTV Slovenija to represent the country in the annual Eurovision Song Contest. Sestre did not win the international contest in Estonia later that year, but their selection triggered public debate over gay rights and tolerance.

Problems

In the coming years, a set of important issues faces Slovene voters, politicians, social scientists, and activists of various types. The hard climb into NATO and the EU notwithstanding, the biggest challenges Slovenia has faced, and still faces, are domestic. These concerns include the decline in civil society; attitudes towards government; resolution or at least clarity about crimes committed during World War II; the early years of communist rule; government scandals; a set of civil rights issues and fundamental freedoms including the independence of the press and protection for minorities; an increase in intolerance; and regional disputes.

In a trend common to countries in transition, there has been a significant drop in the activity and size of Slovenia's civil society since 1991. The term civil society refers to non-governmental organizations in a society, whether they are of a professional, political, economic, religious, or even recreational nature, or related to health or social justice; the vigor of the "horizontal" connections in a society, as opposed to the "vertical" (state-controlled) ones, has been widely taken as a measure of the capacity of a society to resist authoritarianism and build a democratic society. Unions, charitable organizations, and small business associations of course exist, as do independent groups concerned with rape, sexual harassment, and domestic violence; refugee assistance; the environment; gay and lesbian rights; and suicide and drug use. But Slovenes' increasing focus on economic well-being, a paucity of galvanizing political issues such as those provided by the demise of Yugoslavia, and the fact that many earlier independent activists have become politicians, have left civil society considerably less vigorous. Even by 1992, Slovenia "had the lowest levels of membership in NGOs in Central and Eastern Europe" and today these levels are "among the lowest of all developed countries."[20]

Given the sometimes traumatic but always constant evolution of their society in the twentieth century, Slovenes tend to view government with a mixture of emotions and expectations. Mistrust of the state apparatus results from perceptions that it has, in the past, been connected with outside forces considered exploitative or that it is currently being used by scheming politicians for personal gain.[21] This mistrust can create alienation which then reduces the state's legitimacy and ability to be effective. But the greatest internal challenge in Slovene politics remains the creation of stable political parties that reflect more than the personalities and ambitions of their prominent members. At times it has seemed that coalition-building seems to be the government's main preoccupation, and no party has enough votes to lead decisively. Economic restructuring must continue, and at a more rapid pace, while Slovenia must also prove it is a reliable partner to other European countries by fighting organized crime (in drugs and prostitution) and carefully managing its nuclear power industry. While the dearth, though not total absence, of painfully divisive issues is in many ways positive, a political realm based more on programs, platforms, and policies rather than personalities will help Slovenia weather future crises by providing clear alternatives and the capacity for more decisive action; it may also help stem the growing trend of voter apathy. It will also be important for long-term economic development and foreign policy consistency.

Meanwhile, the lack of scholarly consensus and public catharsis on the World War II-era conflicts between Slovenia's leftist and rightist forces, which resulted in collaboration by the anticommunists and assassinations and large-scale executions by the communists, continues to bedevil national unity. The search for a "balanced" view of collaboration with the Axis during World War II and with communist violence in the 1940s and 1950s continues. These important issues for Slovenes were only seldom referred to inside the country until the 1990s, as in the other Yugoslav republics. The "bad blood" of these yet unresolved controversies is still a low hum or undercurrent in Slovenia today, and, until some sort of scholarly consensus is reached on an evaluation of events in wartime Slovenia, the potential for old grievances and misunderstandings to poison politics in the twenty-first century remains. It is impossible to say whether simply airing the grievances on both sides will resolve anything; some observers argue that reconciliation must await generational change and that exchanges nowadays accomplish little. At times, the efforts of collaborators and victims to gain a fair hearing can turn into revisionism or a whitewashing of the historical record, just as the official communist version of events was one-sided for decades. Meanwhile, the number of publications about bloody persecutions, which continued on a large scale into 1946, continues, as does the bitterness of invective directed at former reform communists who are still active in politics.

For his part, President Kučan remarked in 2002 that: "Both the collaboration and the killings have caused great damage to our nation."[22] The discussions have begun to include the destruction of cultural heritage in the form of castles and churches, and memorial gatherings are being held and statues and plaques are appearing at cemeteries, in churchyards, and around battle and burial sites across the country. There are dozens of mass grave sites now known. These issues are fertile ground for the activities of various NGOs, though the issues themselves tend to polarize Slovene society still, and many of the groups that pursue them overtly support rightist political parties. The Nova Slovenska Zaveza, a postcommunist organization which takes its name from the wartime anticommunist movement, has contributed greatly to the memorial activities. In 2003, the National Assembly passed a controversial War Graves Act which standardized the inscriptions and type of memorials for victims of political violence. This nexus of issues, along with Church–state relations, tends to be the most divisive in the Slovene polity. Many cities and towns have retained their old street names or statues of communists like Boris Kidric, Edvard Kardelj, and even Tito, arguing that these things are part of the past that has produced the Slovenia of today.[23] Tito, along with more expected figures such as Primoz Trubar, still ranks high in many polls listing the most important figures in Slovene history; he is also still posthumously popular – always for varying reasons – in the other former Yugoslav republics as well. An interesting comment and admonition about this struggle over memory and victimization from an era sixty years gone was written by a famous Bosnian journalist during the dissolution of Yugoslavia:

> From the Vardar to Triglav, thousands of Partisan and other monuments dating from the previous regime have been destroyed or removed – fewest in Slovenia, most in Croatia – which should facilitate the task of the reinventors of history. It was a revenge against those who wanted to create a world without God. Perhaps one could believe that this destructive rage was justifiable were it not for one discomfiting fact. The barbarians who destroyed anti-fascist monuments also blew churches and mosques sky high with the same zeal in both Croatia and Bosnia–Hercegovina.[24]

There have been a number of scandals so far in the politics of independent Slovenia. For example, in 1993, President Kučan was accused of complicity in the shipment of arms through Slovenia to the forces of the beleaguered independent country of Bosnia–Hercegovina, a position that would not necessarily have made him unpopular in Slovenia or in much of the rest of Europe; in 1994, Defense Minister Janša was removed from his post for abuse of office (and he would remain a controversial and volatile public figure); and also in 1994 the Minister of the Interior, Ivan Bizjak, met a similar fate due to criminal activities of his operatives abroad.

Most of the other scandals involved charges of financial corruption or illegal surveillance; the United List and the People's Party, *inter alia*, have been accused of wrongdoing. If the wave of scandals should continue, or if fallen government ministers should continue to garner significant public support and act as lightning rods for amorphous discontent, the coalition's task of governance will be made increasingly difficult and Slovenia could see a rise in political violence.

Civil rights issues are an important test of the rootedness and strength of any democracy. Many international bodies produce global human rights reports, and usually Slovenia gets high marks for what are called "fundamental freedoms" or civil liberties. Some problems, such as police abuse and the overcrowding and slowness of the justice system, are not deliberate and can be solved with structural changes. There are also indications that political influence over RTVS is still too great. But, increasingly, attention is coming to focus on the various religious and national minority groups discussed in this chapter, and on public attitudes towards them. Discrimination against gays and lesbians and also many forms of violence against women are other lingering problems. Groups as various as the United Nations and the Council of Europe have urged the Slovene government – so far, successfully – to study discrimination against the Roma, for instance, and suggest action plans by which it can be combatted. Most recently, the case of the non-existent Ljubljana mosque and the *izbrisani* (erased) non-citizens have captured world attention and unleashed heated exchanges inside Slovenia.

The civil rights issue that has to do with residents of Slovenia who are being called "the erased" really started in 1992. At that time, just after Slovenia gained its independence, many names were removed from the lists of potential citizens of the country. This was a time when citizenship requirements were in flux, and originally about 30,000 people's names were erased – people who, for the most part, are not ethnically Slovene. That is to say, these people are mostly from other Yugoslav republics who were living in Slovenia at the time of independence but who could not, or would not, pursue citizenship at that time. Their names were "erased" from the lists of potential new citizens after one year. Some were refugees, but others were not, since movement between the republics was common in Yugoslavia. Complicating the public's perception of this issue is the fact that many Yugoslavs of Slovene origin had lived for years outside the republic and some could not even speak Slovene, yet were quickly accepted as citizens of the new state.

With Slovenia's accession to the EU, this denial of citizenship, which today means that the remaining members of the group in question (estimates vary from 5,000 to 18,000) have a hard time getting work permits and health care or governmental benefits, not to mention a passport, came under increasing scrutiny by other European countries. In 2002, Slovenia's highest court, the Constitutional Court, held that the "erasure" was illegal.

Since then, the political wrangling inside the country over just how to undo the measure has grown steadily.

It was decided to hold a public referendum in February 2004, to gain public support for the government's plan to restore the rights to citizenship to "the erased." The Constitutional Court, Slovenia's highest judicial body, intervened, however, on January 9 by putting the planned referendum on hold. The motion to delay the vote was put before the court, surprisingly perhaps, by members of Parliament who are part of the ruling coalition, seemingly in an effort to avoid revealing fault lines in the coalition or even an embarrassing defeat on the issue; the public reason given was to avoid a backlash of intolerance. But conservatives in Parliament also welcomed the stay and began suggesting modifications to the policy and the referendum issue. Opponents of the planned rectification of the status of "the erased" have three objections: anxiety over the current lack of limits on the amount of compensation that applicants can claim, fears that former members of the Yugoslav National Army (JNA) who fought against Slovenia in 1991 might end up winning citizenship, and resentment of the opportunism of people who were at first uncertain if they wanted to become Slovene citizens.

The court quickly reversed itself on January 26, 2004, but Parliament did not set a new date for a binding referendum. A non-binding referendum was held in April 2004, shortly before Slovenia joined the European Union. Although voter turnout for the plebiscite was typically low, at least in part because the ruling coalition urged voters to boycott what they found to be an exercise in offensiveness, the margin of votes against the erased was quite large. Immigration to Slovenia is not uncommon, both because of the country's low birth rate and the instability of the nearby Balkan states. The European Union finds this issue unpalatable and has urged Slovenia to resolve it quickly. Meanwhile, accusations swirl above both camps in Slovenia, with questions flying about historical precedent (the fate of other emigrants and immigrants in the area), the manipulation of both sides of the issue for political gain, racism, and the legitimate difficulty of people obtaining documents from war-torn Bosnia.[25]

The issue of the *izbrisani* is obviously part and parcel of a phenomenon of intolerance that many would argue has been present since 1991 and is gradually growing to potentially dangerous proportions. From initial, politically inspired resentment of other Yugoslavs, especially Serbs, to jealousy at having to share scarce economic resources with refugees, to indignation at being lumped together in Western public opinion with less fortunate successor states such as Croatia, this intolerance is intertwined with many of the minority issues already discussed in this chapter. Most frightening of all, an upsurge in populism and right-wing politics is eroding the legacy of Slovenia's famed "civil society," whose members advocated ethnic and lifestyle tolerance, nonviolence, and limitation of governmental powers.

The final problematic area of Slovene politics and society consists of regional disputes. The EU has already noted Slovenia's lack of regional government – more importantly, Slovenes have already noted that they will not be eligible for certain important EU development funds without instituting levels of effective new administration between the capital city and the local *opčine*. The national government has now organized the townships into twelve "statistical regions," but it is unclear what powers these will have. There are ongoing disputes over how much control Ljubljana has over budgets and the hiring of local officials. There has also been a considerable tug of war of late between Maribor and Ljubljana; the mayor of Slovenia's "second city," Boris Sovič of the *Združena lista*, has pressed for more government offices to be located in Maribor. Debate also continues about whether to found a third university in Slovenia. It would presumably be called Primorska University because it would combine and expand upon a variety of existing educational facilities in the coastal region, which include a polytechnic institute, a teachers' college, and specialized schools for tourism and maritime studies.

5 Independent Slovenia

Economics and foreign policy

Introduction

Since 1991, Slovenia has been in the process of what scholars and politicians call "transition." This term originated with studies of the changes in authoritarian regimes in Latin America and Africa in the 1980s; it has also been applied to "southern European" countries, such as Spain, Portugal, and Greece, that left the realm of dictatorship even earlier. With the fall of communist governments starting in Eastern Europe in 1989 – with Yugoslavia and Albania officially breaking with that model a few years later – and in the Soviet Union in 1991, the set of possible subjects for "transition studies" grew tremendously. The transition has been described and analyzed from all sorts of academic perspectives, from history to economics, political science to sociology, with a healthy admixture of other perspectives thrown in by scholars specializing in nationalism, feminism, and environmental studies. Considerations of the pace and mandate of reform are important, as are international influences such as access to economic assistance from the IMF and World Bank and the lure of admission to the EU and NATO; of course, the historical legacy of the previous system is also of great significance because it determines the starting point of change and helps set the intellectual and emotional framework of transition. Many policy-makers have sought predictions about the future of countries in transition, creating a demand for comparative studies between countries and, most intriguingly, across regions.

In transition studies, or "transitology," the scope of concerns and, especially, the definitions of terms, vary considerably, but the main themes are agreed upon. Most transition studies focus on politics and economics. Specifically, they look at the creation of democratic governments and cultures and the construction of market economies. These two components are really just umbrella concepts for a wide variety of issues, attitudes, and institutions. For instance, democracy can be examined in any number of ways; analytical approaches or political phenomena associated with democracy include representative government, free and fair elections, human rights or fundamental freedoms, civil rights or civil liberties, the rule of law, an independent judiciary, control of corruption, tolerance, separation of Church and state, equality before the law, and the competition of interest groups for resources. The concept of a market economy includes the philosophy and international structure of capitalism in its several forms; a social safety net such as medical care, pensions, disability insurance and unemployment assistance; and laws about trade, property ownership, taxes, advertising and banking.

A simplistic definition of democracy as "rule by the people" is not very useful, either in political life or in the study of history.[1] It is too vague, and one must recall that the basis of that term, popular sovereignty, is also a foundation of nationalism. Nationalism and democracy are very distinct political phenomena. On the one hand, democracy emphasizes how a country is governed at least as much as what actually happens in that country, while nationalism has very often been fused with states that are authoritarian at home and imperialistic abroad; second is the question of "whose democracy?" In countries where ethnic nationalism and traditional patriarchal culture predominate, outgroups can easily be excluded from political rights; for various kinds of minorities, including ethnic or national ones, this exclusion can translate into a dehumanization and great persecution, as the Nazi example most infamously shows. In addition, most scholars now agree that the causal connection between democracy and capitalism is also limited. Democracy seems not to be able to exist without some form of capitalism, but capitalism can quite readily exist without democracy.

Slovenia has a special type of transition because it consists of three main elements rather than two. The other former Yugoslav states are in a similar situation, as are the successor states to the Soviet Union and Czechoslovakia. These countries are all, to some degree, "new" states, in that they were not politically independent before their transition began. Therefore, they have what might be called a "national" agenda as well as the political and economic ones discussed above. Slovenia, then, has been undergoing a triple or "three-way" transition into democracy, independence, and a market economy.[2] There are links between these categories, of course; for instance, as we saw in the discussion of civil society in the 1980s, political democracy and national sovereignty came to be linked in many Slovenes' minds. Likewise, part of the economic transition of the country involves shifting from a Balkan perspective to a national one, at least as a way station on the road to European integration. But the fundamental tripartite division is a useful academic and practical paradigm for viewing the events and trends since 1991. Indeed, it is useful even for the period before that date, since Slovenia's evolution in the twentieth century has been gradual but consistent.

A vast scholarly literature on transition has sprung up in the past two decades. Interested readers can consult special issues of *Slavic Review* (Winter 1999) and *East European Politics and Societies* (Winter 2003) for a wealth of general perspectives and references that also bear on the Slovene case. Other comprehensive or ground-breaking works are mentioned in the notes to this section.[3]

The bottom line on Slovenia's transitions is that they have mostly been successful and are largely, though not completely, finished. In economic terms observers frequently note that the structural transformations have been, for the most part, gradual, due to Slovenes' unwillingness to disrupt the country's social fabric and to the unique and vague nature of socially owned (as opposed to state-owned) property in Yugoslavia. Slovenia's rejection of "big bang" economic reform (often called "shock therapy" because it espouses rapid transition based on austerity measures that produce considerable unemployment, deterioration in public services, and other social distress) has been validated but, some economists caution, may have been possible in Slovenia only because it was starting from a fairly high level of development[4] and because the political mandate to continue reforms over the long term was secure. Slovenia consistently ranks among the most free, stable, and democratic countries in Eastern Europe, and its economy evinces among the highest levels of both reform and growth in gross domestic product since the fall of communism. It joined in the upper echelon of a wide variety of indicators in the twenty-eight countries of Eurasia undergoing transition along with Poland and the Czech Republic. It is no accident, then, that these three countries, along with Hungary, constituted the first wave of new postcommunist members of NATO and were in the vanguard of the EU expansion.

The end of communism in Eastern Europe was preceded by the fall of many authoritarian states across the world, from Latin America and southern Europe to Africa. The combined effect of so much regime change produced a feeling of euphoria and triumphalism in some quarters. The most famous expression of these sentiments was the book *The End of History and The Last Man*, written in 1992 by Francis Fukuyama of the RAND Corporation. In an article written in 1989, when he worked in the US Department of State, Fukuyama had first put forth the idea that "[w]ith the collapse of Communism there is no coherent ideological alternative to capitalism and liberal democracy."[5]

Although fellow conservatives have questioned parts of Fukuyama's argument, it set off a wave of "optimistic" (or self-congratulatory) affirmation and speculation about everything from the ability of technology to satisfy all human wants to the Western military superiority which forced the Soviet Union to spend itself into oblivion, from the ability of free trade to bring global peace by creating functional webs between all people to the "portability" of market ideas for felicitous use in any cultural setting. Most basic of all, and perhaps most important, was the idea that capitalism and democracy were invariably linked. If capitalism produces a middle class, the argument went, then that middle class will have a natural interest in democratic government, as English, American, and French political history have already proven.

Reality has proven more complicated than this, however. History, whether or not it really rolls forward along a Hegelian dialectic, did not stop or disappear. In fact, with popular freedom in Eastern Europe came a revival of historical conflicts, especially by the renewed manipulation of old rivalries; these were not "ancient ethnic hatreds" so much as scape-goating and rabble-rousing to gain political power or explain away economic backwardness. But it is true that they had mostly been taboo in the communist one-party states. Minorities now experienced various degrees of discomfort or danger, and the reactions to persecution raise the specter of territorial revanchism: the Hungarians in Slovakia and Romania, the Roma in the Czech Republic and elsewhere, the Serbs in Croatia, the Albanians in Kosovo and Macedonia, etc. The fall of the Wall, it is often said, lifted the lid off the pot. The metaphor holds, as long as one is willing to allow that key media and economic catalysts were added to the mix after the fall of communism. There are other historically conditioned phenomena to consider, as well. The discredited communist parties recon-structed themselves and were re-elected to leading roles in the 1990s in most of these countries. Now generally transformed into fans of NATO and the EU, they were popular due to their administrative expertise and their willingness to tone down the imported "shock therapies."

Actually, theory has also proven more complicated than the neo-liberals expected. On the one hand, to assert that capitalism or democracy has enjoyed a complete and basically inevitable triumph over communism rides roughshod over accurate definitions. Was it one ideal type or pure form vanquishing another? In other words, which historically conditioned variant of capitalism or democracy won, and which historically condi-tioned variant of socialism lost? On the other hand, one can certainly argue that capitalism did indeed "beat" communism, and that both command economies and one-party systems are now absent from Europe. But what about the degree to which capitalism might now threaten liberal democracy? If the many currents of liberalism have in common the desire to liberate the individual and limit the powers of government, what might the social and political effects of massive, multinational wealth be on demo-cratic countries? Finally, the appearance of global terror networks which culminated in the attacks in the US on September 11, 2001, and the vicis-situdes of coalition-building and military action against them, demonstrate that democracy and capitalism are not operating today in a vacuum. It remains to be seen whether the economics of globalization and the mili-tary presence and power of the US and its allies will engender other forms of local opposition than Islamism, but it is possible.

Even with the apparent triumph of capitalism and the long-sought victory of political democracy, elements of variety and choice remain in the config-uration of social systems. The American model, for instance, sometimes called "winner-take-all" or "Wild West" capitalism, is characterized by its minimal social safety net, its volatile atmosphere of mergers and take-overs, and an increasing concentration of wealth and political power in elite hands. This style of capitalism is not universally embraced. Many countries in Europe prefer some type of what has been called, ironically but positively, "capitalism with a human face" or, less flatteringly to American ears, the "welfare state." Historically, the term "social democracy" comes closest to this idea; many European political parties bear this name, with some even retaining the label socialist (as opposed to the revolutionary label communist). The term "social market economy" is perhaps the most neutral for this important phenomenon; one can also refer to citizens' "social rights" in addition to "social safety net" or "social services sector." Slovenia is an example of this type of system, in which social harmony or cohesion, if not social justice, is a goal of state involvement. Slovenes are determined not to allow great differences in wealth to erode their social cohesion, and most parties are committed to keeping a strong social "safety net," including pensions, protection against unemployment, national medical insurance, and subsidized education. This approach presents an intriguing, if increasingly expensive, alternative to both laissez-faire capitalism and command economies.[6] Even social market economies, though, can be born of distinct philosophical impulses: on the one hand, the belief that true democracy requires the sharing of economic as well as political power, or immediate pragmatic or humanitarian considerations on the other.

Economic issues of the transition

Both the starting point and the results of Slovenia's embrace of market economics have been, as we have seen, good. A wealth of specialized publications make data about the Slovene economy available in English,[7] but the general trends have already been addressed earlier in this chapter. Of the greatest importance to most non-specialists, however, are four issues that will be examined in somewhat more detail here. The first is privatization. This move away from state or social ownership of companies and land is, indeed, a fundamental issue in all of Eastern Europe; given the cultural and political importance of property rights in Western countries and the need for a stable legal environment in postcommunist ones to enable outside investment, there is hardly a more important issue. A second widely discussed issue is Slovenia's profile as a leader in economic recovery and reform among postcommunist states. This status results not only from Slovenia's advanced starting point but also from its large set of successful reforms in areas other than privatization. The third issue that also tends to interest non-economists is the set of changes that were necessary specifically for Slovenia to be accepted into the EU. Finally, this section will look at some problems, past, current, and potential, of the Slovene economy.

Slovenia's first major privatization act was passed in 1992.[8] It was called the Law on Ownership Transformation, and it has been supplemented by other legal acts covering the funding of restitution, the distribution of shares of ownership, hostile take-overs, and the retention of energy production in the government's portfolio. There has been no shortage of criticism of the government's privatization strategy, and the process is still not complete. Undoubtedly, party politics have played a role in the pace, but so have other important considerations. After all, what was the nature of social property? Whose was it, really, since neither the state nor individuals owned it, and who should have a say or a share in its disposition? The slow pace has also allowed legislators to look carefully for the fairest way to privatize for Slovenes, rather than a shock-therapy approach that might benefit insiders with connections or outsiders with money. It is safe to say that Slovenes took their privatization very seriously; parliamentary compromises were a way of seeking to maintain social harmony, not avoid the inevitable.

The original approach for privatization was that the value of the socially owned enterprises, of which there were about 2,600, was split into three amounts. Forty percent was to be distributed to the citizens of the country by means of vouchers or ownership certificates, which they could then buy or sell for shares in companies. Another 40 percent was distributed to the employees of the socially owned enterprises themselves; they could be given out as shares or sold. The final 20 percent was used by the government to fund pensions and the compensation or restitution fund. Only 150 of these companies, those having over 500 employees, were classified as large; medium-sized companies have over 125.[9] That leaves the vast majority as small. Privatization of the media was contentious, and in banking it was quite slow, but today the process is virtually complete, save for the energy, utilities, and social services sectors.

Slovenia's 8,000 manufacturing enterprises include some with international reputations. French automaker Renault has had a major impact with its acquisition of Slovenia's only car production facility, Revoz, in Novo Mesto. American tire producer Goodyear bought 60 percent of the Sava tire plant in 1998 and completed its acquisition in 2004, while the Swiss pharmaceutical manufacturer Novartis took over Slovenia's Lek recently as well. Producers such as Elan (skis), Krka (medicines), Gorenje (appliances), and Iskra (electronic components for cars) continue to do well. In addition, Slovenia retains its specialized operations in printing and in the production of pulp, paper, and specialized steel and aluminum. There have been prominent failures in Slovene industry, however. The TAM bus factory in Maribor, which formerly made tanks, closed in 1996; in 2004, British Imperial Tobacco shut down the famous Tobačna Ljubljana, a large and long-running tobacco production facility, one of several sites it had purchased in Central Europe.

Slovenia's economic profile is decidedly positive. It is, quite simply, "the richest postcommunist state."[10] But that is not all: many observers also assert that "Slovenia is the most successful transition economy in Europe because it has succeeded in ensuring prosperity and stability."[11] Slovenia had not only developed a sound manufacturing base and infrastructure over the two centuries, but it had also been a successful exporter to the West for decades, accounting for nearly a third of Yugoslavia's exports while making up only 8 percent of the population. This showed that the Slovenes had technological expertise, personal contacts in other countries, and an understanding of trade and marketing practices. But Yugoslavia was an economic wreck by the late 1980s. Inflation topped 1,300 percent. The foreign debt soared to $20 billion, which made further borrowing impossible. Unemployment was high, at 15 percent or more, and personal income was falling precipitously. Yugoslav budgets were a sham, and Slovenes were much rankled by the fact that they had increasingly less say over how their financial contributions for defense, security, and development funds at the federal level were spent. It was not just the redistributive nature of some of the Yugoslav fiscal programs so much as their inefficiency and, especially, their exploitation for political ends, especially in Serbia, that disillusioned Slovenes. It has often been pointed out that Slovenia's declaration of independence was a victory not just for nationalism but for financial and monetary sovereignty; that, in turn, enabled the economy to stabilize so that drastic further changes could be pursued.

Although the Slovene Gross Domestic Product (GDP) fell by about 20 percent between 1987 and 1992,[12] it quickly recovered thereafter. By the mid-1990s, inflation and unemployment were also contained, hard currency reserves were climbing, and the structure of the economy itself was changing in a positive direction. By 1996, nearly 60 percent of the GDP was produced in the services sector, while the industrial or manufacturing sector was falling. This meant that Slovenia was following the pattern of other "post-industrial" developed economies. Slovene agriculture is productive, especially in milk and wheat, even though the amount of land in use and the average farm size are by far the smallest in the new, twenty-five-member EU and although about 7 percent of the population is involved in agriculture, a figure that is higher than many developed economies.[13]

On October 8, 1991, the day after the Brioni Agreement's cooling-off period expired, Slovenia stopped using the Yugoslav dinar. It introduced its own currency, the tolar; the word tolar, like dollar, is derived from an old Habsburg currency, the thaler. Slovenia also moved quickly to found a National Bank and its own airline, Adria. The next month, a major law on denationalization was passed; it provided restitution, either in kind or in money, for much of the property nationalized by the communists in the 1940s. Since then, the Slovenes have pursued restructuring and reform on multiple fronts, from encouraging direct foreign investment and joint ventures to approving new VAT and excise taxes, privatizing banks, and initiating pension reform. Throughout the 1990s, Slovenia's per capita GDP remained at double, or more, that of other East European countries, and by 2003 it was at 73 percent of the current (fifteen-member)

EU average; this was the highest ratio of any prospective EU member and it was also higher than that of EU member Portugal. Economic growth remained steady throughout the decade. At the start of the twenty-first century, Slovenia was poised to make greater investments in former Yugoslavia. It also stood to benefit from its location as the jumping-off point for foreign companies expanding their trade in the Balkans as well. The Slovene GDP per capita in 1998 was $10,404, as compared to $3,960 and $6,437 in neighboring Croatia and Hungary, respectively. By way of comparison, Slovenia's other neighbors, Italy and Austria, had figures of $19,363 and $28,667. The figure for the United Kingdom was $18,620 and for the US $26,397. Slovenia's leading trading partner is Germany, which receives over 30 percent of Slovenia's exports and provides over 20 percent of its imports. Other important trading partners are Italy, Austria, France, and Croatia. Austria accounts for the most direct investment, followed by Croatia and Germany.[14]

Slovenia is credited with having a well-trained work force, good roads, considerable budget discipline, and many natural resources. Tourism, along the coast and at ski resorts, has recovered and is once again a major source of foreign currency earnings. Slovenia in general has an excellent record on corruption and has a far lower percentage of its citizens living under the poverty line than Portugal, Greece, Italy, and Spain.[15] In 2001 Slovenia also ranked twenty-ninth out of 174 countries in the United Nations' Human Development Index; by 2004 it had risen to twenty-seventh out of 177. (Over the same period, the US fell from the sixth position to eighth, while Norway remained at the summit.) This significant assessment, which combines analysis of all sorts of standard of living issues, including life expectancy, literacy, crime rates, education, and economic and consumer life, shows Slovenia is ahead of the rest of Eastern Europe and immediately behind Portugal.[16]

Obviously, Slovenia's entire economic transition was also part of its admission process to the European Union. Even before the EU Association Agreement between Ljubljana and Brussels was signed in 1996, and then ratified in 1998, it was clear that restructuring would serve two goals, one domestic and one international. The EU's *acquis communitaire* comprises twenty-nine "chapters" or legal subject areas. By 2004, Slovenia had brought its laws into line with all of these chapters. Some of the most publicized changes required by the accession process involved constitutional amendments. For instance, Slovenia has had to alter some of its laws on elections, duty-free shops, regional government, the judiciary, sovereignty, employment of foreign nationals,[17] extradition, organized crime, and, perhaps best known of all, the rights of foreigners to buy land in the country. This process, often called "harmonization," seemed to many to be lagging in Slovenia by about 2000, and the EU sent the country a stern warning via the progress reports that it issued for the top ten candidate countries.

At its secession, Slovenia not only inherited the old problems mentioned above but incurred new ones. The reorientation of trade, roughly from south and east to the north and west, took several years; most economists today hold that the loss of the ready markets of Yugoslavia was, indeed, more of a problem than the loss of the raw materials originating there. There were also tens of thousands of refugees from Bosnia and Croatia in Slovenia in the early 1990s, and they had to be provided for or resettled. Tourism came pretty much to a halt in 1991, thereby drying up a major source of income for Slovenes. Even when the situation in Slovenia stabilized, and the day shoppers resumed their movement back and forth across the borders to Italy and Austria, the three years of warfare in Croatia meant that transit traffic across Slovenia to Dalmatia remained scant.

Slovene unemployment has proved tough to combat, even though it has been reasonably under control since the mid-1990s. The reason for this is that most economic growth has been in the service sector, where high-skilled jobs are the norm; most of the jobs eliminated have been in manual labor. It takes time and resources to retrain workers to fit into the new economy.[18] Some economists have expressed concern that Slovenia is too dependent on Germany for both imports and exports. Mixed results have also been charted in foreign investment. The need to fight inflation and overvaluation of the Slovene tolar hurt Slovene exports and made conditions less appealing to investors from abroad; later, the slow pace of privatization failed to encourage outside investment. There is also some worry that the slow pace of privatization will hurt Slovenia's competitiveness, especially as compared to other postcommunist countries.[19] Slovenia's "gray economy," or unregulated and untaxed businesses, is also growing and is more widespread than the EU average.[20]

Another of the potential problems the Slovene economy faces is energy. Certainly, the country is not alone among industrialized nations in this regard, but ultimately the cause of Slovene national independence would be strengthened by the development now of a bold and, if need be, experimental diversification of energy supplies. Currently, Slovenia derives 70 percent of its energy in the form of oil and natural gas imports. The overall profile of energy production for Slovenia is 43 percent thermal, 31 percent hydroelectric, and 26 percent nuclear. Slovenia's mining sector is still active, but the future of the nuclear reactor at Krško is in doubt; Austria is wary of it, as it is of the Czech reactor at Temelin as well, but Croatia is dependent upon it. Renewable resources such as hydroelectric, wind, and solar power could be developed further.

In addition to indelible anxiety over the competitiveness of Slovene firms in the general European economy, to the rising costs of social services, and to the issue of government efficiency, perennial in every country around the globe, in the short term the Slovene economy must also deal with being a net contributor to, rather than recipient of, fund transfers to the European Union. Admission to the EU also means that Slovenia's position in Balkan trade, enhanced over the past decade by Ljubljana's expertise on the region and by free-trade agreements with the Yugoslav successor states, will now be eroded. In addition, nearly all Slovenes will be keeping an eye on that interface of economics and culture where new trends might emerge. Will the continued economic changes, now within an EU context, still produce "transition losers" or newly marginalized groups who will be attracted to more radical political programs, especially on the far right? And how will Slovene identity itself fare with so much economic and pop culture competition from the German- and English-speaking worlds?

General contours and issues in foreign policy

The first, and in many ways all-important, item on Slovenia's foreign policy agenda was recognition as an independent state. Once that was achieved in 1992, as we have seen, a veritable march onto the international scene began, as Slovenia applied for and gained acceptance into one group after another. Slovenia joined the United Nations, the Council of Europe, the OSCE, the World Trade Organization, and of course took up relations with economic institutions like the IMF and World Bank, which were in a position to help with the country's debt and restructuring. Slovenia had long been a member of some important regional organizations, such as the Alps–Adriatic Working Community, founded in 1979 along with Croatia and nearby states and counties within Austria, Germany, Hungary, and Italy, but it was not a member of the famous Visegrad group of four former Warsaw Pact states in Central Europe with whom it otherwise had much in common: Hungary, the Czech Republic, Poland, and Slovakia. The pinnacle of international political fora was reached in 1998, when Slovenia moved into one of the two-year rotating seats on the UN Security Council. Another early priority was the normalization of relations with Slovenia's most powerful neighbors, Austria and Italy, both of whom have significant Slovene minority populations and both of whom were capable of hamstringing Ljubljana's gradual move towards membership of the European Union. The goal with Croatia, to Slovenia's south and east, was to achieve at least stabilization. Slovene–Croatian relations, increasingly strained in the 1990s, needed careful management. Slovenia wanted to avoid incurring the wrath of Croatia's large military, but also to short-circuit any spillover of the Croat–Serb conflict and to prevent further tarnishing of Slovenia's reputation by association with the embattled and, at first, rather authoritarian fellow Yugoslav successor state.

By the end of the millennium, Slovenia had become a fascinating case study of a country whose two major foreign policy goals, admission to the European Union (EU) and to the North Atlantic Treaty Organization

(NATO), were bringing along with them very large and concrete domestic agendas. Maintaining the status quo was not considered an option in Slovene foreign policy, since these ideas for change had broad support across the spectrum of Slovene political parties, the status quo was not really an option in Slovene domestic politics either. This was ironic, in a way, because Slovene attitudes and the country's political system constantly encourage consensual change, coalition-building, and compromise, so much so that some outside observers have begun to grow impatient with the pace of change there.

This internal–external linkage was occasioned by the fact that Slovenia had to prove itself in certain ways before the European Union and NATO would offer it membership. First of all, of course, these two organizations had to have a clear intention of expanding and a definite procedure for doing so. Indeed, NATO did accept new members in the late 1990s. There were no guarantees that expansion would continue, and there were mechanisms in place in the legal and organizational structure of the EU and NATO that could halt the groups' growth. But expansion seemed increasingly likely and it was a perennially hot topic for politicians, journalists, pollsters, and pundits, especially in the so-called "candidate" countries. The second step was for Slovenia to be found important enough – according to whatever criteria obtain at the moment – to be considered for admission. Third, the Slovenes would have to clear many hurdles. For Slovenia, to gain admission to Euro-Atlantic institutions would not only increase its prosperity, security, and credibility, but it would also be an unmistakable mark of a decisive break with its Balkan past. As it was to turn out, in 2004 Slovenia would become the first former Yugoslav state to join NATO and the EU, causing a leading Serbian foreign policy expert to note that Europe had, in effect, given the Western Balkans a new name: "Euroslavia," which consists of the former Yugoslavia "minus Slovenia, plus Albania."[21]

Some of these hurdles were akin to an endurance test. Slovenia's decade-old democratic political system was required to demonstrate its stability, control corruption, and keep the peace within the country; the EU and NATO also wanted assurances that Slovenia was not going to zig-zag radically in terms of foreign or economic policy. Simply put, the Euro-Atlantic institutions did not want to bring a potential liability or "problem child" on board. With open borders, a common currency, and common armaments and defense policies, any unknown quantity or "wild card" among member states could cause the existing members great hassle and expense.

Other hurdles involved reform. Obviously, the EU and NATO are alliances of states with liberal democratic political systems and capitalist economic systems. So candidates must demonstrate that one-party rule has been abolished and replaced by a multi-party system in which civil rights are guaranteed; they must also (and this usually proves to be a more complicated task) privatize their economies and enact legislation – unneeded in socialist systems – covering banking, advertising, foreign trade, and insurance needs. There is also an entire "package" of legislation that all EU members must accede to: it includes provisions as diverse as the abolition of the death penalty and a limit on budget deficits at 3 percent of a country's GNP.

NATO and EU membership are two bedrock themes now linking the politics and economies of Poland, Hungary, the Czech Republic, and Slovenia. Obviously, the transition of former communist countries is well advanced and the "West" has developed increasing confidence in the "East" since 1989.

Many Slovenes, like people in other candidate countries, have reservations or even fears about what accession to the two Euro-Atlantic institutions will mean for them. Especially in the case of the EU, Slovenes are uneasy about possible infringement of their sovereignty in both domestic and international affairs; a growth of bureaucracy; an excess of foreign ownership of businesses and land in the country; a forced reduction in agricultural subsidies and in production of key products like milk, along with increased agricultural competition; and neglect of the port at Koper in favor of Trieste.[22] Many key legal issues took a long time to work out, such as disagreements over future agricultural subsidies and over when foreigners may buy property in the new members, while many people in the eastern countries still worry about losing their hard-won national identities in a common culture dominated by the French, English, and German languages. They also resented the possibility of being treated like second-class Europeans by wealthy Westerners and expressed concern about the future costs of adapting their economies and governments to EU standards. In many existing EU countries there is still anxiety about the effects of large amounts of immigration from Eastern Europe on the labor market and over where infrastructure subsidies will come from in a time of strapped budgets all over the continent.

Some objections are, of course, specific as well to NATO membership. Many Slovenes see their country as secure, especially since relations with Italy and Austria are generally excellent. Cost could be a problem, since the Slovene per capita defense expenditure is about one-third that of NATO members. Throughout Europe, many individuals and organizations object to NATO's stationing of nuclear weapons in the country, and more have reacted negatively, since September 11, 2001, to the American emphases that an attack on one member is an attack on all and that the Alliance should be readily used for "out of area" operations. Other critics around the world have argued that the expansion unnecessarily provokes Russia while stoking growth in local military establishments at the expense of social and infrastructure spending; Russia under President Vladimir Putin, for its part, did not seriously oppose the second round of NATO expansion, perhaps in an effort to win Western approval for Moscow's bitter war against secessionist Chechen rebels.

Slovenia's move into NATO

On March 30, 1994, Slovenia joined a brand new NATO project called Partnership for Peace. This was basically an association agreement to signal the two parties' interest in each other. It was also designed to strengthen trust and cooperation and to foster military reform in candidate states. Slovenia quickly developed a close working relationship with the US military, including mutual visits and joint exercises. Slovenes very much believed that they were on the short list for the first wave of NATO expansion, since their political system was stable, their economy healthy, and their strategic value – proximity to conflict zones in the Balkans – clear. The run-up to admission to the North Atlantic Treaty Organization began in earnest in 1996. In that year, Washington included Ljubljana in the Warsaw Initiative. This was a program that provided funds for military training and equipment to postcommunist states. By 2004, Slovenia had received $18 million through this program. Yet, when NATO made its decisions on whom to admit in 1997, it chose only Poland, Hungary, and the Czech Republic. A number of explanations for Slovenia's failure to win an invitation have been advanced.[23] These include the passivity of Slovene diplomats who failed in various ways to clinch the deal with NATO; the limited usefulness of Slovenia's military itself, aside from strategic considerations; the inactivity of the Slovene diaspora in the US, especially in comparison with Poland's; intra-NATO politics, whereby France had to be allowed to save face over the rejection of its favorite candidate, the militarily strong Romania; and a calculation by US President Clinton that Congress would approve only three important new members. Thus, governments in Warsaw, Prague, and Budapest, former Warsaw Pact enemies of the US, came to enjoy the benefits of NATO membership in 1999, five years before Slovenia.

Slovenia and other postcommunist states were alerted to the fact, however, that another wave of candidates would be courted and accepted. In 1998 NATO exercises were held in Slovenia, and in June 1999 President Clinton visited the country, expressing gratitude for Slovenia's cooperation with the air campaign against Serbia and confirming US support for Slovenia's transitions. Clinton's visit was an important milestone for Slovenia in another way, too, because he met there with Montenegrin President Milo Djukanović, who was then a prominent opponent of the Serbian dictator Slobodan Milošević; President Kučan proudly proclaimed Slovenia's role as good neighbor, intermediary, and role model. Slovenia had also recently sent small numbers of peacekeepers and support troops on various multilateral missions to Albania, Cyprus, Kosovo, Macedonia, and Bosnia; veteran diplomat and legal expert Danilo Turk, who had been Slovenia's UN ambassador during its time on the Security Council, played a prominent role in the UN Mission in Kosovo in 2000 and 2001. In 1997, Slovenia began cooperating with SHIRBRIG, the UN's Stand-by High Readiness Brigade which is to be capable of responding to emergencies around the world within thirty days; Slovenia did not officially join the organization right away, as did Poland, Romania, and Lithuania, but it was another indication of Slovenia's strengthening profile. In June 2001, Slovenia hosted its most important diplomatic gathering to date: the first meeting between President Bush of the US and President Vladimir Putin of Russia. Slovenia and many other states also stepped up cooperation with the US and NATO after the terrorist attacks of September 2001. Then, in November 2002, at the now-famous Prague summit, NATO extended another, much broader invitation than the one from 1997. Seven new states were invited to join, boosting the number of members of the Alliance from nineteen to twenty-six.[24] The new candidate countries were Slovenia, Slovakia, Romania, Bulgaria, Estonia, Latvia, and Lithuania. Many Slovenes breathed a sigh of relief; the government, having proven the country's worth to NATO, was especially elated and now set to work gaining the popular support necessary to finish the process.

Another major decision taken at the Prague meeting was the creation of a Rapid Deployment Force. The group came into being in October 2002, with 9,000 soldiers and plans to raise that number to 20,000. The unit is supposed to be deployable to anywhere in the world within seven days. Another important result of this NATO summit was recognition of the need to make individual militaries fit together in a more efficient way and work together in a more modern, mobile fashion. This is to be achieved largely through the designation of niche specializations, narrow areas of specific expertise to be cultivated, especially by smaller states; these will fit realistically into state budgets and avoid repetition inside the Alliance. Slovenia, for instance, will probably eventually provide many crack mountain troops, and perhaps expertise on Balkan conditions and convenient staging areas for Balkan operations. The Czechs foresee specializing in defense against nuclear, biological, and chemical attacks, while Germany will develop a heavy air transport capability and the Baltic states will put together a northern radar shield.

As anti-NATO protestors gathered outside, in an atmosphere reminiscent of anti-globalization demonstrations at world economic gatherings, other important debates about NATO's future were taking place. Although it is likely that NATO will expand again, an essential issue of qualifications remains unclarified, perhaps deliberately so: are new members accepted on the basis of shared democratic and other values, or because they are useful to the Alliance in security terms – by dint of either their military power or their location?[25] A second debate was specifically about mission: although some in the Bush administration preferred an approach so unilateral that it sidelined NATO as well as the UN, other American officials wanted the Alliance updated to fight terrorism world-wide. Many Europeans see other ways to do that and would rather keep NATO close to home. They see a greater need for stabilizing the Balkans and fostering a secure and democratic Russia.[26]

Other concrete issues face NATO. How can the Alliance discipline or expel its members for poor military performance or for backsliding on their democratization? Such issues are unlikely to apply to Slovenia, but concerns have been raised – but not adjudicated upon – in one context or another about Romania, Bulgaria, Slovakia, and Hungary. How can European armies be made more interoperable or even interchangeable by the adoption of common equipment, training, and organization? How can they be made more efficient, with a reduction in the duplication of tasks and research? Recently, NATO launched a new initiative to improve ties with Russia was launched. It was hoped that the NATO–Russia Council would be able to pick up where other cooperative agreements broke off in the 1999 war in Kosovo.

The motivations for NATO's existence and expansion were once simple: the Cold War revealed common values and, especially, patent regional defense needs. Now, however, more factors come into play, although the concept of anchoring a general "zone of stability" across Europe is key. The relative weight of each one in this mix is still uncertain, but it will certainly form an important topic for future scholarly inquiry. Possible spurs to NATO's enlargement, then, include eliminating a power vacuum that might attract Russian imperialism or, more pressingly at the moment, transnational terrorism; securing democratic and free-market reforms in the postcommunist lands; putting a damper on territorial and ethnic disputes in the region; access to additional air corridors, cheaper bases, and live-fire training grounds; markets for Western military hardware, such as the forty-eight F-16s purchased by Poland for $3.5 billion; and a larger pool of potential allies for the US to recruit from in putting together future coalitions for ad hoc missions around the world. The US might also, in the spirit of the 2003 buzz in Washington about the "new" versus the "old" Europe, have sought to dilute the power of Germany and France by cultivating close relationships with first Poland and then Romania.

For the candidate states, the picture is clearer. Above all, NATO means security. For most, that means security vis-à-vis their immediate neighbors, especially if Russia is close by; Russia, in either its imperial or Soviet incarnation, dominated most of Central Europe and the Balkans from 1945 to 1989 and the Baltic states, much of Poland, and parts of the Balkans for long periods before that. There is also a sense, as with the part of the attractiveness of the EU that is not purely economic, of acceptance into a community of shared values. This is NATO as something more than military: something European, liberal, democratic, and both historic and modern. Finally, there is the benefit of boosted prestige and increased connections with Western Europe and North America, which could be parlayed into other benefits in both bilateral and multilateral contexts.

Technically, the membership criteria set forth in the 1949 North Atlantic Treaty are straightforward. But in reality, of course, a great deal of change in the postcommunist states' armed forces and government structures had to be negotiated and then effected. This process usually began with down-sizing the military while also increasing defense expenditures. Other important concerns are guarantees of civilian control over the military, compatibility with NATO's existing forces, and transparency, or lack of corruption. In Slovenia's case, NATO communicated that improvements should be made in command and control, mobility, and logistical flexi-bility. Other former Yugoslav states have a much harder road to travel before admission: both Bosnia and Serbia must fight a great deal of corrup-tion and organized crime, while in addition Bosnia must establish an effective joint Defense Ministry for the Bosniak, Serbian, and Croatian communities, and Serbia still needs to cooperate more fully in the prose-cution of war crimes suspects at the Hague Tribunal and at home.

By early 2002, indications that Slovenia would receive an invitation were strong. In April that year, the government established a telephone hotline to answer citizens' questions about NATO; an expensive mass mailing of pro-NATO brochures to people's homes followed. Nearly all political parties backed entry, but the population was split almost evenly, with a large undecided bloc. The public opinion situation would remain largely the same right up to the eventual referendum. But President Kučan spoke out clearly in favor of joining the Alliance, noting that terrorism, organized crime, and ecological concerns are all international and could still hit Slovenia hard. Consultations with the US were frequent. In May, Prime Minister Drnovšek visited President Bush in the White House, while US Secretary of Defense Donald Rumsfeld visited Slovenia right after the Prague summit.

At this time there were ten countries actively campaigning to join NATO. They called themselves the "Vilnius 10" after a meeting they held in Lithuania; in NATO parlance they were members of MAP, or the Membership Action Plan, which gave advice and support to candidate states. Relations with this group presented Slovene diplomats with some interesting dilemmas. Following on the heels of support for the coming invasion of Iraq offered by the leaders of Hungary, the Czech Republic, Poland, and even Kosovo, the Vilnius 10 offered its endorsement of the US approach. Yet Slovenia remained very coy about its actual relationship with the US on Iraq, and some members of the government distanced themselves from the Vilnius 10 statement. Furthermore, Slovene officials demurred, and then denied being part of the forty-eight member "coalition of the will-ing." Yet, there were fifteen unnamed countries that the US included on its list of allies for Operation Iraqi Freedom. Shortly before the war began in March 2003, Slovenia gave permission only for humanitarian US over-flights. At times, the Vilnius 10 have also called for simultaneous acceptance of the whole group into NATO; Slovenia preferred looser wording, as it had also done with such linkages among EU candidates, because it was such a strong candidate for both Euro-Atlantic institutions. Simply put, Slovenia understandably saw no need to hitch its star to less prepared or less fortunate countries. The three countries of the Vilnius 10 that have not yet been taken into NATO are Albania, Croatia, and Macedonia. These states, known as the Ohrid–Adriatic group, are making rapid political improvements and are eagerly awaiting the next round of expansion.

The year 2003 began with more dilemmas for Ljubljana. Between February and April it became apparent that Slovenia neither fully supported the US-led war in Iraq nor was willing to break with the US over it in public. Eighty percent of the population opposed the war; the government, not eager to sabotage its new NATO relationship, hemmed and hawed. The Slovene government picked the date of March 23, 2003 to hold a legally binding referendum on membership in both the EU and NATO. It wanted to validate its accession by gaining public approval, but it was decided to wait until after NATO's official invitation came in November 2002. Then the government wanted to hurry up the referendum, before the bad press that would be generated by the likely outbreak of the unpopular US-led war in Iraq. Defense Minister Anton Grizold staked his reputation, or at least his job, on the outcome of the vote; the gangster assassination of Serbian Prime Minister Zoran Djindjić less than two weeks before the vote may have inadvertently aided the Slovene government's cause, because it underscored in the public mind the instability of the nearby Balkans. Slovenia was, nonetheless, the only one of the seven candidate countries to hold such a vote. When all was said and done, 66 percent of Slovene voters had opted for inclusion in NATO. The turnout of 60 percent, which might seem low, was actually the highest of any referendum since independence. A drastically higher percentage of Slovenes approved EU membership (90 percent), indicating many Slovenes' unease over the military and foreign policy direction of the US-driven alliance.

Another controversy quickly emerged. The Bush administration, angry that the US was not granted an exemption from the International Criminal Court, had been insisting since mid-2002 on signing bilateral treaties with dozens of countries, providing mutual immunity from extradition. Albania and Bosnia, for instance, were willing to sign such arrangements with the US, but most EU states were indignant at Washington's attempt to circumvent an important innovation in international law, aimed at curtailing war crimes. Croatia denounced the US effort, and Slovenia also refused to cave in. On July 1, the US announced that it was blocking military aid to an unspecified number of uncooperative countries on this issue; the number of affected states was estimated to be between thirty and fifty. Croatia stood to lose $19 million in assistance, and Slovenia something on the order of $2 to 4 million. Meanwhile, Slovenia pushed ahead with its increasing international commitments, making plans to join NATO's Rapid Deployment Force, sending a few more peacekeepers to Kosovo and Bosnia, supplying five experts to help train the new Iraqi police force, and pledging to support Albania's military reforms. Then, in November 2003, the military aid for Slovenia and several other postcommunist states was released after all, with Washington stressing their cooperation in Operation Enduring Freedom in Afghanistan and in the so-called "war on terror" in general. In December, Slovenia sent twenty more peace-keepers to Afghanistan.

Finally, the big and – originally, at least – somewhat controversial day came. On March 29, 2004, the prime ministers of the new member states brought their ratified accession documents to Washington, DC, where US Secretary of State Colin Powell accepted them for NATO. Welcome cere-monies were held at that time at the White House and then again in late June, at NATO's next summit in Istanbul.

Slovenia's neighbors

Croatia

Slovenia has unresolved difficulties with each of its neighbors. While short-lived problems with Italy and Austria caused headaches in Slovenia's plans to integrate with the rest of Europe, problems with Croatia have continued to smolder. They include the operation and finances of the Krško nuclear power plant (in Slovenia, but near Zagreb) and the status of the Slovene minority in Croatia. Most important, however, are the land and maritime border disputes. Some actual territory has been in dispute, in Istria and in the interior, but so are fishing rights and – most urgently, from the point of view of the Slovenes, who have a very limited section of coastline – sea boundaries. Slovenia insists on direct access to Adriatic shipping lanes, a common-sense claim which any notion of "strategic rights" (such as the Croats themselves put forth in their dispute with Montenegro over the Prevlaka Peninsula in southern Dalmatia) would seem to support.

Slovenes started the new century optimistic that improved relations were possible with the new, more democratic Croatian government of President Stipe Mesić and Prime Minister Ivica Račan, which was elected after President Tuđman's death in December 1999. These men run a five-party coalition that includes Mesić's National Party (HNS, or Hrvatska Narodna Stranka, on the center-right) and Račan's Social Democrats (Socijaldemo-kratska Partija Hrvatske, or SDP, on the center-left). Mesić, who visited Ljubljana early in his presidency to initiate a dialog between the two coun-tries, has also downplayed nationalism, curtailed the power of Croatia's "imperial" presidency, emphasized economic development, and begun close cooperation with The Hague war crimes tribunal. Negotiations have thus intensified since 2000 and have been carried out at the level of both presidents and prime ministers and also by parliamentary delegations and expert commissions.

The biggest single source of friction between Ljubljana and Zagreb is sea access for Slovenia in the Gulf of Piran. The maritime boundaries of Croatia and Italy abut one another in the Gulf, located at the north end of the Adriatic Sea just a stone's throw from Trieste and also close to Venice. Slovenia, with its narrow coastline, has no route of its own into international waters; traffic to and from the important port of Koper depends upon the goodwill of Slovenia's neighbors and must use their sea lanes. To an outside observer, Croatia, with its huge Dalmatian littoral, should be able to relinquish a sea lane to its small neighbor, even with the valuable fishing resources in the area. But, there may be natural gas or oil under those waters, and right-wing political parties in Italy might view any boundary alteration as a green light to seek border "rectifications" of their own. Croatia is planning to build a terminal from a Russian oil pipeline nearby, too. There may be a temptation for Slovene leaders to "link" this issue to others as well, so as to increase their leverage with Croatia. In late 2001, Mesić floated the new idea of a horizontal split in the sea lanes, with Croatia retaining rights to the sea floor. The issue could still end up in international arbitration, since a provisional agreement reached in July of that same year has not yet been ratified by the Croatian parliament, although the Slovenes were pleased with both 2001 drafts. The July agreement would have traded a 12-kilometer sea corridor to Slovenia for 1.3 kilometers of territory on land.

In the summer of 2002, the problems around Piran heated up considerably from May through August. Fishers from the two countries confronted each other frequently, police patrol boats faced off each other, and the governments in Ljubljana and Zagreb exchanged protest notes and held several meetings to try to defuse tensions. Still, though, despite temporary "truces" designed to keep fighting fishermen apart, the fishing and transportation issues in the Bay of Piran remained unresolved. Internationalization of the issue, through the creation of some sort of mediating body, might be the only way out of the impasse. Indeed, it is possible, as Slovenia's prime minister-designate Anton Rop stated in December 2002, that only Croatia's accession to the EU will provide preconditions for a comprehensive resolution of all issues separating the two former Yugoslav neighbors, although it is also possible that the EU will insist on a resolution of the thornier issues before admitting Croatia. Meanwhile, Slovenia's membership in the EU, effective in May 2004, will require it to tighten border controls with Croatia; this could increase low-grade tensions somewhat, though probably not as much as other new EU members are expecting to have to deal with in regard to their eastern neighbors, such as Poland with Ukraine and Hungary with Romania. In 2003, Croatia brazenly announced its intention to declare a legally binding Exclusive Economic Zone in the northern Adriatic. After serious, loud protests from the EU, Italy, and Slovenia, which even recalled its ambassador, Zagreb changed its tune to a "fishing and ecological zone" that would still exclude Slovenes.

Croatia's claim is illogical for many reasons: it lacks the naval resources to patrol such a zone, it is already engaging in environmentally damaging fishing practices, and it seems to be picking a fight with a new EU member and its longtime ally, Slovenia. It is possible that the Croatian government is pursuing this admittedly popular conflict with Slovenia to distract domestic attention from its unpopular program of cooperation with The Hague tribunal; the Croatian public could be feeling jealous of the Slovenes, as when the latter country began erecting its required EU-style border and visa regimes. Whatever the Croatian motivation, the refusal to allow Slovenia permanent access to the open sea is at strong odds with Croatia's longing to join the EU, which insists the two countries settle their disputes quickly and peacefully.

In late August 2002, the troubles moved inland when Croat police arrested a local Slovenian politician. Josko Joras, who serves on the town council in Piran, claims that his house and land are actually in Slovenia, but he must cross an international boundary to get to work. Known for his flamboyant Slovene nationalism, Joras has been the victim of abuse by Croatian rowdies. He was arrested for refusing to show his travel documents at a Croatian border crossing and then sentenced to a month in jail for ignoring a previous court order. After his incarceration on August 21, the Slovene media vociferously took up his case. Joras was released on September 6, 2002, after a hunger strike; the two governments and fishers' associations also endorsed temporary "truces" to share the waters of the Bay of Piran.

Border disputes are not limited to the coastal region, either. Inland, along the Kolpa river, there is a disputed frontier, and there has been a small amount of military activity (though no fighting) by both countries to shore up their claims. Residents of the area, of both nationalities, have held meetings to stress their friendly local relations and to urge their governments to work out the problems peacefully and swiftly.

These types of problems with Croatia are all the more disheartening because they would have seemed so unlikely fifteen years ago. The Leagues of Communists in Slovenia and Croatia had usually been allies in the socialist period in the fight for more market mechanisms and republican political autonomy; certainly the two republics were equally alarmed by the Milošević phenomenon and by Serbia's harsh treatment of its Albanian minority by the late 1980s. Many historical similarities – stemming from a common Central European, Roman Catholic, and Habsburg past – link the two peoples; their experiences with everything from staving off the Turks in the Middle Ages to stamping out the Reformation in the 1500s to industrial policies in the nineteenth century gave them shared ground. Even language is a bridge – the Croatian dialect around Zagreb, known as *kajkavian*, is amazingly similar to Slovene. And Tito, after all, was a Croat with a Slovene mother, and he had grown up within shouting distance of the border in an ethnically mixed area.

But there are traditional sources of conflict, or rivalry, as well, and new ones have certainly emerged since independence. At the level of cultural stereotyping, many Slovenes still view Croats as primitive Balkan nationalists with questionable work ethics, more akin to Serbs than Central Europeans; meanwhile, many Croats often think of Slovenes as uptight and tight-fisted peasants lacking any significant cultural traditions. In early 2002, President Kučan publicly expressed his bafflement "at how much mistrust there is among the Croatian public, and in political life there, toward Slovenia."[27] A familiar joke in the form of a jingle, widely circulated on the internet around 2000, plays on these stereotypes: the old SFRY (Socialist Federal Republic of Yugoslavia) would be re-established, it chimes, on that impossible day when, *inter alia*, "the Serb calls the Croat 'brother' and the Slovenes pay for your drinks." At the level of political extremism, hard-core Croatian nationalists have, for 150 years, sometimes denied that Slovenes even exist, calling them "mountain Croats" in the way that some Serbs deny Bosnian nationality and some Bulgarians that of the Macedonians. More recently, a small patch of territory along the Mirna river in Istria was transferred by the Tito government from Slovenia to Croatia in 1954, "stranding" some Slovenes in the neighboring republic.

Notwithstanding the simultaneous secession from Serb-dominated Yugoslavia in the summer of 1991, the Slovene and Croatian paths parted almost immediately, because neither country helped the other one in its war for independence. Croatia allowed the Yugoslav People's Army (the federal force, often known by its Serbo-Croatian acronym of JNA) to roll through on its way to the short but sharp Ten-day War with Slovenia. Shortly thereafter, Slovenia concentrated on its own state-building as Serbian paramilitaries and the JNA tore large swaths of Croatian territory from the control of the Tuđman regime. Since this parting of the ways, Slovenia has moved more rapidly into political democracy and economic reform and long seemed to be moving more rapidly towards EU and NATO membership than Croatia. Relations between individuals in the two countries remain good, and for years in the mid-1990s there were few formalities for travelers at their border. But Croatia's burden of war, destruction, and refugees, and the authoritarian legacy of Tuđman have created resentment over Slovenia's "easier road to hoe."

Another major issue between the two former Yugoslav republics is the disposition of the Slovene nuclear power plant at Krško in eastern Slovenia. It was a joint Slovene–Croatian investment. Today, Slovenia is more dependent on this nuclear power than Croatia, but Krško does supply much of the electricity for the Croatian capital, Zagreb. Since 1991, the two countries have bickered over the running of the plant. Added pressure on Slovenia comes from the fact that many Austrians want to see Krško shut down for good for environmental reasons (in the way they even more vociferously want the Czechs to shut down their plant at Temelin), and the government in Vienna can drag its feet on endorsing Slovenia's accession to the EU if Ljubljana stubbornly keeps the plant open.

After over a decade of negotiations, the prime ministers of Slovenia and Croatia, Janez Drnovšek and Ivica Račan, hammered out an accord in December 2001. It was to govern the management of the facility and it stipulated its ultimate shutdown in 2024. Until that distant date, the plant's spent nuclear fuel will be stored on-site; it will later be disposed of by Croatia. These arrangements were unlikely to mollify environmentalists in any country of the region. But the accord never became valid because it was not approved by the Croatian parliament, and the Croatian role in running the plant was eliminated in July 2002.

Another potentially thorny issue is the money that Croatian citizens deposited in Slovene banks before 1991. Slovenia has refused to negotiate with Croatia, or with any other former Yugoslav republic, on this issue, preferring instead to settle all such claims as part of a general post-Yugoslav settlement. More minor, but still irksome, issues involve customs duties and border traffic (especially for people whose homes are linked to the rest of their own countries by roads that go through the other country). There are also some spots where the exact delineation of the border is disputed. This confusion, resulting from the changing course of rivers and from disagreements in maps, has led to conflicts in jurisdiction and to tension over military outposts.

In July 2001, the two governments worked out a set of agreements on many outstanding issues. The Croatian parliament, or *Sabor*, has yet to approve many of the proposals, however, despite Slovene grumblings that the delay could provoke Slovene foot-dragging on other issues. The agreements between the prime ministers would have granted Slovenia a substantial sea corridor (3.6 km wide) into the open waters of the Adriatic; Slovene shipping concerns and fishermen would be delighted with this amount of territory, which would also presumably include Slovene control over the floor of the Gulf of Piran as well. The deals were a sort of compromise, and both governments have come under fire from nationalists at home for "giving away" sovereign territory. Confusion in border demarcations in four different areas have been settled, mostly in favor of Croatia, although the two governments emphasized that guaranteeing the rights of each other's minorities and improving their lives simply by putting these issues behind them outweigh any calculation of "who got what." One uncontroversial aspect of the agreements was the establishment of over two dozen additional border crossings. Good relations between the two neighbors also bolstered their cases for admission to the EU and NATO.

In 1998, Prime Minister Račan returned to the Slovenes a vehicle used for "intelligence-gathering" that had been impounded after crossing the border illegally. Whether the vehicle was in use by the Slovene government or had been stolen remains unclear. In June 1991, the anniversary of the first decade of Croatian and Slovene independence was celebrated by a gathering in Zagreb of political and military leaders who had played important roles in the wars of independence.

In the winter of 2002, a new crisis with Croatia came to the fore. It was an economic dispute, and not a grave one, though it serves as a reminder of the volatility of relations between the former Yugoslav republics and also the importance of the ties that remain between them. On January 16, Croatia banned road transportation of petroleum products,[28] supposedly for environmental and anti-smuggling reasons. The Slovene government immediately cried foul, stating that the goal was to increase Croatia's share of the important fuel market in Bosnia–Hercegovina at Slovenia's expense. Evidence for this assertion was the fact that the leading Croatian oil company (a government-owned enterprise called INA) was allowed to continue delivering by truck.

As a countermeasure, the Bosnian government promptly instituted a ban of its own – it forbade *all* oil-truck traffic, which Slovenia did not like but which also hurt Croatia, because INA received no exemption. Then the Slovene government complained to the EU and the World Trade Organization; Croatia, also vying for admission to NATO and the EU, would, it was hoped, wilt under the international pressure.

Five days after the crisis began, the Croats did indeed agree to retract most of the restrictions, but the bad feeling (and the Bosnian ban) lingered. On January 30, the Slovene Foreign Minister Rupel visited Sarajevo and tried to convince the Bosnian government to allow overland oil traffic again, since Slovene as well as Croatian trucks were now barred from the country. Finally, the Bosnian government announced that it, too, planned to limit smuggling and environmental damage by allowing foreign oil trucks to enter the country only through a limited number of border crossings. By February 2, traffic was rolling again. Oil is an important part of Croatia's economy, and INA has done well financially. Its privatization began in 2003, and it still dominates the Bosnian market.

After reaching their low point in 2001 and 2002, Slovene–Croatian relations began to improve, albeit slowly. Both countries are taking major steps to improve their highway network. Two different pan-European transport corridors, as they are known, will link the two countries soon, and this will strengthen economic ties. In addition, since both countries rely heavily on tourism, and since tourism withers in the glare of unfavorable international media coverage, it is in their interest to bury the hatchet as quickly as possible over border issues. Ljubljana and Zagreb have recently signed agreements on issues from education to military cooperation, with Slovenia supporting Croatia's candidacy for both NATO and the EU. Slovenia has also hosted a number of high-level meetings of leaders from the immediate region (the Quadrilateral, which includes Slovenia, Croatia, Italy, and Hungary), the Balkans, and all of Central Europe, providing chances for personal contacts between leaders. Most importantly in this regard, though, President Mesić visited Slovenia in May 2003, for talks with Slovene President Drnovšek and former President Kučan.

The international scene has provided Slovenia and Croatia with an opportunity for new cooperation: both countries opposed the US invasion of Iraq in the spring of 2003, and both resisted US pressure to sign bilateral agreements with Washington nullifying the mandate of the International Criminal Court. As part of what the Bush administration terms "the new Europe," Slovenia and Croatia are being both courted and pressured by Washington to break ranks with the majority of European opinion and of EU members. Although countries like Albania, Macedonia, Romania, and Poland are proving amenable to US demands, Slovenia and Croatia have thus far refused to heed Bush's calls. Thus, both countries are slated to be punished with the loss of millions in US bilateral military assistance.

Other important issues remain open as well. Neither country gives official recognition to the other's co-nationals as indigenous or authochthonous minorities, leading to the impression abroad that the groups' identities might be endangered. This causes great consternation among Slovenes, because Croatia's small Slovene minority (as well as its "Istrian" nationality, a cultural hybrid often praised as a symbol of tolerance and diversity) did have official recognition until 1997; following its declassification, the Slovene minority was reported in the next Croatian census to have shrunk by nearly half, to just over 13,000.[29] On the other hand, Croatia's minority is much larger and, like Albanians and other former Yugoslavs, has oddly enough never enjoyed official status in Slovenia.

A final concern for Slovenes is the revival of Franjo Tuđman's old political party, the Croatian Democratic Community (HDZ in Croatian, for Hrvatska Demokratska Zajednica). In late 2002, the fortunes of this highly nationalistic and, at least previously, authoritarian political grouping buoyed and it became the single biggest party again. The ruling coalition is riven by infighting and has already lost one of its members, the Istrian Democratic Assembly. Only with a stable coalition can the progressive leadership in Croatia, such as President Mesić and Prime Minister Račan, continue to improve relations with Slovenia and the rest of Europe.

Hungary

For decades after the Tito–Stalin rupture of 1948, there was great tension and little contact along the Hungarian–Yugoslav border. Tito's acquiescence in the brutal Soviet suppression of the Hungarian reform movement in 1956 contributed to a further, informal chill in relations. Relations improved between them in the 1960s because, although Hungary remained a member of the Soviet bloc, both countries developed relatively liberal regimes. Today, Slovenia's grievances with Hungary are definitely minor, although their relationship in general is not extensive. There is, potentially, a great deal of common ground between them. Hungary is already a member of NATO, both countries are EU candidates, they have faced similar tasks of economic and political reform since the fall of communism, and each state contains a small number of the other's co-nationals. The border region is home to 5,000 Slovenes in seven villages on the Hungarian side and to 9,000 Hungarians in Slovenia's Prekmurje region, with its capital of Lendava (Lendva in Hungarian). Slovenia is a significantly smaller country than Hungary; indeed, Slovenes are numerically the smallest people in the region, and the treatment of their co-nationals in Italy, Austria, and Hungary is quite a popular issue with Slovene voters. As both governments work at improving rail and road links, Ljubljana is calling upon Budapest to offer more TV, radio, and school subjects in the Slovenian language. Slovenia currently offers its Hungarian – and Italian – minorities greater political rights and cultural support than Hungary, rights that include a guaranteed seat in the Parliament.[30]

There was a flap in 2001 over a TV ad run by the Slovene branch of Amnesty International. The spot criticized Hungary for police brutality; after Hungarian protest that the ad was unfair, and following the resignation of Amnesty officials in Budapest, it was withdrawn. But, that same year, the two countries' prime ministers, Drnovšek and Viktor Orban, celebrated the opening of a new rail connection across their frontier. The tracks are part of a new network called the Fifth Pan-European corridor, which links the Ukrainian city of Lviv with Venice in Italy.[31]

For some two years it was uncertain how one final potential issue between the two countries would work out: Hungary's "Status Law." This bill was passed by the Parliament in Budapest in 2001 and it grants many benefits, such as access to social services and the right to work, to Hungarians who live in other countries. Some of Hungary's neighbors, especially Romania, worry that this access will dilute the sense of belonging that their Hungarian minorities feel, or even that it infringes on their states' sovereignty. The selectively "porous" border proved difficult, also, for the EU to swallow. The number of Slovene Hungarians is so small that this is unlikely to become controversial, at least from the Slovene point of view. Hungary, like Slovenia, was invited in November 2002 to join the EU in 2004. The EU then pressured Hungary into changing the law in early 2003, so that it would not apply to Hungarians in other EU countries. This means that it no longer applies to Slovenia or Slovakia, but it will still apply to Romania, Serbia, and Ukraine.

The Status Law is connected to the issue of reviving Hungarian nationalism. Premier Viktor Orban, in office from 1997 to 2002, made many strident appeals to Hungarian "national pride" and "family values" and he ignited controversy with his emphasis on building connections to Hungarian communities beyond the country's borders. Slovenia had less to fear from Orban's rhetoric than Hungary's other neighbors, but any contemporary Hungarian chauvinism awakens memories of Hungary's sometimes rough treatment of its minorities in the past, including the land grab in eastern Slovenia during World War II. One other painful nationalist issue inconveniencing the two countries is the memory of the Hungarian government's use of the term Wendish to describe local Slovenes. This attempt to fragment Slovene identity, eliminate any justification for border alterations, and hasten assimilation was also used frequently in Austria in the twentieth century. The current Hungarian government is considerably more moderate on national issues, preferring now to note that the EU will eventually contain most or all of Europe's Hungarians, and that that is reunification enough.[32]

Austria

For Slovenes the main source of concern with Austria since 1991 has been the political scene. Slovenes in the former Yugoslavia and in the Austrian provinces of Carinthia and Styria alike have been alarmed by the electoral success of the Austrian Freedom Party (Freiheitliche Partei Österreichs, or FPÖ) since early 2000. At that time the FPÖ became part of the ruling coalition in Vienna, with the conservative Austrian People's Party (ÖVP, or Österreichische Volkspartei). Concern over the FPÖ centered on its leader, a controversial figure named Jörg Haider. Haider has been embroiled in many controversies over remarks about Nazis and Jews and strongly opposed Austria's liberal refugee policies of the 1990s and its entrance into the EU in 1995. He has been called a "yuppie fascist"[33] because he is educated, very conservative, and takes a slick, hi-tech approach to campaigning. That use of an ideological epithet is inexact, but Haider is an eccentric, persistent, and brazen populist who has capitalized on many tradition-minded Austrians' searing, soaring anxieties about the rapid changes in their society and in the Europe around them.

Haider was the official party leader in January 2000, but there was such an uproar across Europe – including some sanctions from the EU – that he resigned from that position a few weeks after his party entered the federal coalition. Of course, he retained great influence in the party and remained governor of his home province of Carinthia. He again became head of the FPÖ in September 2002. Slovenes feared that Haider might be in a position to retract some of the Austrian Slovenes' minority rights in his province, and also that he might push the Austrian government into blocking Slovenia's accession to the European Union. Conservatives in Austria have, at times, threatened to do this because many German-speakers were expelled from Yugoslavia in 1945 and their property confiscated earlier in the war by the so-called AVNOJ decrees; this issue carries a similar emotional weight to the expulsions of Germans from Poland and Czechoslovakia; a significant number of this latter group settled in Austria and are politically active. In addition, Germany and Austria are now paying compensation to some of the 60,000-plus Slovenes they deported or interned during the war. The Slovene government has made limited concessions to Austrian demands, but the Czechs have been less pliant. The EU finally ruled that the 1945 expulsions are legally settled. In November 2001, Slovene President Kučan visited Vienna to try to iron over differences with Austria's President Thomas Klestil and its Prime Minister, Wolfgang Schuessel, both of the ÖVP; he was accompanied by Foreign Minister Dimitrij Rupel, who met with his counterpart, Benita Ferrero-Waldner, to discuss the legal and historical research commissioned by the two governments to produce an agreement like the one signed in 1997 by the Czech and German governments.

After the electoral success of 2000, Haider's party soon suffered setbacks at the polls but made periodic recoveries, as in April 2004, when he recaptured public attention by throwing his support behind the ÖVP's candidate for president. That candidate, Ferrero-Waldner, would have been Austria's first female president but was narrowly defeated by Social Democrat Heinz Fischer.

Of longstanding concern to Slovenes all over the world is the position of the Slovene minority in Austria, found mostly in Kärnten (Carinthia) and, to a lesser extent, in Steiermark (Styria). Experts disagree over the numbers of these minority groups. Censuses in Austria do not use ethnicity as a criterion, but rather "language of communication." According to this classification, the 1991 census returned a figure of 16,000 Austrian Slovenes. This would obviously refer to people who considered themselves fluent in Slovene and, apparently, who use it as their primary or preferred mode of communication. The number of people who are familiar with Slovene but not fluent in it and who consider themselves Slovenes by culture or association could be significantly higher. The legacy of the interwar period, and especially the Nazi era, when there were as many as 80,000 Slovenes in Austria, is still painful; they were badly mistreated in those years. The massively important Austrian State Treaty of 1955 created the independent, neutral country of Austria after the tumult of World War II and the tense, four-way occupation of the early Cold War years; this document still serves as Austria's constitution. Its Article 7 guarantees significant rights for national minorities, but these were not consistently under attack by Austrian nationalists until the 1980s. Now Slovene cultural associations and bilingual place names are much more common in southern Austria, even as the pace of assimilation through the "informal" pressure of the media and economic life increases.

Other recent sources of friction with Austria include the lingering demand by some Austrian and German politicians that Slovenia apologize and pay compensation for Yugoslavia's expulsion of German civilians after World War II as part of Slovenia's denationalization program. Austria has also repeatedly expressed its concern over safety at the Slovene nuclear plant in Krško. Since 1998 there has also been a dispute over the rights to the famous breed of show horses known as Lippizaners, originally from the Slovene town of Lipica. Cultural ties between the two countries remain strong (see Chapter 4), and the economic relationship discussed above is vital for Slovenia. Despite the several slow-burning disagreements discussed above, Austria strongly supported Slovenia's admission to the EU. Rumors from 2001 that Austria wanted to sponsor a "former Habsburg caucus" aside, Vienna has shown understanding for the issues that are important to smaller EU members, including the preservation of cultural identity.

Austrian State Radio, the ORF, has sponsored many Slovene programs. But in 2003 it cut funding to the most important one, the 24-hour Slovene service in Carinthia called Radio Dva. Slovenes, as well as artists, academics, and human rights advocates around Europe, protested the measure, which violates EU law. Rumors circulated that it was not just financial exigency at the ORF that occasioned the discontinuation, but that it was a move by an angry Governor Haider, forced by the courts to live up to laws granting bilingual place names and signs in areas where Slovenes formed at least 10 percent of the population. Private alternatives to ORF funding were sought. Eventually Radio Dva's employees worked several months on a voluntary basis, and then the Slovene government in Ljubljana funded the station for six months. By early 2004 a new arrangement was in place, under which the ORF would fund eight hours a day of Slovene programming and Radio Dva and another private station, Radio Agora, the other sixteen hours. The essays, drama, and fiction of two Austrian Slovenes, Janko Messner and Janko Ferk, are also well known, including in some English translations. One well-known Green Party politician in Austria is a Slovene, Karl Smolle. Another Austrian Slovene, Wolfgang Petritsch, who is a historian and diplomat, became well known in his capacity as High Commissioner for Bosnia from 1999 to 2002 and in his earlier work as the EU Special Envoy for Kosovo.

Italy

Italy supported Slovenia's application to join NATO, but Rome at first blocked Ljubljana's efforts to enter the European Union. Above all this was because of revived disputes over former Italian property in the Trieste region. At the end of World War II, some Italians in the area were killed and many others fled or were expelled. Although Yugoslavia had signed two treaties with Italy that supposedly settled this question, by the 1990s Italy was demanding that the issue of compensation from both Slovenia and Croatia be re-opened. Slovenes, in turn, recalled the legacy of forced assimilation in areas occupuied by Italy after World War I and under Mussolini. The rightist Italian government of the early 1990s threatened to hold up Slovenia's admission to the EU and to abrogate the 1975 Treaty of Osimo, which guaranteed rights for the large Slovene minority in northeastern Italy. In the mid-1990s, Italy agreed to settle for the right to buy back property quickly in Slovenia, instead of compensation. The

Slovenes then passed laws enabling Italians to buy land before other EU citizens, and Italy lifted its objections to Slovene accession. Although these issues and some other smaller ones have since faded, many Slovenes fear their revival if the political climate in Italy should change again.

Meanwhile, the large Slovene minority in the northeast has seen a gradual encroachment on its rights for bilingual signage and the public use of the Slovene language; these changes seem also to have been occasioned by increasing Italian nationalism and, ironically, even Italian regionalism which contemplates more autonomy for the wealthier, northern portion of the country. In February 2004, shortly before Slovenia joined the EU, a final section of fence was taken down along the Slovene–Italian border; this opening was widely reported in the media to be the fall of the last bit of the Iron Curtain, the disintegration of which had begun on Hungary's western frontier and along the Berlin Wall in 1989.

Former Yugoslavia

Besides maintaining the sometimes troubled relations with Croatia, Slovenia has also retained or resumed relations with all the regions of former Yugoslavia. Trade ties with the region are of growing, but still modest, significance; free-trade agreements exist with each of the successor states. Slovenia has also tried to assist the governments of Bosnia and Macedonia in various ways, but its resources are limited. Of the greatest importance are the relations with Serbia. Official diplomatic ties were resumed in December 2000, on a visit to Ljubljana by the Yugoslav Foreign Minister Goran Svilanović. Embassies were opened in Ljubljana and Belgrade in the autumn of 2001. The Slovenes and Serbs have also signed agreements on trade and investment; air, road, and river transportation; visas; and property issues. Prime Minister Drnovšek visited Belgrade in June 2002, in a landmark trip for independent Slovenia. In December 2002, the major Slovene retailer, Mercator, opened the largest store in its network in Belgrade. And in early 2003, air service between the capitals was resumed.

Potentially the most important concrete issue involving Serbia, Slovenia, and all the ex-Yugoslav states has been the hammering out of an internationally recognized agreement on how to divide up the former Yugoslavia's debts and assets. The process began in February 2001. A general settlement, covering $645 million in the Yugoslav National Bank, was reached in June 2001, but it then had to be ratified by each new state. Other issues remained unresolved: pensions for former government and military employees, millions of dollars in art from diplomatic missions, money that the Serbs took from the National Bank in 1990, and the payment of the huge debt of over $1 billion to Russia. In December 2001, the parcelling out of the Yugoslav patrimony began. Slovenia got the former embassy in Washington, while Bosnia–Hercegovina took the one in London; the embassy in Paris went to Croatia, while the consulate there went to Macedonia and the Parisian ambassador's residence to Serbia and Montenegro. In October 2002, after a long period of wrangling, representatives from the independent states of Slovenia, Yugoslavia, Croatia, Bosnia–Hercegovina, and Macedonia agreed on a formula for dividing up the former Yugoslavia's $87 million in gold. The formula reflected old Yugoslav budgetary practices and allotted Slovenia 16 percent of the gold, Serbia and Montenegro (still functioning as a kind of third Yugoslavia) 38 percent, Croatia 23 percent, Bosnia 15.5 percent, and Macedonia 7.5 percent. The gold was held for a decade in a bank in Basel, Switzerland, and the International Monetary Fund aided in a search for a solution; throughout the 1990s, Serbia refused to negotiate about the assets because it claimed them all, as the only legitimate successor state to Yugoslavia. The other republics were determined to keep what federal property they had been able to seize during secession, while the Bosnians were upset that Slovenia refused to return their bank assets before a general settlement was reached. The debt to Russia was apportioned in September 2003, along lines very similar to the gold reserves.

In a pair of interesting side notes, both Slovene President Kučan (May 2003) and Croatian President Mesić (October 2002) testified at the trial of Slobodan Milošević in The Hague. Their testimony, and their future interviews and autobiographical writings, will provide a counterweight to the Serbian nationalist version of the breakup of Yugoslavia that is getting so much publicity from the Serbian ex-leader's trial. Meanwhile, on February 4, 2003, the third, or rump, Yugoslavia, expired. On that day the new name for the confederation of the only two remaining republics of Tito's Yugoslavia came into effect: it is called simply "Serbia and Montenegro."

What is the EU?

Over the course of the 1990s, gaining membership of the European Union, or EU (before 1993 known as the European Community, and prior to 1958 as the European Economic Community) became the dominant topic in Slovene foreign policy. This was true for most of the former communist states of Europe. These states saw the EU as a spur to, and a guarantor of, their own democratization, economic prosperity and, in conjunction with NATO, security; among other things, the EU itself saw expanding its membership as a way of increasing its own security by eliminating hotspots of poverty, autocracy, and revanchism. Both sets of states doubtless also view membership in two other ways, too. The first would be as a reward for successful transitions away from one-party states and centrally planned economies. In addition, the EU's prestige has an almost magnetic power on most states. The identity and legitimacy of new states are greatly enhanced by "rejoining Europe," that is, by being deemed worthy of admission to the common European eonomic and political project. After all, this project – whether it is really cause or effect – seems to copper-fasten democracy and prosperity in an increasing number of countries.

To grasp fully why the EU is so important today, one must look back to the early 1950s. It is also essential to remember that the European Union is not about economics alone. In the wake of the brutality and destruction of World War II, politicians across Europe looked for ways to rebuild the continent and provide for future peace and prosperity. Although national leaders are obliged to act in the national interest (or according to their perception of it), the atmosphere in Europe after 1945 was conducive to internationalist, or supra-national, thinking. That is to say, a whole generation of political leaders came to believe that their states' interests would best be served by greatly intensifying cooperation with their neighbors and decisively turning their backs on imperialism and militarism. These two plagues on international relations had been generated by the excessive nationalism and unchecked rivalries of the recent past. Although the racism and aggression of Hitler's Germany and Mussolini's Italy stand out in this regard, we should not forget that World War I had also recently taken ten million European lives, even without the clear conflict of ideologies present in World War II. Thus it is safe to say that there was, indeed, a new factor of idealism – of looking to pioneer a better way rather than try to contain old conflicts – in postwar European politics.

Various multinational groupings were formed in both Western and Eastern Europe. The Cold War stiffened divisions between the respective Washington- and Moscow-dominated military camps known as the North Atlantic Treaty Organization (NATO) and the Warsaw Pact. But there were also more purely regional groupings such as the Council of Europe (founded in 1949), the Western European Union (1954), the Organization for Economic Cooperation and Development, and the European Free Trade Association (both 1960). It is out of one of these, the European Coal and Steel Community (1951), that the EU would eventually emerge.

The six founding members were France, Germany, Italy, Belgium, the Netherlands, and Luxembourg. Although this nucleus would grow continually until reaching a much deepened and broadened network of twenty-five countries by 2004, the 1950s actually brought setbacks. The initial concerns of promoting economic growth and rehabilitating or containing (West) Germany were not enough to lead to what one might call the radical cooperation of today. From 1952 to 1954, plans for a European Defense Community and a European Political Community came to nought. Even so, an International Court of Justice was established in 1952.

But in 1957 the six states signed the Treaties of Rome, which had been hammered out by statesmen such as Konrad Adenauer of West Germany, Jean Monnet of France, and Paul Henri Spaak of Belgium. These arrangements provided for the creation of a "common market" and for much greater cooperation in fields from nuclear energy to agricultural policies to banking.

By 1973 the EC had begun to grow: Great Britain, Denmark, and Ireland joined in that year. Eventually they were joined by Greece (1981), Spain and Portugal (1986), the former German Democratic Republic (merged with West Germany in 1990), and then Austria, Finland, and Sweden (1995).

But the changes to the EC were not just quantitative; they were also qualitative. After years of "Eurosclerosis" (poor administration within the EC and economic and political stagnation in the member states), European Commission President Jacques Delors began moving the organization forward again after 1985. The fall of the Berlin Wall, symbolizing the turning out of communist regimes in Europe, gave great impetus to change. Between 1991 and 1993, the members worked out the Maastricht Treaty. This agreement called for closer relationships and for a name change to the European Union. At the heart of the new arrangements were moves towards a common currency and more coordination of foreign and military policies. By January 1, 2002, the new EU felt very real indeed: in addition to the advance towards acceptance of ten new member states from eastern and southern Europe, on that date eleven of the fifteen members mothballed their individual currencies and adopted the euro. Only Greece was not considered fiscally fit enough to join this currency union, while Great Britain, Denmark, and Sweden chose not to do so.

Following on the heels of NATO's expansion, ten new states joined the EU in May 2004. Slovenia, of course, was among them, along with Poland, the Czech Republic, Hungary, Estonia, Latvia, Lithuania, Slovakia, Cyprus, and Malta. Conditions for their admission, expansion of the "Schengen" standards for internal and external border controls, and new voting (see below) and administrative procedures to be used after enlargement, were agreed upon in the Treaty of Nice (2000) and other fora, though not without the usual drama and complications. This time it was the voters of Ireland who at first soundly rejected the Treaty in June 2001 and then approved it sixteen months later.

There are four general requirements for acceptance into the European Union. They contain a mixture of objective and subjective criteria. A candidate country must have a democratic political system (representative government, civil rights, the rule of law) and a capitalist economic system (variously conceived of on the spectrum of social as opposed to market concerns). Furthermore, as a state it must be able to carry out the *acquis communitaire* (existing EU laws and regulations). Finally, its economy must be robust enough to stand intra-EU competition. Today, the EU is looking ahead to absorbing the rest of the Balkans and establishing higher-profile relationships with Mediterranean and Middle Eastern countries. But it remains to be seen how well the new Union of twenty-five members will function. Issues relating to voting, members' budgets, currency, and a common European Constitution darken the horizon today. Turkey, which was accepted as an associate member way back in 1963 and which is clamoring ever more loudly for admission today, presents challenges which may be emblematic of future candidates: the obvious problem of human rights, and the less often publicly discussed issue of the effect of ethnic (Arab, Turkish, Kurdish) and religious (Muslim) diversity on European identity or even security.

The reasons for the EU's existence and popularity today are manifold. Some of the original justifications, like containing post-Nazi Germany, hardly seem relevant today. But ensuring peace (through functional ties and venues for conflict resolution) among Europe's powerful states and fostering economic and cultural cooperation remain vital. The economic cooperation itself still has as its essence the idea of a common "internal" market (no tariffs, free movement of labor and capital, common policies on subsidies) and a single currency (impact on social and budgetary policies and on trade, since the EU has 19 percent of global foreign trade, compared with 18 percent for the US). In terms of foreign policy, a united Europe has far more prestige and power and can, perhaps, form a healthy counterweight to the US. And the EU also still resonates powerfully as a guarantor of civil rights and liberties. This involves supporting the existence of the smaller or stateless peoples (national minorities) of Western Europe. And, in a more general way, it is linked to the fundamental political and religious freedoms of Central European and Balkan countries in transition. It is obvious that the EU now sees the admission process and the idea of a "common European home" as both a reward and a tool for further change.

Why would the giant organization in Brussels open its doors to ten much poorer states, with a variety of social and ethnic problems, in 2004? The motivations for the continued growth of the European Union are complex. Most importantly, it will take generations for enough scholars to gain access to national and institutional archives for a complete picture to emerge. More autobiographies by statesmen and more polling and political analysis will help. But, doubtless, the set of goals pushing the Union includes the idea of security – both in terms of pushing the Union's (and NATO's) borders into the vacuum of Eastern Europe before chaos, terrorism, or revived Russian imperialism appear there, and in terms of helping the region develop economically so that its poverty does not create an unrelenting flood of immigrants to the West. Optimists about economic growth might well have noted the investment potential of Eastern Europe's raw materials and land, still-ailing infrastructure, and markets hungry for consumer goods. Finally, one should not forget that, in terms of ideology or even idealism, the EU has stressed that it is open to any European state that can meet its admissions criteria; East European states, lured by the prosperity and peace they see in the West, have been unstinting in their enthusiasm and even insistence on joining.

No attempt to assess the significance of the EU can be successful without consideration of how it functions. It is a huge organization, with many of its most important functions centered on Brussels. But many other offices are delegated to other cities around the continent. Its concerns are not limited to major issues of economics and diplomacy but range also to the study of social phenomena and the coordination of policies as varied as worker and consumer safety, the environment, trafficking in drugs and people, terrorism and other crime, and racism. Much of the quotidian work of the EU is directed and carried out by the European Commission in Brussels. This body contains the so-called "Eurocrats" and "comitologists" of the administration and committee systems. Founded in 1958, it consists of Commissioners, their staffs, and a Directorates-General of permanent administrators. The Commissioners, appointed by the member states, are in charge of specific fields (for instance, foreign policy or the environment) and there are working groups on individual issues.

Three other bodies within the EU are important for the establishment and legitimization of the policies that the Commission carries out. The Council of Ministers was founded in 1952. It consists of one high-ranking delegate (at the ministerial level) from each member country. Its president, like so many chairs in the EU, rotates every six months. The Council is a mid-level guidance group to forge operational plans. It does the nuts-and-bolts planning of the EU by putting specifics and muscle into the broad policy decisions of another body known as the European Council. Formed in 1974, this Council "outranks" the first – because it consists of heads of state or government plus the Foreign Ministers of the members. Their job is to set the strategic goals and agenda for the whole EU. This "visionary" role is paralleled by its function of continuing endorsement or legitimization of EU activities, since the Council's members are elected.

The ratification function is carried out as well by the European Parliament. Founded in 1952, this assembly, based in both Strasbourg and Brussels, now has over 700 members. Delegates have been directly elected in their home countries since the late 1970s. There is no other elected, multinational parliament in the world, but this body's significance is far more than its novelty. It is also the only part of the EU establishment that is directly elected, and therefore its importance has grown in recent years in the face of criticism that the Union has a "democracy deficit." The Parliament does more than just ratify and justify decisions from the Commission and the Councils. It disposes over an increasing quotient of budgetary power and can censure and remove Commissioners, as almost happened in 1999. There are some pan-European political parties, and the size of each national delegation depends on the member state's population. Germany, for instance, has ninety-nine delegates; the UK, France, and Italy have seventy-two each; Spain and Poland have fifty; and Slovenia has seven, while Estonia and Malta have six.

The recent expansion of the EU has occasioned changes in voting procedures. In the past, many important decisions (especially on potential new members) required unanimity. This has led to slow or meandering decision-making in the past. Many decisions are now taken according to a process known as "qualified majority voting" (or QMV). A country's vote is now scaled to its population, though not to its economic power. The actual number of votes a country will now have varies according to how many members of the EU there are, but the same proportions among members will be preserved. Germany, France, and the UK all have currently about twenty-nine votes; Spain and Poland both have twenty-seven; and Slovenia and Estonia have four each, while Malta has three. One other important voting mechanism is also new: the system known as "triple-majority voting." Approval no longer consists even of winning (with 50 percent plus one) this revised head-count. Adoption comes after clearing three hurdles: the number of votes in favor must be at least 255 of 345 (74 percent); a majority of member states must vote in favor; and a "demographic majority" of countries representing at least 62 percent of the total EU population must approve the measure as well. Countries may not split their vote. As cumbersome as this system might seem, it will probably prove to be more flexible than the old "liberum veto" approach. How to enforce policies on disputed issues could still be very tricky; in the absence of the goodwill that has recently characterized most EU proceedings, financial penalties of various types seem to be the most likely tools, short of threatening expulsion.

The EU is in many ways a tremendous success story, but member states and outside observers continue to raise some concerns about its future. One of them is about how democratic the organization truly is, since much of its policy is decided by unelected officials. It also remains to be seen whether the currency union will stick or expand, and, even more problematically, whether members will make concrete progress toward creation of a common security policy. Many also worry that the EU reinforces the hegemony of particular varieties of liberal economic thinking to the degree that social policies and the cultural specifity of member states might be in jeopardy.

Slovenia's move into the European Union

Slovenia had many obvious motivations for seeking EU membership, as described above. Polls in 2003 gave specific insights into what Slovenes were thinking: a rise in the country's international prestige, more employment and investment opportunities, greater rule of law, enhanced security, and expanded opportunities for students and researchers.[34]

Slovenia's first approaches to the EU came in 1994, but they were rebuffed, largely at Italy's request. In that same year, however, Slovenia was accepted into the PHARE program, which was the EU vehicle for giving aid and advice to postcommunist countries in their economic transitions. After intense negotiations, Italy agreed to allow Slovenia's candidacy to move forward in 1996, and an association agreement removing most tariffs was signed with the EU that year. Ljubljana then had to pick up the pace of constitutional changes to harmonize Slovene law with that of the EU. From that point on, it was something of a flat-out race to see whether NATO or EU admission would take place first. As it turned out, they would arrive almost simultaneously.

At times Slovene politicians and the public grew grumpy at what they perceived as EU footdragging or bossiness; even foreign diplomats' and EU officials' often diverse, and frequently changing, estimates of when Slovenia would be "ready." Of course, there was also a less visible subtext of when the EU would be ready, and for how many new members. As with NATO membership, the Slovene government liked the idea of individual rather than group admission or "waves." Slovenia's state of development and official preparedness made it eager for an individual approach. After some negative feedback from the EU in 2000, progress reports issued in late 2001 indicated that ten candidate states were essentially ready. In quintessential EU fashion, however, some tasks remained to be completed: by 2004, the new members were supposed to chart further improvements in labor productivity, health care, civil service, and anti-corruption efforts before they would be asked to sign official treaties of accession. In general, the governments of the EU candidate countries strongly supported membership, for both economic and security reasons. All candidate states were assigned a rapporteur to help them through the admissions process, just as each new member would be assigned a commissioner with whom their delegations to Brussels would, more or less, apprentice after May 2004. The rapporteur for Slovenia was an Italian Social Democrat and European Parliament member, Demetrio Volcic, who was actually born in Ljubljana in 1931 and who has also worked on the EU's relations with Armenia and Turkey.

In 2003, the admissions process accelerated greatly. On February 19, the first of the three EU bodies that had to approve new candidates did so. The European Commission gave the nod to ten potential new members: Slovenia, Poland, Hungary, the Czech Republic, Estonia, Latvia, Lithuania, Slovakia, Malta, and Cyprus. On March 7, the Slovenes passed some final constitutional changes about sovereignty, and then on March 23, as part of the legally binding double-track EU–NATO referendum with a 60 percent turnout, 90 percent of Slovene voters endorsed joining the EU. Malta had already held such a vote, and observers credited Slovenia's overwhelming support for the expansion with improving the chances that it would pass in the other eight candidate states, too.

On April 9, the European Parliament voted on and approved each of the ten applicants. Slovenia and Lithuania tied for the most ringing endorsement in terms of the votes cast: 522 for, 22 against. Even the Czechs, still embroiled in some World War II-era controversies with Austria and Germany and bringing up the rear of the endorsements, were easily voted in by a result of 489 to 37. Five days later, the European Council accepted the ten, and on April 16 a major treaty signing took place in the symbolic location of Athens. All twenty-five current and prospective EU states signed Treaties of Accession which came into force on May 1, 2004. The new members then, of course, had to maintain their fiscal standards and finish implementing required legal changes over the next year. In November 2003, the EC President, Romano Prodi, said that Slovenia had only one moderately significant barrier remaining: the recognition of professional and educational credentials from abroad, especially in health care. This was a common shortcoming among the other nine states, too, many of whom also still had more serious concerns to iron out, such as public health and agriculture.

After joining the EU on May 1, 2004, the tempo of negotiations, plans, and press releases in Slovenia barely changed. There was a great deal to be decided, implemented, and managed. One of the most heartening pieces of news for Slovenes is that their standard of living is expected to reach 75 percent of the EU average (a goal of the European Commission) in just one year; for Czechs the waiting period, or rather interval of growth and adjustment, is expected to be fifteen years, while it is much longer for the other new members.[35] Slovenes are also looking forward to long-term transportation projects like the growing system of Trans-European Corridors, highway systems that will run north–south and east–west through the twenty-five EU lands and beyond. Another project advocated by NGOs in former communist countries is a Pan-European Greenway that would link wildlife preserves, parks, and watershed areas along the former path of the Iron Curtain, thereby raising both historical and environmental consciousness.

But Slovenes were not amused by the fact that EU budget projections, released in September 2002, showed that by 2006 Slovenia would be paying out more to the EU than it would be receiving in direct financial benefits, such as development aid. The sum in question was quite large, about 300 million euros, and this was the case despite the fact that the EU was paying out about $42 billion in transition assistance to all ten new members before and after 2004. The reason for Slovenia's meteoric rise from net recipient to net beneficiary is its past and projected economic strength, especially compared to the 73 million other new members in nine other countries, at a time of slow economic growth in Western Europe.

Slovenia must now prepare for the monetary union which will see the tolar eventually replaced by the euro, perhaps by 2008, and more Schengen-level border crossings to Croatia must be built to supplement the first one opened in December 2003. At that point, Slovenia's borders with other EU countries will largely disappear. Temporary restrictions on Slovenes' ability to work in other member states will apply for a few years but, in the meantime, Slovenes will send 335 officials, advisors, and office workers to Brussels to join the EU administration. The chief representative to the European Commission will be Janez Potočnik, who has long been Slovenia's Minister for European Affairs. Slovenes will be called upon in short order to voice their positions on the new European Constitution, voting procedures, the possibility of a permanent presidency of the organization, and moves from some quarters to pursue a more divergent path from the US, especially in environmental and defense policy. Slovenia is now an important front-line state in EU efforts to crack down on the drug trade, human trafficking, money laundering, gun running, illegal immigration, and terrorism.

The European parliamentary elections of June 2004 saw that body grow to 732 members. The EP does not have parties per se, but it has "groupings." The biggest grouping is currently the European People's Party, which is Christian Democratic in direction and won 38 percent of the vote, worth 277 delegates. In second place, as before the last elections, is the Party of European Socialists, which consists of social democrats; they won 27 percent of the vote, or 198 representatives. In third place is the ELDR, a Liberal, centrist group with 9 percent of the vote, or sixty-eight delegates. Next came the European United Left, consisting of other Greens, socialists, and communists, with 5 percent of the vote for thirty-nine seats. The Greens placed fifth, also at 5 percent, or thirty-eight delegates. Two Euro-skeptic groupings finished sixth and seventh, for a total of 6 percent, or forty-two seats; they are the Union for a Europe of Nations and Europe of Democracies and Diversities. Other parties accounted for the remaining 10 percent (seventy seats). Such elections constitute a kind of political barometer for Europe as a whole and for individual states. These most recent results do indeed confirm the shift towards conservatism that has marked European and American politics in the recent past.

A final perspective: the culture of transition

National independence is not the end of Slovenia's political evolution, even if the results of the other two discrete transitions – to a democratic system and a capitalist economy – are fairly certain. A major change in Slovenia's foreign policy establishment, the removal by Prime Minister Rop and Parliament of long-time political figure Dimitrij Rupel from his post as Foreign Minister in July 2004, was unlikely to herald any shift in actual policy. That membership of the European Union will now present Slovenia with new opportunities and pressures, including in the realm of culture, is a topic addressed in the Conclusion of this book. But growth towards a pan-European identity, which some Slovenes find problematic or even perilous, and which evokes varying responses from outside observers as to its desirability or likelihood, is not the only new direction available to Slovenia's evolving political and cultural worlds. There is also the issue of regional identity. Regional associations with neighboring countries have been a part of Slovene thinking for years, as in the Alps–Adria Working Community which brings together nearby regions which are home to Italians, Austrians,

Bavarians, Croats, and Hungarians. But another important locus of identity lies even closer to home.

There has in recent years been a great growth in interest in the regional identity of the major port city of Trieste and the nearby Istrian peninsula. In the nineteenth century, Trieste had the largest Slovene population in the world; the peace settlement after the Great War, of course, severed Trieste's ties to Slovenia and Austria, and eventually the Tito government developed the nearby port of Koper as a quite effective economic substitute. As the Cold War ended, and then many former communist states moved towards admission into Euro-Atlantic institutions, former regional identities began to resurface along the "fault lines" separating Europe's postwar political blocs. One of the zones that has produced intense scholarly and literary, and autobiographical activity is the multi-ethnic, historically rich area around the northern Adriatic, especially greater Trieste and Istria. The legacy of the area retains its mixed nature, blending Italian, Slovene, and Croatian cultural and political presence with the Austrian historical and architectural legacy from Habsburg days.

Some of the new writing from and about the area involves painful memories of World War II and postwar population transfers, but much of it is nostalgic or invokes the cultural and spiritual benefits of the once, and perhaps future, *modus vivendi* of the region. Interested readers can consult the essayistic works *A Ghost in Trieste* by Joseph Cary and *Microcosms* by Claudio Magris, as well as the rich travel literature by Jan Morris, in her *Trieste and the Meaning of Nowhere*. Academic studies of historical memory and diplomacy are the subjects of Glenda Sluga's *The Problem of Trieste and the Italo-Yugoslav Border* and Pamela Ballinger's *History in Exile: Memory and Identity at the Borders of the Balkans*. Fans of fiction may avail themselves of Giuliana Morandini's *Café of Mirrors* or, especially, Fulvio Tomizza's *Materada*; one hopes that the works of the Istrian Croat Nedjeljko Fabrio will soon be more widely available in English. There are also several new studies of James Joyce's time in Trieste around World War I.

But let us return to the most salient issue in Slovene identity at the start of the twenty-first century: Europe in general and Slovenia's place in it. The contemporary writer Drago Jančar has provided, in his short story "Augsburg," both an illustration of, and a commentary on, Slovenia's much-heralded "return" to Europe. Written in the early 1990s in the wake of the violent dissolution of Yugoslavia, this fairly short prose piece is really more of an essay based on a pastiche of images and analogies than a story. But it does show us the carefully studied use Jančar often makes of erudite historical analogies. These analogies often draw on nuanced phenomena or events that are not necessarily familiar to the average North American reader, but his use of history is both evocative and responsible; Jančar thereby achieves a great intellectual – if not emotional – effect with his stories.

"Augsburg" is a monolog by someone living in the former Yugoslavia. It is studded with stark and sometimes brutal images of the breakup of the country and of the civil war raging in Croatia and Bosnia. These images include evidence of national animosity between Serbs and Slovenes, Slovenia's struggle to repair its international reputation for tourism, exhausted diplomats, the slaughter of pigs and Lippizaner stallions, para-militaries, conspiracy theories, barbed-wire and bits of the Berlin Wall for sale as postcommunist souvenirs, and, most shockingly, human carnage. The mélange of images serves as a backdrop to musings and observations about a distant but prosperous and peaceful place to which the author thinks he (and his family or society?) are going. "Augsburg" is thus a utopia for the exhausted post-Yugoslav narrator. In actuality, of course, a great many refugees from Yugoslavia found safe haven in Germany and other European countries during the war. But here the function of Augsburg, a city in southern Germany famous for a very significant sixteenth-century peace treaty, is as an ideal of a way of life and an approach to history: that is to say, it is a powerful symbol that links the lure of material prosperity with the idea of toleration and respect for diversity. But, as we shall see, it is not an entirely comforting or wholesome symbol.

Jančar acknowledges that many Yugoslavs actually set out in these years for exile or asylum in cities like Augsburg when he writes: "Across Europe masses of refugees wander . . . [and] [o]n the other side of the continent millions of emigrants are preparing to set out for Augsburg."[36] He has, however, switched to a non-geographic conception of Augsburg when he states immediately afterwards: "But getting to Augsburg is not easy. We know that now."[37]

Jančar's text provides one clue to the nature of the difficulty for people or countries seeking peace and prosperity à la Augsburg. Visitors must negotiate a complicated system of gates, walls, and moats, and supply appropriate documents, answers to questions, and donations or bribes in order to gain entrance to the city. There is even a large squadron of dragoons held in reserve in a secret location to force out unwanted applicants. As today, in the case of the complicated process for admission to the European Union, not everyone is welcome in utopia and force will be used to keep undesirables out.

But one must go beyond the text to discover the other cautionary note. The Peace of Augsburg (1555) ended much of the religious strife in Central Europe by recognizing Lutheranism's right to exist alongside Catholicism. One can aptly see in it, therefore, a healthy, modern toleration of diversity; this image certainly has resonance in the Balkans in the 1990s. Still, the state of affairs which the Treaty created was far from ideal. First of all, it was arrived at after much blood had been shed and much ill-will generated; the similar suffering in Jančar's narrative was created by nationalism, but yet, ironically, the Peace of Augsburg is today seen by historians as spurring the growth of territorial states (as opposed to the Holy Roman Empire and other "pre-modern" state forms) which, in turn, spurred the growth of nationalism. Second, and more directly, one should hasten to add that although the Peace removed restrictions on official Lutheranism, it was not an embrace of true diversity or individual choice. Princes and kings still decided the official religion of their realms, and no faiths other than Catholicism and Lutheranism were to be tolerated. Is the peace offered by the symbol of Augsburg, then, illusory and unsatisfactory or, at least, ultimately only partial? It is likely that Jančar recognizes that the answer to this question is "yes," since he ends the story by stating that "[w]hen we have finished sleeping, we shall dream on."[38] Evidently, arrival and admittance do not solve all of the travelers' problems.

Jančar, while cosmopolitan in disposition, is obviously comfortable with the theory and practice of nationalism. He has become a major public intellectual in Slovenia, and his views go a long way towards establishing a Slovene profile on various issues in the international arena. His prolific essays and commentaries cover literature, history, and some social and political issues. By international – or at least former Yugoslav – standards, he would have to be accounted a moderate nationalist. Like the Christian Socialist and poet Edvard Kocbek, whom he admires in many ways, Jančar agrees that there is something fundamental and enriching about national loyalties, but he eschews chauvinism. Writing about a specific historical issue that is very important to Slovenes because of the large amount of emigration that took place from both Habsburg and Yugoslav Slovenia, Jančar notes that Slovenes who left their homeland should not be regarded as a group who let down their native "blood, soil, language and culture"[39] but rather as individuals who sought opportunity and self-assertion. It does reflect poorly, however, on Slovenia's state history that there was no country, especially a nation-state, to help protect and empower these people in their homeland.

Jančar's views on the history of communism in Eastern Europe are, not surprisingly, rather gloomy. For him there was no essential difference between Yugoslavia's "liberal" communism and the Stalinistic or stagnant and more repressive regimes he saw in Poland and elsewhere; they were just "the various totalitarian variants of the same idea."[40] Furthermore, he deterministically states that the evolution of these regimes "could not have ended any differently" than in their collapse, starting in 1989.[41] Echoing the sentiments of many other intellectuals, Jančar states that communist governments suffered from "the senselessness which is generated by the absolute authority of mediocrity."[42]

About the transition period following 1989, Jančar, citing the Polish example, is well aware of how stormy the social and ideological atmosphere can become, as countries face "[a]nti-communism with a Bolshevistic face, warnings of encroaching fundamentalism and anti-semitism, the break-up of Solidarity, the messianic error of Lech Walesa, and finally the search for pragmatic solutions."[43]

The transition period is intertwined with important questions of nationalism, of course, and Jančar also takes a dim view of previous "Yugoslav nationalism." He even sounds a rather cautionary note about Slovene nationalism, although he clearly maintains that that republic had a right to secede in 1991. Yugoslavism was "a debacle"[44] because it relied on integralist or assimilationist thinking (usually Serb-driven) which ran roughshod over the traditions of the country's various peoples. Furthermore, in a kind of impatient but well-informed historical reasoning that I am tempted to call "naive realism" or "precipitate empiricism," Jančar argues that Yugoslavia tried and botched every conceivable form of political and economic organization; of course he is talking about the chaotic, one-of-a-kind twentieth century, and one could argue that many of the negative trends in the Balkans were the result of foreign intervention, but there was, in truth, little point in conducting hypothetical historical arguments with Yugoslavia's exhausted citizens by the 1990s. It was also a debacle because by 1990 every major and minor national group in the country (with the possible exception of the Bosnian Muslims) had big grievances against the system. This socialist Yugoslavia, furthermore, to which Slovenia was forced to pay a bloody and unacknowledged "tribute" via the postwar massacres by Tito's Partisans, disappointed the cause of maverick socialism by not supporting Hungarian revolutionaries and Czech reformers in their conflicts with the USSR in 1956 and 1968, respectively.

Jančar is also cautious about the influence of nationalism on writers, especially when nationalistic artists get politically active. He encourages separation between the thematic world of politics, domination, and strength and that of literature; since Jančar, himself a prolific essayist and high-profile public figure, obviously recognizes that an individual may inhabit both worlds, it is apparent that he eschews writing about nationalism. He even singles out some Serbian writers and former colleagues who, basically, went off the deep end in the 1980s and abandoned all humanist and humanitarian concerns. Instead of accepting nationalism, reductionistic history, and gloomy paradigms of state worship and unending bloody conflict, Jančar asks that he "at least be allowed to get out of this debate. It should be permissible for me to be interested in other things on this earth."[45] Furthermore, nationalism is not a guarantee of individual rights, of an appreciation for diversity, or of prosperity via capitalism. Writers in the "new" Central European Slovenia should remain open to cultural influences from the Balkan south and east, while politicians should bear in mind their new and high degree of accountability. From this, we can conclude, as did two British historians recently in a major work about Slovenia,[46] that now, for the first time in history, Slovenia has no foreign occupier or hegemon (such as the earlier Rome, Vienna, Moscow, or Belgrade) on which to blame any tensions or shortcomings that might mar its future. The point is not that Slovenia has indulged in a politics of "passing the buck" but that its politicians and voters need to take their civic responsibilities very seriously.

But thoughts such as these can also spur us on, even beyond the borders of the Slovenes' independent state, to another level of identity and loyalty.

In 1924, the great Chinese revolutionary and statesman Sun Yat-sen wrote that: "We, the wronged races, must first recover our position of national freedom and equality before we are fit to discuss cosmopolitanism."[47] Sun knew that nationalism brought unity[48] to peoples that are otherwise like "a heap of loose sand."[49] He also knew that "cosmopolitanism," like other forms of internationalism and globalization, sounds admirable but readily functions as camouflage for the imperialism of stronger countries. Slovenia as a member of the European Union is now entering a unique situation where its identity, or at least a major part of it, climbs up a level to a plane defined more by common agenda and ideas than cultural, language, or ethnicity.

Slovenes are fortunate that the EU offers a relatively sheltered harbor for Slovene culture during this extension of loyalty. Two other, but related, trends might well interest the next generation of observers of Slovene nationalism, however. How will the development of multiple "nested" or layered identities affect Slovenia's nationalism as its citizens embrace and prioritize their own affinities and values? This essentially post-modern question does not assume that nationalism, which was never monolithic in the first place, will disappear, only that it will have new rivals in terms of individual loyalties and preoccupations. Furthermore, how will the greatly enlarged European Union negotiate its new identity in a global environment filled with conflict and in a continental one filled with economic change and social rifts, some lingering from the past and some emerging at the present time?

6 Conclusion

Slovenia's three transitions are now finished. The "revolutions of 1989" – in Slovenia's case, it was 1991 – presented the communist countries of Eastern Europe with three massive new challenges: to establish independent countries either by escaping Soviet control or calving off from multinational states, to build democratic political systems, and to set up market economies. With Slovenia's accession to the European Union in 2004, these three transitions are complete. Of course Slovenia will still have to react to problems and opportunities at home and abroad, and the EU and NATO will continue to evolve. But at this great turning point, it is time to take stock of some large, long-term issues relating to Slovene identity.

In a sense, of course, one may assert that Slovenia's basic cultural and social loyalties, based on the country's Central European identity, did not change over the twentieth century. But loyalties in the sense of political sovereignty certainly did change from 1900 to 2000: from being a collection of Habsburg crown lands, the Slovene-inhabited parts of Europe evolved – through two state formations both bearing the name Yugoslavia and through the crucibles of two bloody and exhausting world wars – into a small, independent country. Needless to say, Europe also changed around Slovenia: Yugoslavia germinated, withstood a brutal world war, thrived in some ways, and then withered and disappeared; fascism and communism lent their intoxicating and dictatorial energies to an omnibus of conflicts both cold and hot; and the largely imperialistic and militaristic Great Power alliances of 1900 have been replaced by the European Union, stressing mutual prosperity, democracy, and peace.

The plural form "loyalties" is also intended as a reminder that individuals are more than just members of a nation; since Slovenes' – like everyone's, more or less – individual identities are multifaceted and multilayered, involving religious, linguistic, sexual, intellectual, and other considerations, it follows that their actions in society and the world at large do not follow a strictly nationalist hierarchy.

In the fictional works of the great Austrian novelist and journalist Joseph Roth, there is a prominent Slovene family named the Trottas. As World

War I tears apart the Habsburg Empire, and their family with its new-found wealth and fame, one of the younger Trottas laments the fact that the family's home village of Sipolje has disappeared. The village, it seems, has been amalgamated with others into a large trading town, and its children now go to university in the Yugoslav cities of Dubrovnik or Zagreb and not in Vienna. It is true that World War I, which opened the twentieth century in such dramatic fashion, brought enormous changes to Slovenia. Although Roth had his own very understandable reasons for lamenting the passing of the Dual Monarchy, as far as the Slovenes were concerned, these changes were far from disastrous. This century was perilous for most of Central Europe, but the Slovenes left it as a newly independent country, with a stable political system and economy, poised for acceptance into the twin Euro-Atlantic institutions of the European Union and the North Atlantic Treaty Organization.

Perhaps one might consider the political and cultural track of Slovenia in the near future in the following terms: how "pan-European" should or could Slovenia now become? Arguments over subsidiarity and sovereignty in the new Europe aside, the Slovene culture and language are now going to face perhaps their severest tests ever: assimilation through political co-optation and, even more gravely, economic and marketing homogenization via globalization. Politically speaking, of course, the European Union has mechanisms to keep the French, Italians, Germans, or Austrians from running roughshod over Slovenia; likewise, EU member states are free to vary only so far from EU policies on issues from irredentism to minority rights, lest they face financial penalties or, presumably, the new ultimate threat, ejection. Therefore, some observers might be worrying unnecessarily about a recrudescence of *slovenstvo* (usually characterized as a stubborn or defensive adherence to the "Slovene manner of doing things") as a political factor. Relations with the US would seem, all in all, to pose an equally great challenge for Slovenia now. In 2002 and 2003, US pressure to circumvent multilateral agreements about the International Criminal Court and to join the thin ranks of President Bush's coalition against Iraq – in other words, to take sides in the fallacious US-marketed dichotomy between the emerging "new" Europe and the superfluous "old" one – placed the Slovene government in a difficult position. This was so much the case that, in the spring of 2003, a diverse group of protestors assembled outside the American embassy in Ljubljana, chanting "Hlapci, Hlapci! " This rendition of "Servants, servants!" echoes a famous poem by the beloved (albeit radical) poet Srečko Kosovel from the 1920s, and also contains shades of the famous story by Ivan Cankar, and the point was to ponder publicly whether Slovenia is in danger of accepting a new master (Washington) in the wake of the old one (Belgrade, or, in Kosovel's case, Vienna and Rome).

In terms of economics, *slovenstvo* might even prove to be a positive phenomenon in the face of the effects of globalization on the Slovene economy and culture. Globalization is a broad term which refers to at least three different processes at work today: new and powerful mobility of capital, spurred on by the internet; a tidal wave of homogeneous, mostly American, mass popular culture marketed by large corporations; and a neo-imperialistic distribution of investment power that serves the interests of industrialized states in an era when they control international lending institutions and when the countries of the global "south" are being "schooled" in privatization and ever more effectively plugged in as raw material providers to a planet-wide economic division of labor. Obviously, Slovenia alone cannot successfully buck a set of trends this powerful, but Europe as a continent – even though it is also to some degree a purveyor of such trends – can offer a significant counterweight to the unprecedentedly huge American presence on the world scene. Slovenia, fond of offering itself to the West as a diplomatic "bridge to the Balkans," has something else to offer Europe and the world as well: an example of functional and open-minded specificity in an increasingly standardized world. Will the efficient and polyglot Slovenes go on to carve out an economic and cultural niche that could earn them the felicitous nickname of the "Dutch of the Balkans"? Or might they at least remain a case study of capitalism with a human face, banking on social consensus and social justice instead of just the immediate bottom lines of corporate earnings statements?

To turn now to the issue of nationalism once again, many historians, including Miroslav Hroch and Ivo Banac, have noted that the Slovene movement began among a small core of "awakened intellectuals," mostly priests and scholars; it did not originate, as with many other nationalisms, with a sense of popular sovereignty in a territorially defined state or as part of the political agenda of a liberal *bourgeoisie*. We have seen how the Slovene movement grew to have a broader base in the last decades of the Habsburg Empire. Both world wars then helped mobilize Slovenes politically, while the time in the two Yugoslavias brought social and economic modernization that empowered Slovenes with new ideas and options.

Nationalism itself might be usefully defined as a sense of identity and loyalty, residing at both the individual and group levels, based on a common language, culture, territory, and history. It is a modern concept, although ethnic identity is old. Nationalism is connected to the idea of popular sovereignty (the people should rule) but it is definitely not always democratic. It originated in various places in Europe in the eighteenth and nineteenth centuries as a consequence of several types of economic and intellectual change. Since then it has largely come to replace many other types of identity (dynastic, religious, regional); the nation is, for many, *the* community in which they feel most safe, understood, and useful. We should, therefore, try to account for two other prominent features of the Slovene national movement. These related factors are, first, that it has developed more slowly than the nationalism of most of its Central European and Balkan neighbors, and, second, that its nationalism has mostly been of a political or civic nature, rather than ethnic.

With regard to the first point, one should consider that "slowly" here refers ultimately to the demand for statehood, or political self-determination. It is true that until the 1980s most Slovenes were content with their nation developing within one of its traditional multilateral or federalist contexts, but this is not to accuse Slovenes of being vague in their demands or meandering in pursuit of them. Territorial unity and language preservation were most important to Slovenes early on, and the emphasis then switched to making Titoist Yugoslavia safe for federalism by making the LCY more democratic.

With regard to the second point, it is usually noted that, while all nationalism is rooted in various forms of culture and common identity, civic nationalism considers the inhabitants of a country to be a political population, brought together by shared values or a common agenda. Ethnic nationalism, on the other hand, considers those inhabitants an extended kinship group and makes common ancestry indispensable. Political nationalism is mostly a product of the Enlightenment and developed out of socioeconomic changes in existing territorial states. These changes were producing challenges to the political monopoly of the aristocracy, Church, and monarchy in the form of a capitalist, urban middle class. This class conceived of popular sovereignty as a way to consolidate power and, ultimately, mobilize their co-nationals for work in factories and victories in battle. Ethnic nationalism, with its much higher quotient of Romantic thought, was born when the idea of nationalism was imported into less economically developed regions, where people lived in multinational states. It conceived of popular sovereignty as a process of territorial and ethnic exclusion. One of the leading scholars of nationalism today, Anthony D. Smith, has recently re-examined ethnic and civic nationalism in terms of "vernacular mobilization" and "bureaucratic incorporation."[1]

The two forms are not rigidly distinct in practice because, in times of crisis or rapid change, people's reactions to stimuli can change. So can definitions of "outsiders" and "the other." It is true that the late start of Slovene nationalism amid a mostly agricultural people living in a multiethnic empire could have predisposed Slovenes to ethnic nationalism. In addition one can note that Slovenes grew more intolerant of Balkan *jugoviči* in the aftermath of secession in 1991. The graffiti "Burek, nein danke!" scrawled on walls in downtown Ljubljana demonstrated a certain resentment at Slovenia's having "spun its wheels" in Yugoslavia for too long. The recent controversy over the *izbrisani* is a further case in point. Slovenia, like most European countries, has some discrimination against Roma and other minorities, and there are both skinheads and politicians who get mileage out of manipulating paranoia and stereotypes. Although, historically, predictors of radical movements would seem to be largely absent, an increasing number of voices are being raised today charging that Slovene nationalism is hardening into a kind of ethnocentric fixation that supports traditionally authoritarian and patriarchal structures and fosters an intolerant atmosphere within the society, including towards innovations from beyond the country's borders.

Nonetheless, when we consider that the vast majority of Slovenes are anything but xenophobic, that they historically exhibit generally positive feelings about their fellow South Slavs, that the country never had a major fascist movement like all four of its neighbors did, and that it harbors no serious irredentism, and that preference for local customs and cultural inheritance is also present in many other European countries, then the true picture emerges.

What possible explanations, then, exist for this state of affairs? The first factor is that Slovenes escaped the curse of medieval greatness. This sounds ironic, because at some point every people wants the world to take note of its historical significance, and nationalists usually spend a great deal of time unearthing "state traditions" to justify their claims to sovereignty in the modern era. But state traditions also bring claims to territory. Territory, in turn, is often contested; one nation's claim is often contested by the overlapping historical claim of another state or by population changes that have taken place in the meantime. Serbian and Croatian nationalism, for instance, are both very much burdened by such conflicts, especially in Kosovo and Bosnia–Hercegovina, respectively.

A second explanation is that Slovenes also largely escaped the "crusading mentality" of religious struggle. Not only have there traditionally been few religious minorities on Slovene territory, but Roman Catholicism – an international institution, not a nationally specific one – is also shared by their neighbors, the Austrians, Italians, Croats, and Hungarians. Of course, respect for diversity can be demonstrated only where diversity exists, but is it really a bad thing that Slovenes never learned to call all of their Muslim neighbors *Turci* like many Serbs do, to feel themselves to be the *antemurale christianitatis*, or to have confessional rivalry and insecurity poison their relationship with the powers above them that controlled their land, taxes, and armed forces?

Third is the fact that Slovenia's leading political force until 1941 was the clericalist party. One might call this a voluntaristic rather than structural factor, since it depended on ideas and personalities. The Slovene People's Party (SLS) – and even its three smaller rivals, for their own reasons – did not try to ratchet up nationalist fervor and then cash in on it at the polls, as leading parties have done elsewhere. The growth in the franchise was, at any rate, in Vienna's hands. The SLS only gradually overcame its dislike for nationalism, seeing in it a mass movement that smacked of crass modernity and a political force that threatened to dislodge Vienna from its unique position in international affairs: pro-Vatican, anti-Belgrade, and "neither Russian nor Prussian," as the saying goes.

A fourth element is the Slovenes' status inside the Habsburg Empire. This did not always bring satisfaction but it did supply a critical sense of security. Sadly, the danger of assimilation was real in the period between the Counter-Reformation and the Enlightenment, with neither a native aristocracy nor much urban presence to anchor the culture. But Habsburg politics evolved and proved just pliable enough to keep the Slovenes from suffocating. Slovene elites also proved adept enough at filling in the gaps and bending the sharp corners of the Habsburg system to function as pro-Slovene, if not directly pro-Slovenia. If the demands of *realpolitik* brought more aggressive strains of nationalism to the fore in places like Italy, Germany, and Russia, then Slovenes were safely out of the limelight. And economic development and relative prosperity – usually present in the Slovene countryside in just enough measure to prevent the degree of misery that can pervert politics – arrived at the right time and under the right conditions to keep Slovenes from feeling either completely left behind or exploited by "alien" elements.

Saying that one hopes that political exigencies (such as the so-called war on terrorism) and socioeconomic homogenization will not deprive Slovenia of its sovereignty or its uniqueness is another way of wishing for Slovenia to remain both Slovene and European. But another element of that country's identity deserves clarification as this study draws to a close: the important notion of its Central Europeanness. By the 1990s, many Slovenes readily employed the concept of "Central European identity" to distinguish themselves from their Balkan "cousins," with whom they were "trapped" in the Yugoslav state. "Balkan" to a Slovene could conjure up colorful images of southern neighbors – violence, primitive-ness, and lethargy – that fused with feelings of political impotence, just as an urban Czech or Pole might refer to Ukrainians or Russians as "Eastern European." (To be fair, one should add here that most Slovenes retained an enthusiastic appreciation for the food, geography, and climate – and sometimes more – of the neighboring Yugoslav regions, and also that Croats and Romanians are also fond of asserting that the Balkans begin at their southern border but do not include their lands.) So, by clearly differentiating themselves from the political bad habits and historical train wreck that the term "Balkans" is regarded to entail, the Slovenes asserted their adherence to a different cultural pole: Central Europe.

This assertion, whatever the virtues of its political undertones and what-ever the final judgment on its historical contingency, is certainly accurate. Slovenia does not have a Balkan culture. It does have a Central European culture. But what exactly does this statement mean? One of the greatest proponents of the idea of Central European identity in the twentieth century is the Nobel Prize-winning Polish writer Czeslaw Milosz, author of the famous essay "Central European Attitudes."[2] He dismisses a strictly geographical definition of the idea, as something that unites, for instance, what historian Alan Palmer so accurately called "the lands between" Russia and Germany. The similarities reside in human activities and attitudes; they are constructs, not cartographical entries. One thing that Central

European countries share is societal characteristics. Vastly important here is the ethnic and religious diversity of the region, but Milosz also pointed to a later introduction to industrialization and mass urban society than Western Europe had, and a different preceptor (Marxism–Leninism instead of capitalism) for this transition.

A second set of characteristics involves the intelligentsia. Intellectuals in Central Europe tend to be ironic, if not cynical, about the faiths and ideological movements of our day, but yet they burn with commitment for civic projects and tend to be highly respected as a group by society at large. Third, Central Europeans feel the weight of their past on their present; their interest in history, along with their awareness of both the dangers and delights it preserves, tends to prevent the kind of "cultural amnesia" so prevalent in the West. These last two similarities spill over into a fourth criterion, similarities in high and popular culture ranging from architecture to poetry. Fifth, the people of the region share a sense of a common future, one that might involve political or cultural cooperation, or both; Milosz thus designates Central Europe "an act of faith, a project, let us say, even a utopia"[3] which has both multinational and international components. Finally, Central Europeans are united in having been denied their sovereignty for long periods by foreign empires (Romanov, Habsburg, Hohenzollern, Ottoman); as a result they have seen their "national pride" humiliated, and they have stared assimilation and disenfranchisement in the face.

There is a vast literature on the topic of Central Europe. The Hungarian writer György Konrád shares many of Milosz's views, he goes on to stress that it is an "aristocratic metaphor" because it is mostly a mental or "intellectual concept."[4] He also notes, however – while leaning towards a characterization of the region as utopia, like Milosz – the contradictions and even the potential for nationalist violence in the Central European character. One could also briefly note the contribution of the great Czech-French novelist Milan Kundera, who focuses even more explicitly on the heavy hand of politics and war in creating a sense of the region as "a culture or fate."[5] Central Europeans in Kundera's conception inhabit small nations. They are not conquerors or empire-builders; rather, a "small nation can disappear and it knows it."[6] Politically dominated of late by the East, the USSR, Central Europe also, however, has another adversary: the erosion of its culture by the same technology and mass marketing that is eroding the distinct identities and values of Western societies.

Whether one hews more to Milosz's notion of Central European culture as distinct or to Kundera's notion of it as Western but long separated and now eroding, one can find allies among various Slovene writers and commentators. From the mid-1980s on there was a major revival of interest in the Central European idea in Slovenia, exemplified by the establishment of the Vilenica literary awards. The ideas on Central Europe of highly respected poet Edvard Kocbek were often discussed.

Kocbek published an important essay on the theme of Central Europe in 1940.[7] This piece is a brief work, but it is nearly encyclopedic in scope. It begins with two important assertions. The first is that national differentiation in Central Europe, under the influence of German Romanticism, was a natural humanistic process because nations are organic entities that grow out of historical conditions. Even individual freedom, asserts Kocbek (rather daringly, perhaps, from the perspective of West European civic nationalism), depends upon national freedom. The second assertion is that Central Europe is an interconnected region that is a microcosm or laboratory of values, change, and conflicts to which Western Europeans should pay careful attention.

The essay then, as befits an article written after World War II had already broken out, turns quickly to analysis of the threats to the peoples of Central Europe. Obviously, German expansionism is the concrete and immediate danger; Kocbek adds that German interests in the region had turned truly malignant only recently, due to the empire-building pressures of capitalism which pushed many other European states into a scramble for colonies abroad. In addition, a more subtle, and longer-term, danger is pinpointed: the idea that national sovereignty is the *summum bonum* of political life. Kocbek stresses that Central Europeans should never concentrate just on borders and the life of the "state" but should give great attention to cultural and economic issues. In essence he is renewing a call for some sort of federation in the region, at least as far as an economic union entails, with firm and specific guarantees of national cultural autonomy.

The relevance of Kocbek's ideas to contemporary Slovene history is twofold. Like other writers cited here, he underscores both the depth of the connections between the peoples of Central Europe and the general importance of culture. But he also poses a yet unanswered question about what would be best for Slovenia: a regional federation or a pan-European one. He leaves open the possibility that West European hegemony, perhaps mostly economic, could replace the physical menace that Germany represented in his day.

Even more skeptical about the Central European "utopia" is the prominent writer Drago Jančar. Although he rejects the notion attributed, not surprisingly, to Peter Handke of Central Europe as a mere "meteorological phenomenon" and thus socially and politically irrelevant, he also points out negative common features of the region's history and culture. "The consequences of times past are our reality today," Jančar writes in reminding us that it is not just "horizontal" connections (today's similarities) between cultures that matter;[8] it is also "vertical" or chronological elements that can leave us with historical hangovers, both from earlier national disputes and the legacy of communist collaboration and oppression. The good and the bad mixed together in the Central European character and historical experience Jančar characterizes as potent "contradictions" which, although sobering, should not make one dismissive of the region's potential.

In the final analysis Jančar is willing to praise Central Europe as a place that aspires to the free exchange of ideas and esthetic tendencies and to the toleration and even promotion of diversity, but he warns that it has not yet achieved these goals. The Habsburg Empire, ironically enough, has many lessons to offer the current pan-European administrators in Brussels, both in terms of what should be recreated and avoided on the continent; Jančar also singles out Central European intellectuals for praise as possessing a special kind of skepticism that, forged in the long decades of communist dictatorship, has "a special feeling for the criteria – of a classical, a Christian, and an Enlightenment nature – which make Europe into something more than just a common economic space."[9] Such sensibilities will be necessary to create real intellectual unity and to protect cultural diversity under the EU's common legal and economic structures.

Central Europeans do not always shy, he avers, from mediocrity or from settling old scores; threatened as the region is (or has been) by the military "parades on Red Square" on the one side and the legions of McDonald's and Coca-Cola on the other side, Slovenes should not be deluded into thinking that some sort of federation is necessary to protect them:

> I propose that we continue to stick to a type of organization of Central Europe that enables the greatest extent of diversity. For the Slovenes and for several other peoples, this is certainly the fully ramified nation-state. If such does not exist, in its place will be a vacuum, and this vacuum will not merely be a matter of form. Out of a sense of incompleteness will emerge a rupture, a wound, which will bring in tow more and more new difficulties for us and for others.[10]

This thought is at once a justification for exiting Yugoslavia and a Euro-skeptic's caution about how far to plunge into new continental or regional political alliances. It places Jančar in the camp of defenders of the traditional nation-state, although he eschews chauvinism and chides Slovenes to remain open to cultural influences from all over the continent, including their Balkan neighbors and former fellow Yugoslavs.

Scholars who deal with the identities and movements to which we give the collective term "nationalism" are today split between constructivists and perennialists. The former track the growth, or better, the deliberate cultivation, of national feelings and thought by elites in the modern era, while the latter spend their time tracing distinct cultures' popular roots deeper and deeper into the past. It has not been the goal of this book to settle this debate, although the weight of evidence seems to this observer to endorse constructivism; one should consider here above all nationalism's secularism and mass political character as well as its links to the idea of popular sovereignty and to large standing armies and the mobilization of tremendous military power in order to note how it diverges from the patriotism of the past. Whichever school is right, one can, however, assert what this observer calls the phenomenon of "necessary nationalism."

Many observers of modern politics have noted that nationalism is almost impossible for a contemporary society to avoid. This is true even if nationalism is merely a constructed and temporary phenomenon. The validity of this opinion is still being borne out repeatedly, from postcommunist Eastern Europe to post-Indonesian East Timor. It is almost as if, for whatever set of increasingly well-studied reasons (including the oft-ignored power of example), nationalism is a rite of passage or a virus that changing societies simply have to endure.

Without intending to do so, Jančar is expressing the same idea that the Russian Lenin and his Slovene follower Kardelj expressed in the first half of the twentieth century, namely that future social progress inside and outside a given society is contingent upon a final resolution of the local national question. Easier to swallow, nowadays, might be the remarks attributed to Sun Yat-sen, the liberal leader of China's great revolution in 1912, as he began to throw off the yoke of Western imperialism and modernize his country. The "wronged," or unfree, peoples, to paraphrase Sun this time, would not be fit to be cosmopolitan until they had been allowed to become independent.

Fitness, it would seem, translates into recognition and a sense of self-confidence. Conditions in the new Europe are ripe for Slovenia to continue to develop in many positive ways. Slovenia will not be alone in facing great pressures in terms of cultural assimilation and the loss of political sovereignty; the other small states of Europe will face them too. The long-standing anxiousness among many Slovene intellectuals and political leaders about the domestic and international status of the Slovene language may be able to serve as a mirror for many of the challenges of the near future. "Die wahre Heimat ist eigentlich die Sprache," wrote Humboldt. Although layered, nested, and constructed identities may be the order of the day in the twenty-first century, it is doubtful whether the replacement of the nation-state model, bloodied and hierarchical and exclusive as it may be, by a standardized, continental (or globalized), Washington- or Brussels-directed consumer identity should be heralded as progress. European cultures, perhaps especially those of Central Europe, would seem to occupy a vanguard position in the development of post-nationalist identities that are neither completely denatured nor entirely solipsistic.

It is remarkable how closely many of these thoughts hew to the idea expressed nearly a hundred years ago by the great Slovene writer Ivan Cankar, who proclaimed: "Only those peoples are useful to universal humanity who are satisfied and who enjoy the circumstances and space to develop all of their vigor."[11]

Notes

Preface

1 Derek Sayer, *The Coasts of Bohemia: A Czech History* (Princeton: Princeton University Press, 1998).
2 Drago Jančar, "Madžari okupirajo Maribor," in *Sproti: eseji in članki* (Trst: Založništvo Tržaškega Tiska, 1984), pp. 163–167.
3 *Radio Free Europe/Radio Liberty (RFE/RL) Newsline*, (March 28, 2003) 7: 60.
4 *RFE/RL Newsline* (February 9, 2004) 8: 25.

1 The Slovene lands and people to 1918

1 "Slovenski kmečki upori," in *Enciklopedija Slovenije* (Ljubljana: Mladinska Knjiga, 1987–2002). Volume 12, p. 46.
2 Henry R. Cooper, Jr, "Primož Trubar and Slovene Literature of the 16th Century," in *Slovene Studies* (1985), 7/1–2, p. 35.
3 "Primož Trubar," in *Enciklopedija Slovenije* (Ljubljana: Mladinska Knjiga, 1987–2002). Volume 13, p. 374.
4 "Janez Vajkard Valvasor," in *Enciklopedija Slovenije* (Ljubljana: Mladinska Knjiga, 1987–2002). Volume 14, p. 134.
5 A.J.P. Taylor, *The Habsburg Monarchy, 1809–1918. A History of the Austrian Empire and Austria–Hungary* (Chicago: University of Chicago Press, 1976), pp. 127–128 and 202.
6 Ibid., p. 203.
7 Thanks to Prof. Timothy Pogacar of Bowling Green State University for supplying the text of this poem.
8 Henry R. Cooper, Jr, "Afterword" to *France Prešeren: Poems/Pesmi*, sel. and ed. by France Pibernik and Franc Drolc (Klagenfurt: Hermagoras-Verlag, 1999), pp. 175–176.
9 Louis Adamič, *The Eagle and the Roots* (Garden City, NY: Doubleday and Co., 1952), p. 163.
10 Henry R. Cooper, Jr, *France Prešeren* (Boston: Twayne, 1981), p. 59.
11 Cooper, ibid., p. 65.
12 "Josip Jelačić an Miklošič aus Wien, 25. Oktober 1853," in Katja Sturm-Schnabl, ed., *Der Briefwechsel Franz Miklošič's mit den Südslaven* (Maribor: Založba Obzorja, 1991), Letter 33, p. 98.
13 C.A. Macartney, *The House of Austria. The Later Phase, 1790–1918* (Edinburgh: Edinburgh University Press, 1978), p. 153.
14 Arthur May, *The Hapsburg Monarchy, 1867–1914* (Cambridge, MA: Harvard University Press, 1951), p. 29.
15 May, ibid., pp. 47–48.

16 May, ibid., pp. 218–219.

17 Taylor, *op. cit.*, pp. 171–172.

18 Leopoldina Plut-Pregelj and Carole Rogel, "Neo-Illyrism," in *Historical Dictionary of Slovenia* (Lanham, MD: Scarecrow Press, 1996), p. 201.

19 Quoted in Marija Mitrovic, *Geschichte der slowenischen Literatur: Von den Anfangen bis zur Gegenwart*, transl. Katja Sturm-Schnabl (Klagenfurt: Mohorjeva, 2001), p. 218. Many Slovene writers have indeed written on themes of resistance to the Turks, including the Protestant reformers, Josip Jurčič, and Anton Aškerc. It is also interesting to note the recent popular historical interest in Slovenes and war, perhaps occasioned by their well-organized, if small-scale, military success in breaking away from Yugoslavia in 1991; pride in the secession is matched perhaps by a desire to recast the Slovene reputation as something other than bookish, punctual, and frugal. In the 1990s, several historical works were published in Slovenia about Slovenes abroad and in military roles. See also the excellent short story and novel by today's leading figure in Slovene literature, Drago Jančar, "Prikazen iz Rovenske" (1998; The Apparition at Rovenska) and his novel *Galjot* (1978; The Galley Slave).

20 "Duma," transl. by Henry R. Cooper, Jr, in *Slovene Studies* (1986), 8/2, p. 90.

21 Ibid., p. 93.

22 It is easy to forget that the adoption of the goals or tactics of socialism often had, historically speaking, nothing to do with a desire to align oneself or one's country with the Soviet Union. The appeal of socialism as a strategy for social modernization is readily evident, for instance, in Milovan Djilas's *Land Without Justice*, just as its futuristic artistic energy is attested by Aleksander Wat in his *My Century*. One need also consider communist parties' early stances on fighting racism and fascism, and also the tactics of nation-building and anti-imperialism in the developing world after 1945, in order to understand fully how powerful the appeal of socialism was. The works of another writer treated in this article, Louis Adamič, offer yet another permutation on this theme. Paradoxically, the left-leaning Adamič came to eschew socialism in "individualistic" America but gave increasing support to the communist movement in Yugoslavia. He viewed violent revolution as the only likely way out of Yugoslavia's pre-World War II national and class contradictions. See Irena Milanič, "Louis Adamič as Viewed by Slovene-American Writer Mary Jugg Molek," in *Slovene Studies* (1997), 19/1–2, p. 111.

23 Ivan Cankar, "Wie ich zum Sozialisten wurde," in *Vor dem Ziel: Literarische Skizzen aus Wien*, transl. by Erwin Kostler (Klagenfurt: Drava, 1994), p. 35.

24 Ivan Cankar, "Slovenci in Jugoslovani," in Boris Ziherl, *Ivan Cankar in naš čas* (Ljubljana: Cankarjeva Založba, 1976), p. 181.

25 Ibid., pp. 186 and 189.

26 May, *op. cit.*, p. 390.

27 Carole Rogel, *The Slovenes and Yugoslavism* (Boulder: East European Monographs, 1977), p. 64.

28 Vlasta Jalušič, "Women in Interwar Slovenia," in Sabrina P. Ramet, *Gender Politics in the Western Balkans* (University Park, PA: Pennsylvania State University Press, 1999), pp. 51–66.

29 Taylor, *op. cit.*, p. 238.

30 Robert A. Kann, *A History of the Habsburg Empire, 1526–1918* (Berkeley: University of California Press), pp. 514–515.

31 John R. Schindler, *Isonzo: The Forgotten Sacrifice of the Great War* (Westport, CT: Praeger, 2001), p. 52.

32 Ibid., p. 47.

33 See also the article "Slovenski književniki in 1. svetovna vojna" by Ivan Vogrič in *Zgodovinski časopis* (2000), 54/2, pp. 197–232. The following are other fairly

recent novels on the subject of the Great War: Andrej Capuder, *Rapsodija 20*; Miloš Mekeln, *Veliki voz*; Kajetan Kovič, *Pot v Trento*, Makso Šnuderl, *Izgubljena zemlja*; and Miran Jarc, *Novo mesto.*

2   Slovenia in the two Yugoslav states

1 John R. Lampe, *Yugoslavia as History: Twice There Was a Country* (New York: Cambridge University Press, 1996), p. 130.
2 Fred Singleton, *A Short History of the Yugoslav Peoples* (New York: Cambridge University Press, 1985), p. 135.
3 Ibid., p. 137.
4 Borih Jesih, "Parties, Elections, and the Slovene Minority in Austria," in Karl Cordell, ed., *Ethnicity and Democratisation in the New Europe* (New York: Routledge, 1999), pp. 106–116.
5 Singleton, *op. cit.*, p. 131.
6 Joseph Rothschild, *East Central Europe Between the Two World Wars* (Seattle: University of Washington Press, 1983), p. 279.
7 Ibid., p. 208.
8 Leften S. Stavrianos, *The Balkans Since 1453* (New York, 1958), p. 634. See also Jozo Tomasevich, *Peasants, Politics, and Economic Change in Yugoslavia* (Stanford: Stanford University Press, 1955).
9 Srečko Kosovel, *Integrals*, transl. by Nike Kocijančič Pokorn, Katarina Jerin and Philip Burt, *Litterae Slovenicae* (1998), XXXVI: 2, pp. 76–77.
10 Ibid., p. 97.
11 In the edition from footnote 9 above, Kosovel refers, for instance, to a "corporal [who] terrorises" (p. 59), such as Hitler, and he inveighs against "Europe/ and the League of Nations,/ shiny spears/ and gas warfare," (93) possible foreshadowings of the Italian invasion of Abyssinia in 1935. In the poem "Presentiment of the Future," Kosovel even hints at the famous debate about the value of poetry after Auschwitz: "Rhymes have lost their value./ Rhymes do not convince./ ... Whither with your phrases, dear orator?/ Pack them off into a museum./ ... Everything has lots its value./ ... A foreboding of the future draws alongside us." See "Reime," in *Gedichte. Slowenisch-Deutsch*, transl. Ludwig Hartinger (Klagenfurt: Wieser, 1992), s.p.
12 Louis Adamič, *The Native's Return: An American Immigrant Visits Yugoslavia and Discovers His Old Country* (New York: Harper and Brothers, 1934), p. 31.
13 Ibid., p. 31.
14 See discussion in Jerneja Petrič, "Louis Adamič and Slovene Identity," in *Slovene Studies* (1997), 19/1–2, pp. 121–130.
15 Edvard Kardelj, *Razvoj slovenskega narodnega vprašanja* (Ljubljana: DZS, 1970), p. 128.
16 See the forthcoming work by Peter Vodopivec, *Zgodovina Slovenije.*
17 See Edvard Kocbek, "Srednja Evropa," in *Dejanje: Revija za kulturo, gospodarstvo, in politiko* (1940), Volume III, pp. 89–92. See also Peter Vodopivec, "O Kocbekovem prispevku k razpravi o Srednji Evropi," in *Glasnik slovenske matice* (1990), pp. 60–62.
18 See "Dolomitska izjava," in *Slovenska kronika XX. stoletja, 1941–1995* (Ljubljana: Nova Revija, 1996), p. 49.
19 Michael Biggins, "Edvard Kocbek," in Vasa D. Mihailovich, ed., *South Slavic Writers Since World War II* (Detroit: Gale Research, 1997), pp. 79–80.
20 See "Kmetova pesem" (The Peasant's Poem) by Karel Destovnik-Kajuh, *Zbrano Delo: Pesmi* (Ljubljana: Borec, 1966), p. 202; and "Nečisti čas" (Unclean Times) by France Balantič, *Muževna steblika* (Ljubljana: Državna Založba Slovenije, 1984), p. 83.

21 Destovnik-Kajuh, *op. cit.*, p. 202.

22 Ibid., p. 203.

23 See, for example, Will Bartlett, "Communism in Yugoslavia and Albania," in Patrick Heenan and Monique Lamontagne, eds, *The Central and East European Handbook: Prospects onto the 21st Century* (Chicago: Glenlake Publishing, 2000), pp. 80–91. Also John K. Cox, *The History of Serbia* (Westport, CT: Greenwood, 2002), pp. 101–125.

24 Ivo Banac, *With Stalin Against Tito: Cominformist Splits in Yugoslav Communism* (Ithaca: Cornell University Press, 1988), pp. 186–187. Also Leopoldina Plut-Pregelj and Carole Rogel, "Purges, Anti-Cominformist," in *Historical Dictionary of Slovenia* (Lanham, MD: Scarecrow Press, 1996), pp. 228–229.

25 See James Gow and Cathie Carmichael, *Slovenia and the Slovenes: A Small State and the New Europe* (Bloomington: Indiana University Press, 2000), pp. 55–60.

26 Singleton, *op. cit.*, p. 261.

27 For another example of expanded Slovene horizons, see also Mate Dolenc, "The Role of My Boots in the Angolan Revolution," transl. by John K. Cox, in *Slovene Studies* (2001), 23/1–2, pp. 49–71. See also Evald Flisar, *Tales of Wandering*, transl. by the author and Alan McConnell-Duff (Norman, OK: Texture Press, 2001).

28 Plut-Pregelj and Rogel, *op. cit.*, p. 188.

29 Michael Biggins and Janet Crayne, eds, *Publishing in Yugoslavia's Successor States* (Binghamton, NY: Haworth Information Press, 2000), Biggins, "Publishing in Slovenia," p. 10.

30 Tomaž Mastnak in Jim Seroka and Vukašin Pavlović, *The Tragedy of Yugoslavia: The Failure of Democratic Transformation* (Armonk, NY: M.E. Sharpe, 1992), p. 49.

31 Ibid., p. 63.

32 Slavoj Žižek, *Druga smrt Josipa Broza Tita* (Ljubljana: DZS, 1989), p. 115.

33 Singleton, *op. cit.*, p. 270.

34 Gow and Carmichael, *op. cit.*, p. 108.

35 Žarko Lazarevič, "Economic History of Twentieth-century Slovenia," in Jill Benderly and Evan Kraft, eds, *Independent Slovenia: Origins, Movements, Prospects* (New York: St Martin's, 1996), p. 58.

36 Dijana Pleština, *Regional Development in Communist Yugoslavia: Success, Failure, and Consequences* (Boulder: Westview Press, 1992), pp. 180–181.

37 Gow and Carmichael, *op. cit.*, p. 108.

3 Slovenia and the break-up of Yugoslavia

1 Gregor Tomc, "The Politics of Punk," in Jill Benderly and Evan Kraft, eds, *Independent Slovenia: Origins, Movements, Prospects* (New York: St Martin's, 1996), p. 115.

2 For a discussion of Laibach, see Marina Gržinić, "Neue Slowenische Kunst (NSK): The Art Groups Laibach, IRWIN, and Noordung Cosmokinetical Theater Cabinet – New Strategies in the Nineties," in *Slovene Studies* (1993), 15/1–2, (published 1995), pp. 5–16. See also James Gow and Cathie Carmichael, *Slovenia and the Slovenes: A Small State and the New Europe* (Bloomington: Indiana University Press, 2000) and Brian J. Požun, *Shedding the Balkan Skin* (e-book available at www.ce-review.org). Laibach's web sites are www.laibach.nsk.si and www.nskstate.com. For further information on various NSK projects, see www.ljudmila.org/embassy/.

3 Christopher Bennett, *Yugoslavia's Bloody Collapse: Causes, Course and Consequences* (New York: New York University Press, 1995), p. 102.

4 Gojko Vuckovic, *Ethnic Cleavages and Conflict: The Sources of National Cohesion and Disintegration* (Brookfield, VT: Ashgate, 1997), p. 117.

5 Quoted in ibid., p. 120.
6 See Dejan Jović, "Yugoslavism and Yugoslav Communism: From Tito to Kardelj," in Dejan Djokić, ed., *Yugoslavism: Histories of a Failed Idea, 1918–1992* (Madison: University of Wisconsin Press, 2003), pp. 157–181.
7 For an excellent summary of late twentieth-century Serbian political culture, see Veljko Vujacic, "One Hypothesis on the Different Outcomes of Soviet and Yugoslav State Collapse," in *East European Studies, the bulletin of the Woodrow Wilson International Center for Scholars*, September–October 2003, pp. 7–8. See also Tim Judah's *The Serbs* (New Haven: Yale University Press, 1997) and Eric Gordy's *The Culture of Power in Serbia* (University Park, PA: Pennsylvania State University Press, 1999).
8 Quoted in Lenard J. Cohen, *Broken Bonds: The Disintegration of Yugoslavia* (Boulder: Westview, 1993), p. 62.
9 Viktor Meier, *Yugoslavia: A History of Its Demise*, transl. by Sabrina Ramet (New York: Routledge, 1999), p. 149.
10 Gow and Carmichael, *op. cit.*, pp. 176–177.
11 James Gow, *Triumph of the Lack of Will: International Diplomacy and the Yugoslav War* (New York: Columbia University Press, 1997), p. 4.
12 Peter Demetz, *After the Fires: Recent Writing in the Germanies, Austria, and Switzerland* (San Diego: Harcourt Brace Jovanovich, 1992), p. 214.
13 Moray McGowan, "German Writing in the West (1945–1992)," in Helen Watanabe-O'Kelley, ed., *The Cambridge History of German Literature* (New York: Cambridge University Press, 1997), p. 483.
14 William H. Gass, *Tests of Time: Essays* (New York: Knopf, 2002), p. 70.
15 Peter Handke, *A Journey to the Rivers* (NY: Viking, 1997), p. viii.
16 Ibid., p. 27.
17 Peter Handke, *Abschied des Träumers vom Neunten Land. Eine Wirklichkeit, die vergangen ist: Erinnerung an Slowenien* (Frankfurt: Suhrkamp, 1991), p. 7.
18 Peter Handke, *Unter Tränen fragend. Nachträgliche Aufzeichnungen von zwei Jugoslawien-Durchquerungen im Krieg. März und April 1999* (Frankfurt: Suhrkamp, 2000), p. 137.
19 Ibid., p. 118.
20 See "Interview with Alain Finkielkraut," in Niko Grafenauer, ed., *The Case of Slovenia* (Ljubljana: Nova Revija, 1991), pp. 37–40.
21 Alain Finkielkraut, *Dispatches from the Balkan War and Other Writings*, transl. by Peter S. Rogers and Richard Golsan (Lincoln: University of Nebraska Press, 1999), p. 39.
22 Ibid., p. 26.
23 Ibid., p. 52.
24 Ibid., p. 105.
25 Ibid., p. 5.
26 Ibid., p. 143.
27 Ibid., p. 32.
28 Ibid., p. 129. Almost as if to prove the point, all three of the Serbo-Croatian city names given above are misspelled in the English translation.
29 George W. Hoffman and Fred Warner Neal, *Yugoslavia and the New Communism* (New York: Twentieth Century Fund, 1962), pp. 74–75.
30 Fitzroy Maclean, *Eastern Approaches* (New York: Time, 1964), p. 326.
31 Stane Kavčič, *Dnevnik in spomini* (Ljubljana: Časopis za kritiko znanosti, 1988), p. 532.
32 Edmund Wilson used a similar phrase, "the great headmaster," in analyzing Lenin's life and work in his study *To the Finland Station: A Study in the Writing and Acting of History* (New York: Doubleday, 1953), p. 436. One can make instructive comparisons between Kardelj and Lenin. But analysis of the differences

between the bookish, theory-driven Kardelj and Tito as the more active Yugoslav military and diplomatic figure are more instructive in the Yugoslav case.

33 Here "liberal" – in its East European context – denotes greater freedom from capricious or administrative rule, less central authority in politics and economics, some type of pluralism either in the selection or criticism of office-holders, and a degree of profit motive in economic affairs.

34 The mission was to serve the interests of the greater socialist whole, but it nonetheless embraced the national idea as useful for the propagation of anti-hegemonial relations and unity.

35 France Bučar, *The Reality and the Myth*, transl. by Rudolf Čuješ (Antigonish, Nova Scotia: Francis Xavier University Press, 1989), pp. 117–118.

36 Ibid., pp. 177–178.

37 Ibid., p. 295.

38 Ibid., p. 322.

39 Edvard Kocbek, "Who Am I?" in *Edvard Kocbek (Litterae Slovenicae/Slovenian Literary Magazine*, vol. XXXIII, 1995: 2, p. 86), transl. by Michael Biggins.

40 Edvard Kocbek, "In a Torched Village," in *Embers in the House of Night. Selected Poems of Edvard Kocbek*, transl. by Sonja Kravanja (Santa Fe: Lumen Books, 1999), p. 54.

41 Michael Biggins, "Edvard Kocbek," in Vasa Mihailovich, ed., *South Slavic Writers Since World War II* (*Dictionary of Literary Biography*, vol. 147), (Detroit: Gale Research, 1997), p. 80.

42 Thomas Eekman, *Yugoslav Literature (1945–1975)*, (Ann Arbor: Michigan Slavic Publications, 1978), p. 143.

43 Michael Biggins, "Edvard Kocbek," in Mihailovich, *op. cit.*, p. 82.

44 Marjan Drnovšek, France Rozman, and Peter Vodopivec, eds, *Slovenska kronika XX stoletja, 1900–1941* (Ljubljana: Nova Revija, 1995), p. 392.

45 Michael Biggins, "Edvard Kocbek," in Mihailovich, *op. cit.*, p. 81.

46 Marjan Drnovšek, France Rozman, and Peter Vodopivec, eds, *Slovenska kronika XX stoletja, 1941–1995* (Ljubljana: Nova Revija, 1996), p. 22.

47 Ibid., p. 49.

48 Ibid., p. 123.

49 Ibid., p. 74.

50 Edvard Kocbek, "Smuggling," in *Edvard Kocbek (Litterae Slovenicae/Slovenian Literary Magazine*, vol. XXXIII, 1995: 2, p. 66), transl. by Michael Biggins.

51 Ivan Cesar, "Od rane proze Edvarda Kocbeka do *Straha i hrabrosti*," in *Strah i hrabrost: četiri novele* (Zagreb: Globus, 1985), p. 6.

52 Josip Vidmar, *O slovenstvu i jugoslavenstvu: izbor iz radova*, ed. Josip Šentilja and transl. from Slovene into Croatian by Kamilo Burger *et al.* (Zagreb: Globus, 1986), p. 235.

53 Ibid., p. 320.

54 Ibid., p. 466.

55 Ibid., p. 341.

56 Ibid., p. 320.

57 Ibid., p. 341.

58 France Bernik and Marjan Dolgan, *Slovenska vojna proza* (Ljubljana: Slovenska matica, 1988), p. 335. This passage was in English in the original.

59 Edvard Kocbek, "Premišljevanje o Španiji," in *Svoboda in nujnost: pričevanja*. Second, revised edition (Celje: Mohorjeva, 1989), p. 45.

60 Ibid.

61 Edvard Kocbek, "The Lippizzaners," in *Embers in the House of Night. Selected Poems of Edvard Kocbek*, transl. by Sonja Kravanja (Santa Fe: Lumen Books, 1999), p. 16.

62 Edvard Kocbek, "Slovene Hymn," in *Edvard Kocbek (Litterae Slovenicae/Slovenian Literary Magazine*, vol. XXXIII, 1995: 2, p. 38), transl. by Michael Biggins.

63 Danilo Kiš, "The Gingerbread Heart, or Nationalism," in Susan Sontag, ed., *Homo Poeticus: Essays and Interviews* (New York: Farrar Straus Giroux, 1995), p. 18.
64 Josip Vidmar, *op. cit.*, p. 341.
65 Michael Biggins, "Edvard Kocbek," in Mihailovich, *op. cit.*, p. 79.
66 Ibid., p. 86.
67 Ibid., p. 80.

4 Independent Slovenia: politics, culture, and society

1 The old Yugoslav term for parliament, *Skupščina* in its Slovene variant, has fallen into disuse. Today the word *Parlament* in Slovene typically refers to the *Državni zbor*, though technically the *Državni svet* is also subsumed under that designation.
2 Donald Reindl, "Slovenia: Making Way for Women," in *Balkan Report*, (March 5, 2004) 8: 9. Available online at the Radio Free Europe web site (www.rferl.org).
3 James Gow and Cathie Carmichael, *Slovenia and the Slovenes: A Small State and the New Europe* (Bloomington: Indiana University Press, 2000), p. 147.
4 See, for instance, comments by Slovene sociologist Rudolf Rizman in Jolyon Naegele, "Political Extremism in Eastern Europe: On the Wane or Going Mainstream?" *(Un)Civil Societies* (15 May, 2002) 3: 20. Available online at the Radio Free Europe web site (www.rferl.org).
5 By comparison, one should remember that after parliamentary elections in 1996 it took the LDS well over three months to form a coalition government. At that time accusations flew that the rudderless condition of the ship of state had slowed Slovenia's march into NATO.
6 Lea Plut-Pregelj and Carole Rogel, *Historical Dictionary of Slovenia* (Lanham, MD: Scarecrow Press, 1996), p. 186.
7 See www.nationalitiescouncil.org/sister_piran.html. The five groups are the local branches of the SNPJ and KSKJ, as well as the Slovenian Women's Union of America, the Slovenian National Home, and the Slovenian Cultural Society.
8 See Donald Reindl, "The Mixed Feelings of Slovenian Emigrants," *Balkan Report* (July 11, 2003) 7: 21.
9 One of the other most prominent aspects of traditional Slovene culture still in evidence is the drying frame for hay, grains, and other agricultural products known as the *kozolec*. See Marjan Mušič, *Arhitektura slovenskega kozolca/The Architecture of the Slovene Kozolec* (Ljubljana: Cankarjeva založba, 1970). For other intriguing examples of Slovene vernacular architecture, see Plut-Pregelj and Rogel, *op. cit.*, pp. 18–20. For a study of decorated bee-hives, see Claude Rivals, *L'Art et l'abeille: ruches décorées en Slovénie: essai de l'iconologie populaire* (Paris: Etudes et communication, 1999).
10 See Donald Reindl, "St. Nick, Santa, and Father Frost Duke It Out in Slovenia," *Balkan Report* (December 19, 2003) 7: 41.
11 See Donald Reindl, "Slovenia Says Sunday is Special," *Balkan Report* (October 3, 2003) 7: 33.
12 Marija Mitrović, *Geschichte der slowenischen Literatur: Von den Anfängen bis zur Gegenwart*, transl. by Katja Sturm-Schnabl (Klagenfurt: Mohorjeva, 2001), p. 529.
13 Karl-Markus Gauß, *Die Vernichtung Mitteleuropas* (Klagenfurt: Wieser, 1991), p. 136.
14 Ibid., p. 150.
15 See *Balkan Report* (November 30, 2001) 5: 79.
16 Information on many other publications, selection tools for librarians, and online catalogs can be found in Michael Biggins and Janet Crayne, eds, *Publishing in Yugoslavia's Successor States* (New York: Haworth, 2000).
17 See Rebecca Mead, "The Marx Brother: How a Philosopher from Slovenia Became an International Star," *The New Yorker*, May 5, 2003, pp. 38–47.

18 *Radio Free Europe/Radio Liberty Newsline* (January 10, 2001) 5: 6.
19 Brian Pozun, "Siddharta: Aiming at the World," in *Ljubljana Life* (September 2003). Available at http://www.geocities.com/ljubljanalife/Siddharta.htm. See also www.siddharta.net.
20 Brian Pozun, "Slovenia," in Freedom House's *Nations in Transit* (2002), p. 363. Available online at http://www.freedomhouse.org/research/nattransit.htm.
21 See sociologist Rudi Rizman's discussion of "zones of uncertainty" in Slovene political life in "Slovenia's Path Towards Democratic Consolidation (Part B)," *East European Perspectives* (May 30, 2001) 3: 10.
22 Quoted in Donald Reindl, "Slovenia and Its World War II Legacy," *Balkan Report* (January 18, 2002) 6: 5.
23 This author recalls querying several librarians in Slovenia in 1991 and 1992 about the future of the numerous volumes on their shelves by communist luminaries such as Kardelj. One very telling answer came from a librarian in Prekmurje, whose answer was, paraphrased, "We will keep them, because they are part of our history; but we will only keep one copy of each, not the many mandatory duplicates we had before."
24 Gojko Berić, "Did We Exist?" from *Letters to the Celestial Serbs*, transl. by Saba Risaluddin (London: Saqi Books and the Bosnian Institute, 2002), p. 22.
25 "Slovenes Restoring Rights," *New York Times*, February 4, 2004, online version.

5 Independent Slovenia: economics and foreign policy

1 Naturally enough for a topic this important, there is a genuine plethora of definitions of democracy available to the interested student. One way of conceptualizing democracy, based on the work of Adam Przeworski, is used by Valerie A. Bunce and applied to Slovenia and other states in her article "The Political Economy of Postsocialism," in *Slavic Review* (Winter 1999) 58: 4, pp. 756–793. She proposes that democracy is a "system of governance that combines freedom, uncertain results, and certain procedures" (p. 773). Freedom here includes both human rights and political representation, and "procedural certainty" refers among other things to the rule of law. The most intriguing aspect of this definition is embodied in the notion of "uncertain results," signifying competition and the accountability of the parties and government to the will of the people.
2 See, for instance, "Overview: Slovenia's Threefold Transition," in Mojmir Mrak, Matija Rojec, and Carlos Silva-Jáuregui, eds, *Slovenia: From Yugoslavia to the European Union* (Washington: The World Bank, 2004), pp. xix–lvi. See also Philip G. Roeder, "The Revolution of 1989: Postcommunism and the Social Sciences," in *Slavic Review* (Winter 1999) 58: 4, pp. 743–755.
3 See Valerie Bunce, *Subversive Institutions: The Design and Destruction of Socialism and the State* (New York: Cambridge University Press, 1999); Renée De Nevers, *Comrades No More: The Seeds of Change in Eastern Europe* (Cambridge, MA: MIT Press, 2003); John Feffer, *Shock Waves: Eastern Europe after the Revolutions* (Cambridge, MA: South End Press, 1992); Bela Greskovits, *The Political Economy of Protest and Patience* (Budapest: Central European University Press, 1998); Samuel Huntington, *The Third Wave: Democratization in the Late Twentieth Century* (Norman, OK: University of Oklahoma Press, 1991); Juan Linz and Alfred Stepan, *Problems of Democratic Transition and Consolidation: Southern Europe, South America, and Post-Communist Europe* (Baltimore: Johns Hopkins University Press, 1996); Adam Przeworski, *Democracy and the Market: Political and Economic Reforms in Eastern Europe and Latin America* (New York: Cambridge University Press, 1991); Vladimir Tismaneanu, *Fantasies of Salvation: Democracy, Nationalism and Myth in Post-Communist Europe* (Princeton: Princeton University Press, 1998). Useful works on the revolutions of 1989 themselves include Padraic Kennedy, *A Carnival of Revolution: Central Europe, 1989*

(Princeton: Princeton University Press, 2002); Ralf Dahrendorf, *Reflections on the Revolution in Europe* (New York: Random House, 1990); Gale Stokes, *The Walls Came Tumbling Down: The Collapse of Communism in Eastern Europe* (New York: Oxford University Press, 1993); and Timothy Garton Ash, *The Magic Lantern: The Revolution of '89 Witnessed in Warsaw, Budapest, Berlin and Prague* (New York: Vintage, 1993). For information-rich essays on individual European countries, see the many works by J.F. Brown and the four-volume series edited by Karen Dawisha and Bruce Parrott entitled *Democratization and Authoritarianism in Postcommunist Societies*. Especially useful for observers of Slovenia are the volumes *Politics, Power, and the Struggle for Democracy in South-East Europe* and *The Consolidation of Democracy in East-Central Europe* (both from Cambridge University Press, 1997). Several scholarly presses have brought out large lists of books on transitology, and the interest in transition studies on the part of academics and practitioners in government, economics, and the NGO sector has been so great that it has even led to the launch of new presses and journals.

4 See Mrak, Rojec and Silva-Jauregai, *op. cit.*, p. xxiii.

5 Robert Skidelsky, *The Road from Serfdom: The Economic and Political Consequences of the End of Communism* (New York: Penguin, 1995), p. 165.

6 A perennial simplification of these two systems has it that capitalist liberal democracy offers people equality of *opportunity* while the communist leviathan – both a political and economic system – tries by hook or crook to engineer an equality of *results*. A more useful historical characterization is that the first system strives to offer citizens formal legal equality, with all of its virtues and limitations, and to contain social conflict, while the second system, in the theory of its non-Stalinist variants, attempts to increase the public's access to educational, health, economic, and other resources while eliminating social conflict.

7 Interested readers can consult the various reports published by the Eurostat office of the European Union, the Organization for European Cooperation and Development (OECD), the European Bank for Reconstruction and Development (EBRD), the International Monetary Fund, and the World Bank, as well as the Economist Intelligence Unit's Country Profiles. See also the many relevant sections of James Gow and Cathie Carmichael, *Slovenia and the Slovenes: A Small State and the New Europe* (Bloomington: Indiana University Press, 2000); Leopoldina Plut-Pregelj and Carole Rogel, *Historical Dictionary of Slovenia* (Lanham, MD: Scarecrow, 1996); Bogomil Ferfila and Paul Phillips, *Slovenia: On the Edge of the European Union* (Lanham, MD: University Press of America, 2000); Danica Fink-Hafner and John R. Robbins, eds, *Making a New Nation: The Formation of Slovenia* (Brookfield, VT: Dartmouth Publishing, 1997); Jill Benderly and Evan Kraft, eds, *Independent Slovenia: Origins, Movements, Prospects* (New York: St Martin's, 1996); and Mrak *et al.*, *op. cit.*

8 See Skidelsky, *op. cit.*, p. 170 for a discussion of capitalism's "core institutions" and of the important Harvard economist Jeffrey Sachs's views on shock therapy. How did countries in transition know where to begin? Advice from Western governments and academics and international lending institutions began the discussion of restructuring priorities. According to Skidelsky, the capitalist minimum comprises "stable, convertible national currencies; freedom of international trade and foreign investment; private property rights; private ownership; corporate control of large enterprises; and a social safety net."

9 Plut-Pregelj and Rogel, *op. cit.*, p. 225.

10 Evan Kraft, Milan Vodopivec, and Milan Cvikl, "On Its Own: The Economy of Independent Slovenia," in Benderly and Kraft, *op. cit.*, p. 220.

11 See the report on the comments of Jean Lemierre, President of the European Bank for Reconstruction and Development, of March 7, 2002. In "European Bank Singles Out Slovenia for Praise," *RFE/RL Newsline* (March 8, 2002) 6: 45.

12 Plut-Pregelj and Rogel, *op. cit.*, p. 85.
13 Andrew H. Dawson, "Agriculture," in Patrick Heenan and Monique Lamontagne, eds, *The Central and East European Handbook: Prospects onto the 21st Century* (Chicago: Glenlake, 2000), p. 145.
14 Ferfila, *op. cit.*, p. 152.
15 Brian Pozun, *Nations in Transit* (New York: Freedom House, 2002), p. 371.
16 See http://hdr.undp.org.
17 This process, involving recognition of foreign educational credentials, is called *nostrifikacija* in Slovene. It is the subject of Donald Reindl's report "Sclerotic Labor Market Burdens Slovenia," in Radio Free Europe's *Balkan Report* (November 14, 2003) 7: 37, available at www.rferl.org.
18 Gow and Carmichael, *op. cit.*, p. 125.
19 Janez Šušteršič, "Political Economy of Slovenia's Transition," in Mrak *et al.*, *op. cit.*, p. 406.
20 See Reindl, ibid.
21 See comments of Predrag Simić in Patrick Moore, "At the Back of Europe's Bus," *Balkan Report* (June 14, 2002) 6: 22.
22 See Donald Reindl, "Slovenes Assess Pros and Cons of EU Membership," *Balkan Report* (January 10, 2003) 7: 1; and "Slovenes Weigh Up EU Pros and Cons," *Balkan Report* (August 8, 2003) 7: 25.
23 See Gow and Carmichael, *op. cit.*, pp. 191–202.
24 NATO was formed at the start of the Cold War in 1949 by the North Atlantic Treaty. Its chief goal was to prevent a communist take-over of Western Europe. The original members were Belgium, Canada, Denmark, France, Iceland, Italy, Luxembourg, the Netherlands, Norway, Portugal, the UK, and the US. New members were added later: Greece and Turkey (1952), West Germany (1955), and Spain (1982). In effect, the former East Germany became a member too in 1990 when the reunification of Germany occurred.
25 Samuel Charap, "NATO Expansion: Changing the Debate," *RFE/RL Newsline* (January 9, 2002) 7: 5.
26 See Stephen F. Szabo, "After Prague: American Views of the New NATO," *East European Perspectives* (December 4, 2002) 4: 24.
27 See *RFE/RL Newsline* (February 1, 2002) 6: 21.
28 See *RFE/RL Newsline* (January 16, 2002) 6: 10, and ff.
29 *Balkan Report* (July 19, 2002) 6: 26.
30 *Balkan Report* (August 29, 2000) 4: 65.
31 *RFE/RL Newsline* (May 17, 2001) 5: 94.
32 *RFE/RL Newsline* (January 3, 2003) 7: 1.
33 Kate Connolly, "Remember Jorg Haider?" in *The Guardian*, January 29, 2001, available online at: www.guardian.co.uk.
34 See note 22 above.
35 See Valentinas Mite, "Baltic States Coping with Decade-long Decreases in Population," *RFE/RL Newsline* (April 16, 2002) 6: 71.
36 Drago Jančar, "Augsburg," in Joanna Labon, ed., *Balkan Blues: Writing Out of Yugoslavia* (Evanston: Northwestern University Press, 1995), pp. 83–84.
37 Jančar, "Augsburg," p. 84.
38 Jančar, "Augsburg," p. 86.
39 Drago Jančar, "Slovene Exile," in *Nationalities Papers* (Special Issue), ed. Henry R. Huttenbach and Peter Vodopivec, XXXI:1 (Spring, 1993), p. 95.
40 Drago Jančar, "Reflecting on Poland," in *The Slovenian Essay of the Nineties*, selected by Matevž Kos (Ljubljana: Slovene Writers' Association, 2000), p. 143.
41 Ibid.
42 Jančar, "Poland," p. 147.
43 Jančar, "Poland," p. 150.

44 Drago Jančar, "Erinnerungen an Jugoslawien," in *Erinnerungen an Jugoslawien: Essays*, transl. into German by Horst Ogris (Klagenfurt/Celovec: Hermagoras/ Mohorjeva, 1991), p. 11.
45 Jančar, "Erinnerungen," p. 28.
46 Gow and Carmichael, *op. cit.*, pp. 211–214.
47 Sun Yat-sen, *The Three Principles of the People*, abridged from the translation by Frank W. Price (Taipei: China Publishing Company 1981), p. 21. If Sun's idea is examined in modern vocabulary, i.e. "nation" instead of "race," and with a recognition of the historical differences between the Chinese and Slovene experiences, this concept has a certain application to Slovenia.
48 See Anthony D. Smith, *Nationalism and Modernism: A Critical Survey of Recent Theories of Nations and Nationalism* (New York: Routledge, 1998), pp. 1–2, for a reminder of the positive historical legacy of nationalism and thus its potential benefits. These are often ignored by scholars today. On the one hand, this is because of nationalism's indisputable and often outrageous track record of imperialism, exclusion, violence, and patriarchy. Nationalism's credibility, on the other hand, has also been attenuated because it has so often been falsely represented in popular and political literature as an inherently democratic awakening of a people rather than the construction and mobilization of an identity and a political program.
49 Sun Yat-sen, "The Three People's Principles," in William Theodore de Bary, ed., *Sources of Chinese Tradition* (NY: Columbia UP, 1960), pp. 768–769.

6   Conclusion

1 Anthony D. Smith, *Nationalism and Modernism: A Critical Survey of Recent Theories of Nations and Nationalisms* (New York: Routledge, 1998), pp. 193–194.
2 Czeslaw Milosz, "Central European Attitudes," in Ladislav Matejka, ed., *Cross Currents 5: A Yearbook of Central European Culture* (Ann Arbor: University of Michigan, 1986), pp. 101–109.
3 Ibid., p. 107.
4 George Konrád, "Central Europe Redivivus," in *The Melancholy of Rebirth: Essays from Post-Communist Central Europe, 1989–1994* (San Diego: Harcourt Brace and Co., 1995), pp. 156–163.
5 Milan Kundera, "The Tragedy of Central Europe," in *The New York Review of Books*, April 26, 1984, pp. 33–38. Reprinted in Gale Stokes, ed., *From Stalinism to Pluralism: A Documentary History of Eastern Europe Since 1945*, 2nd edition (NY: Oxford University Press, 1996), pp. 217–223.
6 Ibid., p. 221.
7 Edvard Kocbek, "Srednja Evropa," in *Dejanje: Revija za kulturo, gospodarstvo, in politiko* (1940), Volume III, pp. 89–92. See also Peter Vodopivec, "O Kocbekovem prispevku k razpravi o Srednji Evropi," in *Glasnik slovenske matice* (1990), pp. 60–62.
8 Drago Jančar, "Mitteleuropa zwischen Meteorologie und Utopie," in *Erinnerungen an Jugoslawien: Essays*, transl. into German by Peter Wieser (Klagenfurt/Celovec: Hermagoras/Mohorjeva, 1991), p. 57.
9 Drago Jančar, "Die Welt als Gegensatz begreifen. Mitteleuropa – eine Idee von gestern?" in *Brioni und andere Essays*, translated from the Slovene by Klaus Detlef Olof *et al.*, (Wien: Folio, 2002), 24–33, p. 29.
10 Drago Jančar, "Mitteleuropa," p. 64.
11 Ivan Cankar, "Slovenci in jugoslovani," in Boris Ziherl, *Ivan Cankar in naš čas* (Ljubljana: Cankarjeva Založba, 1976), pp. 181–182.

Select bibliography

Allcock, John B. "Aspects of the Development of Capitalism in Yugoslavia: The Role of the State in the Formation of a 'Satellite' Economy," in Francis W. Carter, ed., *An Historical Geography of the Balkans*. London: Academic Press, 1977, pp. 535–580.

Antič, Milica. *Ženske v parlamentu*. Ljubljana: Znanstveno in publicisticno sredisce, 1998.

Arnez, John. *Slovenia in European Affairs: Reflections on Slovenian Political History*. New York: League of CSA, 1958.

Badovinac, Zdenka. *Body and the East: From the 1960s to the Present. Moderna Galerija Ljubljana/Museum of Modern Art*. Cambridge, MA: MIT Press, 1999.

Banac, Ivo. *The National Question in Yugoslavia: Origins, History, Politics*. Ithaca: Cornell University Press, 1984.

Barker, Thomas M. *The Slovene Minority of Carinthia*. Boulder, CO: East European Monographs, 1984.

—— *Social Revolutionaries and Secret Agents: The Carinthian Slovene Partisans and Britain's Special Operations Executive*. Boulder, CO: East European Monographs, 1990.

Bazlen, Bobi. "Interview über Triest," in Karl-Markus Gauss, ed., *Das Buch der Ränder – Prosa*. Klagenfurt: Wieser, 1992, pp. 240–250.

Benderly, Jill and Kraft, Evan. *Independent Slovenia: Origins, Movements, Prospects*. New York: St Martin's, 1994.

Bennett, Christopher. *Yugoslavia's Bloody Collapse: Causes, Course and Consequences*. New York: New York University Press, 1996.

Bernik, France and Dolgan, Marjan. *Slovenska vojna proza*. Ljubljana: Slovenska matica, 1988.

Biggins, Michael. "Edvard Kocbek," in Vasa Mihailovich, ed., *South Slavic Writers Since World War II (Dictionary of Literary Biography*, vol. 147), Detroit, MI: Gale Research, 1997, pp. 79–86.

Biggins, Michael and Crayne, Janet, eds. *Publishing in Yugoslavia's Successor States*. New York: Haworth, 2000.

Bogataj, Janez. *Handicrafts of Slovenia: Encounters with Contemporary Slovene Craftsmen*. Ljubljana: Rokus, 1999.

Bokovoy, Melissa, Irvine, Jill A. and Lilly, Carol S., eds. *State–Society Relations in Yugoslavia, 1945–1992*. New York: St Martin's, 1996.

Bučar, Bojko and Kuhnle, Stein, eds. *Small States Compared: Politics of Norway and Slovenia*. Bergen: Alma Mater, 1994.

Bučar, France. *The Reality and the Myth*. Transl. Rudolf Čuješ. Antigonish: St Francis Xavier University Press, 1989.

—— *Prehod čez rdee morje*. Ljubljana: Mihelac, 1993.

—— "Slovenia in Europe," in Henry R. Huttenbach and Peter Vodopivec, eds, *Voices from the Slovene Nation, 1990–1992*, special issue of *Nationalities Papers*, XXI: 1 (Spring 1993), pp. 33–41.

Budna, Nataša. "Feministično delo splošnega ženskega društva," *Journal for History, Literature, and Anthropology* (1994) 46: 535–537, pp. 1232–1257.

Cankar, Ivan. *Dream Visions and Other Selected Stories*. Translated by Anton Druzina. Willoughby Hills, OH: Slovenian Research Center of America, 1982.

Carmichael, Cathie. *Slovenia* (World Bibliographical Series, v. 186). Santa Barbara, CA: ABC-Clio, 1996.

Cohen, Lenard. *Broken Bonds: Yugoslavia's Disintegration and Balkan Politics in Transition*. 2nd edn. Boulder: Westview Press, 1995.

Cox, John K. *The History of Serbia*. Westport, CT: Greenwood, 2002.

Deak, Istvan. *Beyond Nationalism: A Social and Political History of the Habsburg Officer Corps, 1848–1918*. NY: Oxford University Press, 1990.

Debeljak, Ales. *Twilight of the Idols: Recollections of a Lost Yugoslavia*. Buffalo: White Pine Press, 1994.

Djokić, Dejan, ed. *Yugoslavism: Histories of a Failed Idea, 1918–1992*. Madison, WI: University of Wisconsin Press, 2003.

Dolenc, Ervin. *Kulturni boj: slovenska kulturna politika v Kraljevini SHS 1918–1929*. Ljubljana: Cankarjeva založba, 1996.

Dolenc, Mate. "The Role of My Boots in the Angolan Revolution." Translated by John K. Cox. *Slovene Studies* (2001, published 2003) 23: 1–2, pp. 49–72.

Dolgan, Marjan, ed. *Kriza revije "Dom in Svet" leta 1937: zbornik dokumentov*. Ljubljana: Založba ZRC, 2001.

Dragović-Soso, Jasna. *"Saviours of the Nation": Serbia's Intellectual Opposition and the Revival of Nationalism*. Montreal: McGill-Queen's University Press, 2002.

Duhaček, Daša. "Women's Time in Former Yugoslavia," in Nanette Funk and Magda Mueller, eds, *Gender Politics and Post-Communism: Reflections from Eastern Europe and the Former Soviet Union*. New York: Routledge, 1993.

Duša, Zdravko, ed. *The Veiled Landscape: Slovenian Women Writing*. Ljubljana: Slovenian Office for Women's Policy, 1995.

Dyker, David A. and Vejvoda, Ivan. *Yugoslavia and After: A Study in Fragmentation, Despair, and Rebirth*. New York: Addison-Wesley Longman, 1997.

Englefield, Greg. *Yugoslavia, Croatia, Slovenia: Re-emerging Boundaries*. Durham: University of Durham, 1992.

Fallon, Steve. *Lonely Planet: Slovenia*. Oakland: Lonely Planet Publications, 1998.

Fink-Hafner, Danica and Robbins, John R. *Making a New Nation: The Formation of Slovenia*. Brookfield, VT: Dartmouth Publishing, 1997.

Fischer, Jasna, Lazarevi, Žarko, and Prinčič, Jože. *The Economic History of Slovenia, 1750–1991*. Vrhnika: Razum, 1999.

Glušič, Helga. "Drago Jančar," in Vasa D. Mihailovich, ed., *South Slavic Writers Since World War II* (*Dictionary of Literary Biography*, vol. 181). Detroit, MI: Gale Research, 1997, pp. 84–90.

Gow, James and Carmichael, Cathie. *Slovenia and the Slovenes: A Small State in the New Europe*. Bloomington, IN: Indiana University Press, 2000.

Grafenauer, Niko, ed. *The Case of Slovenia: Writer's Journal Special Edition*. Ljubljana: Nova Revija, 1991.

—— ed. *Jaz, čas in zgodovina: izbor slovenskih avtoportretov*. Ljubljana: Nova Revija, 1999.

Granda, Stane and Šatej, Barbara eds. *Slovenija 1848–1998: iskanje lastne poti*. Ljubljana: Zveza zgodovinskih društev Slovenije, 1998.

Hall, Brian. *The Impossible Country: A Journey Through the Last Days of Yugoslavia.* Boston, MA: David R. Godine, 1994.

Harriman, Helga H. *Slovenia under Nazi Occupation, 1941–1945.* New York: Studia Slovenica, 1977.

Heuberger, Valeria, Riegler, Henriette and Vidovic, Hermine, eds. *At the Crossroads: Disaster or Normalization? The Yugoslav Successor States in the 1990s.* Frankfurt: Peter Lang, 1999.

Hribar, Tine. *Slovenci kot nacija. Soočanja s sodobniki.* Ljubljana: Enotnost, 1995.

Huttenbach, Henry and Vodopivec, Peter, eds. *Voices from the Slovene Nation,* special issue of *Nationality Papers,* XXI: 1 (Spring 1993).

Jančar, Drago. *Mocking Desire.* Translated by Michael Biggins. Evanston, IL: Northwestern University Press, 1998.

—— *Northern Lights.* Translated by Michael Biggins. Evanston, IL: Northwestern University Press, 2000.

Janša, Janez. *Premiki: Nastajanje in obramba slovenske države, 1988–1992.* 2nd edn. Ljubljana: Mladinska knjiga, 1992.

Janša-Zorn, Olga. *Slovenian Historiography in Foreign Languages Published from 1918–1993.* Translated by Cvetka Vode. Ljubljana: Institute of Contemporary History, 1995.

Jelavich, Barbara. *History of the Balkans.* 2 vols. New York: Cambridge University Press, 1983.

Jelavich, Charles. *South Slav Nationalisms: Textbooks and Yugoslav Union Before 1914.* Columbus: Ohio State University Press, 1990.

Jesih, Boris, Klopčič, Vera and Stergar, Janez, *Ethnic Minorities in Slovenia.* 2nd edn. Ljubljana: Institute for Ethnic Studies, 1994.

Jurak, Mirko, ed. *Cross-Cultural Studies. American, Canadian and European Literatures: 1945–1985.* Ljubljana: Edvard Kardelj University of Ljubljana, 1988.

Kann, Robert A., Kiraly, Bela K., and Fichtner, Paula S., eds. *The Habsburg Empire in World War I: Essays on the Intellectual, Military, Political and Economic Aspects of the Habsburg War Effort* (East European Monographs XXIII), New York: East European Quarterly/Columbia University Press, 1977.

Kardelj, Edvard. *Socialism and War: A Survey of the Chinese Criticism of the Policy of Coexistence.* London: Methuen, 1961.

—— *Reminiscences. The Struggle for Recognition and Independence: The New Yugoslavia, 1944–1957.* London: Blond and Briggs, 1982.

Kavčič, Stane. *Dnevnik in spomini (1972–1987).* 3rd edn. Ljubljana: Casopis za kritiko znanosti, 1988.

Lampe, John. *Yugoslavia as History: Twice There Was a Country.* New York: Cambridge University Press, 1996.

Lively, Penelope. "The Slovenian Giantess," in *The Five Thousand and One Nights.* Seattle: Fjord Press, 1997, pp. 20–38.

Lydall, Harold. *Yugoslav Socialism: Theory and Practice.* New York: Oxford University Press, 1984.

—— *Yugoslavia in Crisis.* New York: Oxford University Press, 1989.

Magas, Branka. *The Destruction of Yugoslavia: Tracking the Break-up, 1980–92.* New York: Verso, 1993.

Mastnak, Tomaz. *Vzhodno od raja: civilna druzba pod komunizmom i po njem.* Ljubljana: DZS, 1992.

Milač, Metod. *Resistance, Imprisonment, and Forced Labor: A Slovene Student in World War II.* New York: Peter Lang, 2002.

Miladinovič, Mira and Droschl, Max, eds. *Schnellstrasse, Fernlicht: Orte der Literatur: Ljubljana 1991*. Vienna: Droschl Literaturverlag KEG, s.d.

Mrak, Mojmir, Rojec, Matija, and Silva-Jáuregui, Carlos, eds. *Slovenia: From Yugoslavia to the European Union*. Washington, DC: The World Bank, 2004.

Muser, Erna. "Slovenke do leta 1941," in *Borbeni put žena Jugoslavije*. Beograd: Leksikografski zavod, 1972.

Neuhäuser, Rudolf, Olof, Klaus D., and Glusic, Helga, eds. *Zeichen und Wege: Slowenische Erzaehler der Gegenwart*. Klagenfurt: Drava, 1986.

Olof, Klaus and Okuka, Milos, eds. *Traumreisen und Grenzermessungen: Reisende aus fuenf Jahrhunderten ueber Slowenien*. Klagenfurt: Drava.

Pahor, Boris. *Pilgrim among the Shadows. A Memoir*. Translated by Michael Biggins. New York: Harcourt Brace and Company, 1995.

Pirjevec, Joze. *Jugoslavija 1918–1992: nastanek, razvoj ter razpad Karadjordjeviceve in Titove Jugoslavije*. Koper: Lipa, 1995.

Plut-Pregelj, Leopoldina and Rogel, Carole. *Historical Dictionary of Slovenia*. Lanham, MD: Scarecrow Press, 1996.

Potrč, Ivan. *The Land and the Flesh*. Translated by H. Leeming. London: Peter Owen, 1969.

Požun, Brian J. *Shedding the Balkan Skin: Slovenia's Quiet Emergence in the New Europe*. E-book from Central Europe Review, 2000.

Prisland, Marie. *From Slovenia to America*. Chicago: Slovenia Women's Union of America, 1968.

Prunk, Janko. *Slovenski narodni programi: narodni programi v slovenski politični misli od 1848 do 1945*. 2nd edn. Ljubljana: Društvo 2000, 1987.

—— *A Brief History of Slovenia: Historical Background of the Republic of Slovenia*. Ljubljana: Mihelač, 1994.

Ramet, Sabrina Petra. *Nationalism and Federalism in Yugoslavia, 1963–1983*. Bloomington, IN: Indiana University Press, 1984.

—— ed. *Yugoslavia in the 1980s*. Boulder, CO: Westview Press, 1985.

—— *Balkan Babel: The Disintegration of Yugoslavia from the Death of Tito to the War for Kosovo*. 3rd edn. Boulder, CO: Westview Press, 1999.

Repe, Božo. *"Liberalizem" v Sloveniji*. Ljubljana: Borec, 1992.

Rogel, Carole. *The Slovenes and Yugoslavism, 1890–1914*. Boulder, CO: East European Monographs, 1977.

Rupel, Dimitrij. *Slovenska pot do samostojnosti in priznanja*. Ljubljana: Kres, 1992.

—— *Odcarana Slovenija. Knjiga o slovenski pomladi in jeseni*. Ljubljana: Mihelač, 1993.

—— *Edinost, sreca, sprava*. Ljubljana: Mihelač, 1996.

Rusinow, Dennison. *The Yugoslav Experiment, 1948–1974*. Berkeley, CA: University of California Press, 1977.

Sabic, Zlatko and Bukowski, Charles, eds. *Small States in the Post-Cold War World: Slovenia and NATO Enlargement*. Westport, CT: Praeger, 2002.

Scammell, Michael. "Slovenia and Its Poet" and "Four Poems by Edvard Kocbek," *New York Review of Books* (October 24) 38: 17, 1991.

Schindler, John. *Isonzo: The Forgotten Sacrifice of the Great War*. New York: Praeger, 2001.

Selhaus, Edi. *Evasion and Repatriation: Slovene Partisans and Rescued American Airmen in World War II*. Manhattan, KS: Sunflower University Press, 1994.

Seroka, Jim and Pavlovic, Vukasin, eds. *The Tragedy of Yugoslavia: The Failure of Democratic Transformation*. Armonk, NY: M.E. Sharpe, 1992.

Shoup, Paul. *Communism and the Yugoslav National Question*. New York: Columbia University Press, 1968.

Silber, Laura and Little, Allan. *Yugoslavia: Death of a Nation*. Rev. edn. New York: Penguin, 1997.

Singleton, Fred. *A Short History of the Yugoslav Peoples*. New York: Cambridge University Press, 1985.

Sitar, Sandi. *Sto pričevanj o slovenski zgodovini*. Ljubljana: Prešernova družba, 1999.

Skrbiš, Zlatko. *Long-distance Nationalism: Diasporas, Homelands and Identities*. Brookfield, VT: Ashgate, 1999.

Stele, France. *Slovene Impressionists*. St Paul: Control Date Arts, 1980.

Švajncer, Janez. *Vojna in vojaška zgodovina slovencev*. Ljubljana: Prešernova družba, 1992.

Tomc, Gregor and Adam, Frane, eds. *Small Societies in Transition: The Case of Slovenia*. Ljubljana: Faculty of Social Sciences, 1994; special issue of *Druzbene razprave*.

Tomšič, Vida. *A Selection of Articles and Speeches on the Status of Women and Family Planning in Yugoslavia*. Belgrade: Federal Council for Family Planning, 1975.

—— *Woman in the Development of Socialist Self-managing Yugoslavia*. Belgrade: Jugoslovenska stvarnost, 1980.

—— *Women, Development, and the Non-aligned Movement*. New Delhi: Centre for Women's Development Studies, 1988.

Udovički, Jasminka and Ridgeway, James, eds. *Burn This House: The Making and Unmaking of Yugoslavia*. Durham, NC: Duke University Press, 1997.

Vilfan, Jože. *Delo, spomini, srečanja*. Koper: Lipa, 1978.

Vilfan, Sergij, ed. *Ethnic Groups and Language Rights*. New York: New York University Press, 1993.

—— *Pravna zgodovina slovencev*. Ljubljana: Slovenska matica, 1996.

Vodopivec, Peter and Mahnič, Joža, eds. *Slovenska tridesta leta: simpozij 1995*. Ljubljana: Slovenska matica, 1997.

Vratuša, Anton. "Development of the Slovene National Question," *Socialist Thought and Practice* (March/April 1988) 28: 2.

Wachtel, Andrew Baruch. *Making a Nation, Breaking a Nation. Literature and Cultural Politics in Yugoslavia*. Stanford, CA: Stanford University Press, 1998.

Zawacki, Andrew, ed. *Afterwards: Slovenian Writing, 1945–1995*. Buffalo, NY: White Pine Press, 1997.

Žižek, Slavoj. "Eastern Europe's Republics of Gilead," *New Left Review* (Sept/Oct. 1990) 30: 183, pp. 50–62.

Zlobec, Ciril. *Lepo je biti Slovenec, ni pa lahko*. Ljubljana: Mihelač, 1992.

Zwitter, Fran. "The Slovenes and the Habsburg Monarchy," *Austrian History Yearbook* (1967) 3: 2, pp. 157–188.

—— *O slovenskem narodnem vprasanju*. Ljubljana: Slovenska matica, 1990.

Websites with information on Slovenia

www.tol.cz and www.ce-review.org First-rate news sites for all of Central Europe and the Balkans.

www.state.gov/g/drl/hr/c1470.htm US State Department Human Rights Reports from 1993 to the present.

www.stat.si Slovenia's government statistical office.

www.hrw.org Human Rights Watch.

www.ljubljanalife.com General news and features in English. The "News" section includes links to resources such as Mladina, Delo, and 24ur.com.

www.rferl.org Radio Free Europe's site with many relevant resources.

www.sta.si/en/ Slovenia's government press agency's site in English.

http://www.ijs.si/lit/ Resources for the study of Slovene literature.

www.sigov.si Official site of the Slovene government.

www.uvi.si/eng/ Official site of the Slovene Ministry of Information (in English).

www.matkurja.si A "guide to virtual Slovenia" with a wide range of English-language features.

www.ljudmila.org Alternative web site for pop culture, high culture, environmental causes, and more.

Index